BROKEN
AND
CHAINED

MY FIRST THIRTY DAYS
IN THE HELL CALLED DETOX

Lori L. Gottula

outskirts
press

Outskirts Press, Inc.
http://www.outskirtspress.com

Paperback ISBN: 978-1-4327-2996-7
Hardback ISBN: 978-1-9772-7030-6

Outskirts Press and the "OP" logo are trademarks belonging to Outskirts Press, Inc.

PRINTED IN THE UNITED STATES OF AMERICA

I am so thankful....

For God, who wrapped His arms around me
when I came running home.

For my husband, Randy, who loved me even when I didn't.

For my family and friends, whose faith in and
support of me never wavered.

For my counselor, Brad Shay, whose guidance
brought me out of the darkness and into the light.

For the person I call "My Friend," whom God used to reach me.
Without the role that she played in my life,
I would not be alive today.

For you, for picking up this book.

I wrote this book eleven years before
I sought publication. Fear kept me from it.
I share it now to bring hope to the broken and addicted,
and to help loved ones understand what happens to the body
and mind during detox. This is not a pretty story.
But it has a beautiful ending.

A NEW LIFE IS POSSIBLE.

In my second book, *Breaking the Chains,*
I will detail my climb out of the dark hole of
addiction and codependency
in hopes that it will lead to your own.

*Some names in this book have been changed, and so noted with
an asterisk. The book details MY story, from my perception at the
time. To name others would not be fair or prudent. I have also

tamed some of the language so that tweens and teenagers might be allowed to read it. We have to fight harder for kids than drug dealers do, so we need to arm them with the truth.

Lastly, this book portrays who my husband and I were at the time. It in no way represents who we are today.

Table of Contents

Introduction

Tick, tick, tick, tick.

I braced myself against the counter between my kitchen and living room, and looked up at the clock on the wall. The second hand ticked off like a timebomb as it counted down the five minutes until feeding time.

Tick, tick, tick, tick.

I looked back down at my bottle of prescription painkillers, sitting there on the counter, all smug and in control. Hydrocodone. My reason for living. The love of my life. I was ten days into self-imposed detox, and had taken one pill per day for the first five days, then a half per day for the next four, and would continue doing so until I ran out. I took my allotment at 8:00 p.m. because I knew, if I couldn't make it to that time, I would never kick this habit for good. Eight p.m. was now four-and-a-half minutes away.

Tick, tick, tick, tick.

I picked up the rust-colored bottle and shook it. There were six pills remaining. I listened as they clinked against the sides of the bottle, and that clink sent a shot of dopamine into my brain. It meant that I still had painkillers left. No matter what I was going through, I could take one at any time, and end some of this horror.

I set the bottle back down. I knew I wasn't going to make it. I hadn't slept in thirty-three hours, and that was after sleeping just six hours over a period of three days. I was delirious and dehydrated. I'd just been to the bathroom for the twentieth time since noon because the toxins were literally draining out my body. I stunk like rotting flesh. Sweat beaded on my forehead and slid down my nose. More sweat snaked like a river down my back. I was so hot that I felt like I was being microwaved, then within minutes, shook with feverish chills. Every inch of my body—from the roots of my hair to the soles of my feet—ached to the core. I couldn't breathe because my nose was stuffed up yet ran without warning. When it did, a thin stream of watery mucus trickled into my mouth, so I dashed to the stinking, dirty toilet in the bathroom, where I hurled pink chunks. Again.

My heart raced. The room where I stood breathed in and out, then tapped *rat-a-tat-tat*. Sometimes, I crashed into things because my focus and balance had been beaten by the fists of twelve years of addiction. But it was the anxiety that drove me to my knees. It shot through my nerves like electrical jolts. My arms convulsed in the air. I shook my head, my hands, my arms, trying to force the electricity out. It wouldn't go! It wouldn't go! It just kept frying my insides. Bzzzzzzt bzzzzzzzt bzzzzzzzzzzzzzzzzzzzzzt. I couldn't stand it! The anxiety was going to break me!

Tick, tick, tick, tick.

Oh my God! Why had I done this to myself? No one had even known I had a problem! I was really involved in my community, so I was very visible, but I'd hidden my problems well. Why hadn't I continued to do so? Why hadn't I just weaned myself off the painkillers? Why had I felt the need to go to drug rehab, then leave after the first night to detox on my own at home?

My anxiety shot to level orange. Panic! No, this was worse than panic! It was sheer terror, and it bolted through my veins! I felt like someone was chasing me with a knife! I had to hide! I had to get away! Surely, I could do something, go somewhere to escape this!

Oh God, please make it stop! I thought. My heart pounded. *I can't get away! I'm going to die! This is going to kill me! Withdrawal is going to kill me! I'm never going to make it through three more minutes!*

"Just take one early!" the pills hissed. "It will make the sickness and anxiety go away for a while. Just take one!" *Bzzzzzt. Bzzzzt.* The anxiety lit up my fingertips. I twitched and squirmed. I ran into the living room and felt the house twirl. I was in a tornado! I couldn't stand up! The house was spinning!

"I can't take it anymore!" I screamed. I no longer had the strength to fight it on my own. There was no way I was going to make it. How had I done this to myself? How had I spiraled this far down?

Chapter One

In September 2012, my husband, Randy, was sixty-one years old, and I was fifty-one. We lived in Falls City, Nebraska, population 4,300. We were part owners of the only grocery store in town, and had the support of a region that we'd called home for twenty-two years. At any given time, we employed forty to fifty people, and were very involved in the community, organizing and sponsoring activities and events. Randy worked sixty to seventy-hour weeks at the grocery store, and a few nights a week, called football or basketball play-by-play on a local radio station. When he wasn't doing either, he was attending a ballgame, and taking pictures that he then gave away. I did volunteer work, reared our daughter, and wrote feature articles for the Falls City Journal, our local newspaper. I'd also written seven screenplays, three of which had reached the finals of five international contests. In addition, I was working on what I'd hoped would be my first book, a nonfiction story titled *Misty**. The title character was legally blind, a champion barrel racer and a certified equine massage therapist. She and her mother, Jane*, had overcome incredible obstacles together. Misty's blindness was just one of them. Jane had endured a tumultuous marriage for more than twenty years—finally divorcing, and she had lost two of her sons in separate, tragic incidents. The fact that she could even get out of bed was amazing. The two women leaned on each other. I couldn't wait to tell their story to the world.

Because of my commitment to the book, I eventually left some of the organizations that I had once supported or led—like the Chamber of Commerce—but I still ran our community's annual parade every August; one that attracted thousands of spectators.

Randy and I also had a wide social circle, so we loved living in Falls City. Plus, our family members all lived within a four-hour radius. We had three grandsons who were active in sports, so we often traveled the three hours to Schuyler, Nebraska, to watch their games. Their parents, Andy and Shanda (Randy's daughter from a previous marriage) were teachers in the Schuyler school system, so their family was busy all the time. Randy's son, Todd, lived in Kearney, Nebraska, where he was the director of the Viero Event Center. He and his wife, Kristin, also led very busy lives. We didn't get to see those two as often as we wanted either.

The child we saw most often was our daughter, Cassie, who lived just ninety minutes from us, in Bellevue, Nebraska. She lived in an apartment with her then boyfriend (now husband), Brian Shaw. She worked at Peru State College, which was halfway between her apartment and our home, so when Brian worked out of town, she came home for a few days to see us and her friends.

Whenever we could, Randy and I enjoyed visiting our kids and other family members, particularly my mom. She still resided in the home where I was raised in Auburn, Nebraska. (My dad, who'd been the love of my mom's life since she was twelve years old, had died in 1998 from esophageal cancer.) My three siblings all lived in eastern Nebraska, too, so everyone was close to me.

In Falls City, I had a group of friends who were all professionals in their fields. We called our group the Quilting Club, but we neither quilted nor were a club. We just called ourselves that because it was more acceptable to call a member's office and say we were going quilting than it was to say we were going drinking. But we did much more than drink. We also helped each other through the pressures of daily life. When the child of a Quilter got married, our group hosted the bridal shower and assisted with the wedding; helping with decorations, rehearsal dinners, and anything else that the mother of the bride or groom needed. When loved ones died, the Quilters descended on the family with enough food and paper products to take care of everyone for days. When a member of our group was ill, we provided dinners or help until she was well. We also donated money to local charities, and one time painted a home for a needy family. But our primary aims were stress relief and just plain fun. And man, did we have a great time! Plus, spending time with the Quilters was the cheapest therapy I'd ever had.

The Quilters in a 2010 photo, *left to right*: Gail Froeschl, Debbie Witt, Linda Jones, Sue Harmon, Betty Maze, Lynne Davis, me, Kathy Martin, Renee Kopf, and Karen Sailors.

When the women and I were in our early thirties and forties, we went out one night during the week, then again on Friday or Saturday night with our husbands. If our kids were with grandparents or friends, we closed down the bars, then gathered at our friend Linda's house to finish the night away in the hot tub. Now that we were all in our fifties and sixties, we went out at 5:00 p.m., stayed out until 7:00 or 8:00 p.m., and finished our drinks before the "young crowd" showed up. We still loved getting together, but went home early, feeling good and having caught up with each other's news before our kids and/or grandkids showed up for the weekend. Each time we left the bar, we drove home to lives that looked perfect from the outside. Maybe their lives were, but mine certainly wasn't. If it had been, I wouldn't have written this book about my first thirty days in the hell called detox. But to understand how far I had spiraled, and even more importantly, how high I had to climb to get out, one has to know where I started. So, let me back up a little.

I was raised in Auburn, Nebraska during the 1960s and '70s, the second of four children of Richard and Judy Kimball. Our family had very little that we wanted but everything we needed, including an abundance of love. We kids knew that God came first, the family unit second, and our parents' relationship third. We were also raised in a spiritual home, where church was required. That was O.K. with me, though. I was the outgoing, chubby little girl who praised Jesus at the top of her lungs. I talked to adults as if I was one, and, at church, helped with collection or any other volunteer job for which I could raise my hand. I was also very headstrong, loved to be in charge, saw the good in everyone, and wanted everybody to get along. I was obsessed with people-pleasing, so I did everything I could to please Jesus, my mom and dad, teachers, minister, and every little old lady who sat in pews six through eight. The more I could do to help, the happier I was.

Although I was very active in church, I grew up thinking that Christianity was a set of rules and regulations, and that I had to be good enough for God to love me. I thought my salvation came through my actions, not His gift. I believed I had to be worthy. And inside, I felt like I didn't measure up. I was constantly trying to prove myself—so I could earn God's love and everyone else's.

In my little-girl social circle, I was the best friend and constant sidekick to the beautiful popular girl. She was Sandra Bullock, I was Melissa McCarthy. I was the hilarious supporting actress to the leading lady. She was the girl every other little girl wanted to be, and the one with whom every boy wanted to be. The fact that she wanted to be with me became a large part of my identity. My world was just brighter when she was around. We did silly, goofy things together, and I made her laugh! The bonus was, I made the other kids laugh, too! The kids also thought I was one of the smart chicks, the organizer, and the therapist. They told me their problems because I kept everything confidential, and I genuinely cared. On the inside, though, I was in a constant state of upheaval. I was physically chunky, so I was sometimes pitied by adults who said things like, "You're not fat! You're just pleasingly plump." Yeah, like that was better? Plus, I was the butt of jokes brought on by my brothers' friends. By the time I was in the sixth grade, the jabs started to chip away at my self-esteem and pride. They made me self-conscious and often depressed. But I couldn't tell anyone! I was a good little Christian girl! Christians weren't supposed to be depressed, were we? But sometimes, I was. Of course, I wasn't always that way. When I was in front of people, or do-ing something with friends, I really was the person they saw. I felt better when I was out among the living. But when I was alone, I just felt hol-low. I tumbled down a big black hole and couldn't get out. I didn't want anyone to know, so I hid my emotions until I was alone in my bedroom and could spill them out all over my pillow. That was how I kept my depression to myself. Rarely did anyone see it. Not even my family.

I started yo-yo dieting when I was twelve. I lost twenty pounds and gained it back six months later, plus a little bit more just for cushion. To make up for my lack of willpower and size fourteen jeans, I became a perfectionist and overachiever.

In high school, I was the president or an officer of several organiza-tions—like my class, the choir, band, pep club, Fellowship of Christian Athletes, and more. I liked being in charge because I enjoyed getting things done. I played sports until I had to choose between volleyball and the lead role in the school musical. After that, I was all about the arts. I was still very involved in summer softball, but most of my school-year attention went to musicals, plays, speech, music, band, and extracurricular activities. And I loved to learn. If I got a B on a test, it sent me into a spiral of shame. I worked hard to be the best I could be in every endeavor, and had big dreams for my life.

God was still a central part of my life then, so I attended youth group every Wednesday, led a program called "Children's Church" on Sundays, and was involved in a singing group called Goin' Home. During the summer, when I wasn't lifeguarding at the local pool, I volunteered at a Christian camp, where I also learned American Sign Language. As hard as I tried, though, none of those things fulfilled me for very long. I felt guilty about it, too. I truly believed in God and Jesus, but going to church just wasn't exciting. We sang old hymns and worshipped with a distant reverence. It just didn't make me feel alive. The only thing that did was that relationship that I zeroed in on—usually with someone I had to chase after. Whether it was a friend or love interest, the pull was so strong that I wanted to be with her or him all the time. Our connection made my soul leap with joy when things were going well, and ache with unbearable pain when they weren't.

I loved my high school friends, and had a blast when we were together. I also enjoyed school more than most students did. But when I was with the subject of my codependency, life went from black and white to vibrant color. It was like the opening scenes in The *Wizard of Oz* movie, then the colorful scenes when Dorothy woke up in Oz. Everything in my life was just more exciting when my codependent person was there.

The subject of my attention in high school was a love interest who was older than I was. I wasn't interested in guys my age because they were too much like brothers. I wanted a man who made me feel that surge of electricity when he walked in the room, and I found it in my guy. Our relationship was forbidden by my parents and society, so that added another twinge of excitement. I felt like my man and I had a connection that no one else understood. Our relationship caused a lot of problems between me and my parents, though, and between me and God, so that made my anxiety and depression worse. The ups and downs were like driving on a curvy mountain road in gale-force winds, with no barricades between me and the cliffs. I broke up with my boyfriend, chased after him, got back together, broke up, got back together. He couldn't take the indecision, and I couldn't take the heartache, so I decided to focus on God and leave the electricity behind.

After I graduated from high school, I went to Nebraska Christian

College on academic scholarship, and planned to become a minister. I took classes like Hebrew History, public speaking, the book of Acts, and several other Bible-based courses. I studied hard because each of my classes was more difficult than calculus and physics combined. In my spare time, I joined an acting group called Christ and Company. We performed all over the region in churches and at conventions. When I was performing for or studying about God, I felt good, like I was doing what I was supposed to be doing. But I still felt like something was missing! I tried everything I could think of to fill it. That was how I found the first love of my life the summer after my freshman year at NCC. I found alcohol.

Alcoholism ran through the veins of my father's lineage. Dad didn't drink much himself, but both of his biological parents were alcoholics. Knowing so didn't faze me a bit, though, because WOOO-EEE, I was too busy having fun! When I drank, I let my hair down. I stopped feeling like an old person in a young person's body. I no longer felt responsible for everybody else, like I had to take care of them, please them, fix them, save them. So, I started partying every night. And I had a blast doing it.

When August rolled around, I knew I couldn't go back to NCC to be a minister! Don't get me wrong, I wasn't one of those legalistic Christians who thought that Christ followers couldn't have a few beers on Saturday night. However, I knew I couldn't get plastered every night and still be a minister. As a result, I stayed in Auburn, worked for the Nemaha County (NE) assessor, and left the church completely. I drifted around for two years. During that time, I got involved with a guy who was quite a bit older than I, and when I wasn't working, I wanted to be with him all the time. Fortunately, or unfortunately, depending on how one sees it, he usually felt the same way. However, when he didn't, I was crushed. I always thought he would lose interest in me or find someone else if I wasn't with him all the time. So, I became obsessed. As a result, he broke up with me, chased after me, broke up with me, chased after me...

During one of our breakups, I finally woke up and realized that I needed a college education to get anywhere in life, so I went back to school at the University of Nebraska – Lincoln. I partied every night and frequently skipped class, so I was lucky to pull down Bs and Cs. The only thing I still did well was work. My parents had instilled a strong work ethic in me and my siblings, and I couldn't and wouldn't do a bad job when I was getting paid to do a good one. Besides, I had bills to pay.

When my former boyfriend married someone else, I started dating a guy my own age because it seemed more acceptable to people. We got engaged, but I had a pit in my stomach about that because I felt like I was doing it just to please people. I wasn't really into him unless I was drinking, so I broke up with him, got back together, got pregnant, and got abandoned. He "wasn't ready to be a dad," and that was O.K. with me. I wasn't ready to be his wife. I also knew that, if he was involved in my child's life, he would make me fight for custody. I wasn't about to let that happen, so I let him walk out. I moved back to Auburn, gave birth to my beautiful daughter, Cassie, and worked three jobs while I attended college at the small but perfect (for me) Peru State College in Peru, NE. I was determined to raise my little girl without diving into the quicksand of welfare.

One of the jobs that I held was as a disc jockey and production assistant at a local radio station. Randy worked there part-time as a sports play-by-play announcer, and one night, asked if I wanted to ride to a Peru State College football game to watch my younger brother, David Kimball, play. I went, and Randy and I began dating shortly after. Our relationship was the healthiest I'd ever had. He included my daughter in a lot of the things we did, and he adored his own children. I was sold. I wanted to be with him when we weren't working, but I didn't HAVE to be. I also didn't have to chase after him because he made it very clear that he loved me. He treated me like a queen, plus he was hard-working, highly respected in the community, and crazy about my daughter. I, likewise, loved him and his children. The relationship was a win-win!

I graduated from college in 1986 with a degree in English, speech, and theater, and landed a job with my alma mater. I was the assistant to the president, which meant that I organized everything in which he was involved, and also helped with other projects that he assigned. I got paid to people-please! Talk about a dream job! I started climbing the ladder of success with crushed beer cans beneath my high heels.

On the weekends, I even partied with my boss and his wife, and two of the deans.

One year after I started my job, Randy and I got married. Cassie was three years old, so my new husband became the only father she had ever known. He treated her with the same love and fatherly attention with which he treated his biological kids. She was his. We were his. And his family became our family.

In 1990, Randy and I and two partners from the Hinky Dinky Limited Liability Corporation bought a grocery store in Falls City, Nebraska, so he and I and Cassie moved there. (Randy's kids remained with their mom in Auburn, which was just thirty minutes away.) A certified workaholic, Randy was at the store most of the time. After I left Peru State College in 1991, I started doing public relations/volunteer work, and was active in everything in which Cassie was involved. I also worked out every day, and was trim and fit.

Me, at age thirty, in a photo taken in Acapulco, Mexico

I really liked Falls City and being an at-home wife and mom. I loved volunteering, too, because I enjoyed helping out, so I kept my schedule full with organizations like the Business and Professional Women, Chamber of Commerce, and Ladies' Golf Association, the latter two for which I was president. I made a lot of friends through groups like those. But my most important job was raising Cassie and supporting her events. I was the Kool-Aid mom. I coached her softball teams and invited her friends over to the house often. I was very busy and enjoyed my life, but looked forward to the nights when I could meet up with the Quilters. When I was drinking, I was fun, funny, and confident. But the next day, I usually sank into the pit of guilt and depression. As I had done all my life, though, I held things together until I was alone. Since Randy worked long hours and Cassie was in school, I was alone quite a bit. Some of my days were productive, and others were excruciating.

In 1998, my life changed when I hurt my back just bending over to put my swimming suit on. I was in the hospital for one week, unable to roll onto my side on my own. After I was dismissed, I was in physical therapy for eight months, and had a knot in my back that was like a charley horse in a person's calf. It hardened as the day went on. I couldn't get rid of the pain. It was debilitating and constant.

For the next several years, I was in and out of hospitals and doctors' offices, trying to find an answer for the pain. No one could help me, so to manage it, I took Hydrocodone, an opiate painkiller. Those pills gave me a euphoric high that not only helped my back, they helped the rest of my problems, too! When I added a little alcohol at night, my pain was tolerable, and I was able to drown anything else that bothered me. Until the next day. Then, the agony and depression set in again. They recycled daily. I took the pills, drank at night, and pretended my way through the depression days. I was good at it, too. From the outside looking in, I appeared happy, in control, put together. I did everything I could to stay involved with Cassie's events, attending every activity in which she participated. I directed her high school musicals, and continued to coach her summer softball teams. In the community,

CHAPTER ONE

I ran the town's parade, and organized a few golf tournaments at the country club, even though I could no longer play. I looked like I had the perfect life and had it all together. But behind closed doors, I was taking medication that stole my soul so gradually that I had no idea anything was even happening to me. I just started sinking inside myself. In addition, I began packing on pounds—fifteen the first year, ten the second, another ten the third. And the more I gained, the more I hid. At least once per year, I hurt my back and was in the hospital for a week. Then the vicious cycle began all over again.

During one of my hospital stays, I had what my husband and I determined was an accidental overdose of the painkiller Demerol. The episode left me with extreme anxiety and a wicked, life-changing case of claustrophobia. I had hurt my back again, and was basically immobile. The nurses had to help me do everything, including simple things like changing positions in bed. The charley horse was in the muscle on my lower back, left side, and it wouldn't stretch out or soften. The pain was unbearable. It was so bad, in fact, that I had an IV in the back of my hand and a pain pump that shot Demerol straight into my veins. There was a limit on the pump, so I had no worries about overdosing if I pushed the button too often. But I pushed it every chance I got. The medicine made me loopy and tired but made my suffering more humane.

On my third day in the hospital, I pushed that pump every twenty minutes, so the nurses could place pillows under my side, or slip a bed-pan beneath me. But later in the day, I woke up from a drug-infused nap, and couldn't feel my legs. I was so frightened that I tried to get up on my own. The pain made me scream with horror, but I kept going, and when my legs should have hit the floor, I felt nothing. I slid down onto my butt and shrieked for help. Fortunately, I had been labeled a fall risk, so an alarm went off at the nurses' station. My nurse came running in, called for help, and another one appeared. The two pulled me back into bed while I moaned with gut-wrenching pain. I still couldn't feel my legs. My heart raced, and I felt like I was on fire. I also sensed impending doom, and knew for sure that I was dying from a drug overdose.

"Please, call my husband at the store," I begged. "Please help me. I got too much Demerol, and now I'm going to die. I'm burning up. Please help me."

While one of the nurses ran to find a fan, the other one called Randy at the store, and told him to come immediately. The first nurse hooked up the fan, and the other one cleaned me up because I had lost control of my bowels. I was humiliated and forlorn, but more than anything, I was just plain terrified. As soon as the nurses finished, they pulled the curtain back, and Randy came rushing in.

"I'm going to die," I told him. "I got too much Demerol and I'm going to die." He raced to my bedside and took my hands in his. Then he bent down close to me.

"It's O.K., honey," he said. "You're going to be O.K. You're at the hospital and in good hands."

"I need Life Flight! I'm dying!" I said. I could feel myself drifting away, like I was losing consciousness. I shook my head to ward off the sinking feeling. "Please, I need a helicopter to fly me somewhere that specializes in drug overdoses."

"We don't even know for sure that's what this is," Randy said.

One of the nurses said, "We've summoned the doctor on call. Please hang on. He'll be here in a few minutes."

"I may be gone in a few minutes!" I yelled. I was in certain peril and was petrified that the medicine was going to kill me. I could feel myself floating above the room! Suddenly, I went from unbearably hot to freezing! It was like I was ripped from hell and placed in a deep freeze, with the door closed on top of me. I shook uncontrollably. My teeth literally chattered.

"What's wrong with me?" I screamed. "I'm freezing now!"

One of the nurses turned the fan off, and the other one ran to get warm blankets. When she came back, she and Randy piled four or five on top of me, but my teeth continued to clatter. I could not get warm. She took my temperature then. It was normal. Still, I was so cold that I shook. Randy pulled the blankets up to my chin and tucked me down inside.

Dr. Terry Symonds, the on-call doctor, sauntered in then. Randy and I were social friends of Terry's and sometimes attended the same parties, so we knew him fairly well. Sauntering was one of the words that described him best. Very little ruffled his feathers. However, in my state, I wanted and needed him to run.

"Get me a helicopter, please," I begged. "Please, Terry. I need to be somewhere that deals with drug overdoses."

"You are," he said. Then, he turned to the only nurse still left in the room. "What's going on?" he asked. She handed my chart to him, then he and she took a few steps out the door. My panic hit a new level. They acted like there was time to discuss my case, and there wasn't! I was going to die while they talked about it! My husband walked away from the bed then, to see what they were talking about.

"No!" I yelled. "Don't leave me here alone! I'm going to die! I don't want to die alone!" He rushed back over. The bed rails were raised on both sides, just in case I tried to get out again, or maybe because the nurses didn't want me to fall out, since I couldn't feel my legs. Suddenly, I went from iceberg cold to on-fire hot, like I was literally standing in a fire.

"Oh my God!" I screamed. "I'm on fire! I'm on fire!" I shoved the blankets as far down as I could, which wasn't very far since I couldn't move. "Terry, please! I'm going to die!"

The nurse rushed back in, and she and Randy quickly yanked the blankets off me. She flew to the fan and turned it on high. I could hear the whir of the blades, so I leaned into the cool blast of air. Dr. Symonds walked back into the room very calmly.

"We don't know for sure what this is," he said, "but I checked your urine counts and the amount of opioids in your system is too high, so we're going to give you a medication called Narcan that will reverse the effects of the painkiller, and the other meds."

"Not more medicine!" I said. "Please, I'm so hot. Can someone get me a cold washcloth?" The nurse raced to the bathroom. I heard the water running.

Randy squeezed my hand and said, "Honey, this Narcan will reverse the painkiller. It will take it out of your system." I nodded. But I felt myself drifting away. My head dropped, and the voices in the room sounded like the adults on Charlie Brown. *Wawawawawa.*

"Lori, stay with us," someone said. I woke up to Dr. Symonds patting my face. "Stay with us," he said. "We need you to be alert and aware." The nurse shimmied in behind him and wiped my face with a cool washcloth. I tried to keep my eyes open, but really struggled. I was so in-and-out that I didn't understand what was happening to me! How could I be so cold and then so hot within seconds? I turned to Dr. Symonds and the nurse, and watched as she pressed a syringe into my IV. "This will only take a few minutes," Dr. Symonds said.

A few minutes later, I *wanted* to die. I shook violently as electricity raced through my limbs.

"Agggghhhhh!" I shouted. "Aagggghhhh!" A lightning bolt zapped inside me. My arms, neck, and hands convulsed. My toes curled. The lightning ripped through my insides, from my toes up through my stomach and into my limbs. My arms flailed uncontrollably.

"Help me!" I screamed. "Help me!"

"Randy," Dr. Symonds said, firmly, "hold her arms down. Do whatever you have to do so she doesn't hurt herself." He and the nurse lowered the side rails, and Randy stepped in close.

"Hold her arms down," Dr. Symonds said, again. I couldn't see him beside me, but could tell by the shakiness in his voice and the look in my husband's eyes that both were very concerned. But I couldn't ask because the electricity made my legs and arms convulse like I was having epileptic seizures. Randy grabbed my arms, then practically lay down on top of me. However, he was no match for the strength of the Demerol as it fought its way out of my body.

"Oh my God!" Randy yelled. "I need help! I can't believe how strong she is! I can't hold her down!" The strength wasn't mine. It was the devil's. It shot jolts through my body and took control of my limbs, as if someone had electrocuted me. But I couldn't explain that. I was too busy trying to stay alive. Meanwhile, my body contorted into impossible pretzel positions. Then, just as quickly as it came, the electricity stopped. I felt Randy's muscles relax, and he stood back up. He took deep breaths, and so did I. I had never been so grateful for anything to be over in my life. I was completely depleted. It was a level of exhaustion that I had never felt before, and hoped I never would again. I turned my head slowly and watched Dr. Symonds pace beside me while the nurse moved the blood pressure machine close to my bed.

"Please," I whispered. "Please help me." Then, I closed my eyes and drifted away again.

The powerful surge gripped me out of the blue and bent my neck sideways. My arms thrust into the air, then I flopped around like a demon-possessed character in a horror film. Dr. Symonds moved away from the bed so the nurse could grab my legs. Randy lay on top of my upper body again, pressing my arms down with his chest.

"My God, I've never felt anything like this before," he said.

"Help me!" I screamed. "Helllllllppp meeeeeee."

The convulsion twisted my arms up so forcefully that it shoved Randy away from me. I worried that I had hurt him, but he came back with a vengeance. The battle was life and death, and he wasn't about to let death win. The convulsion probably lasted two minutes, but to me, it felt like two days. When it lifted, Randy and the nurse stood up and massaged their arms. Then, the nurse walked around my bed and wiped the sweat off my forehead. Randy took his tie off and unbuttoned the top button on his shirt. Dr. Symonds sauntered to the foot of my bed and squeezed my toes.

"Can you feel that?" he asked. I nodded. Thank God I could finally feel something down there! I moved my right leg a little bit, and felt the knot in my back tighten.

"Why is this happening?" I asked. "Please call Life Flight. I don't want to die."

"We're going to make sure you don't," he said. He looked down at me over his bifocals. "This is the Narcan reversing the effects of every drug in your system. It's ugly, I know, but right now, it's necessary."

"I can't do this anymore," I said. "I can't. I'm going to die, Terry. Please fly me to a trauma center that deals with drugs. I need a helicopter." I had no idea what I thought a different facility would do, but at that moment, during that crisis, I just felt like I needed to escape. And then I felt the jolt of instant drug withdrawal travel through my nerves and grab my body.

"Noooooo!" I screamed. Randy and the nurse lay back over me, holding me down as the devil threw me into terror-filled convulsions of biblical proportions. I silently begged God to save me. I asked Him for mercy, and pledged the rest of my life if He would just take it all away. But I continued to thrash around in bed while Randy did his best to keep me from giving myself a black eye.

That same scenario played out for the next ninety minutes. I was cold then hot, freezing then on fire, frigid then in hell. When I was hot, I was suddenly drenched with sweat, so when I got cold, it was ten times worse because I was wet. The nurse and Randy raced around to wipe me off, cover me up, take the covers off, turn on the fan, turn the fan off, then hold me down, hold me down, hold me down. Nurses ran in and out with towels, fresh gowns, bed pans, etc., but MY nurse stayed there the whole time. She had no time for anyone but me. Dr. Symonds stayed there, too. In between jolts of electricity, he assured me he wasn't going anywhere. My poor husband stood by my bedside throughout the whole ordeal, holding me down with every ounce of strength he had, then standing back up to relax and massage his muscles so he could prepare for the next time. Finally, after all of that torture, I fell asleep. When I woke up, the electricity didn't return.

"It's gone," Randy whispered. He leaned down over me and stroked the top of my head. "The convulsions are over. You've been asleep for about half an hour." I could barely stay awake, but I smiled slightly and thanked God that he had sent Randy to love me, and Dr. Symonds to save me. Then I fell asleep again.

At the end of that hospital stay, I was grateful to be alive, but because I'd been held down and confined, I developed a severe case of claustrophobia. I'd been unable to "get out" of that situation on my own, so I couldn't stand any circumstances in which I was out of control. I couldn't even sit in the center of a row of seats at a concert or arena unless I could get out on my own—not even at an outdoor venue. I could ride in an airplane, but only if I was in the aisle seat. If someone blocked me in, I panicked inside until the situation changed. I had to be able to get out on my own.

Those mental barriers took their toll on me throughout the following years, whether I was at home, at a local eatery, or on vacation in a foreign country. I even had to have control when attending or volunteering for my daughter's activities. I just picked and chose events based on whether I could get out on my own. When I directed her musicals, I sat away from the crowd, in the balcony, watching and giving directions to the backstage staff through a microphone and earpiece. I was able to still do a lot of things, but everything had to be on my terms. Otherwise, I felt held down and suffocated. Controlled.

Fast forward to 2003. Cassie graduated from high school that May, and I suddenly lost half of my purpose. I had more time on my hands, so I started writing screenplays again. I just kept plugging away, hoping that my "someday" would come. Meanwhile, the situations with my back and hibernation just got worse. And my weight skyrocketed. By 2009, when I started interviewing Jane and Misty for the *Misty* book, I weighed 200 pounds. I was disgusted with myself, and continued to withdraw from people. I went out with the Quilters sometimes, drank my beer, shared a thousand laughs, and went home.

After my first interview with Misty and Jane, I spent most of my time on interviews and writing. The two women and I also started traveling to give motivational presentations about their story at schools and conventions. Our smallest audience was probably thirty, our largest, five hundred. We began gaining attention for the book, so I didn't want to do anything but write and give our presentations. I left the house occasionally, but often went days at a time without leaving the confines of my bedroom. I lay on my bed and typed. The more I lay down, the more my back hurt, and the more frequently I took my painkillers. I became increasingly withdrawn, more lethargic and heavier. As I did, my back hurt even more. Tsunami waves of depression came washing in. My life became a vicious cycle.

But then, I started spending time with a new friend. (I will call her "My Friend" because it is not my intention to disparage her, but rather to talk about my own brokenness). My Friend and I had a laugh-out-loud blast together. She was hysterically funny, and she said I was, too. We went to movies, shopping, and Broadway shows together, traveled to horse sales, horse shows, and rodeos. I opened up and was myself with her, instead of wearing my mask like I usually did. The more time we spent together, the closer we became. She had a daughter who was out of high school, and the girl went with us to various events as well. Her daughter often said that her mom and I were so much alike that we were like twins. When we were together, we were silly and goofy and laughed until our cheeks hurt. My Friend often told me I was the best friend she'd ever had, and that filled me to the core. My need for that codependent relationship was filled once again.

Nearly a year after we started hanging out, though, something started happening. She continued to tell me things that made me feel like a million bucks, but then days later, completely ignored me or froze me out of conversations. She often stood me up or showed up two hours late. She started ditching me for another friend of hers and her daughter's named Anastasia*, and that gutted me like a fish. If I called to ask what I had done, she didn't answer the phone or return my calls, so I sent rambling emails to try to fix everything. The emails sounded obsessive and desperate and just made me feel as crazy as she tried to convince me I was. I started losing sleep. I wanted to tell her to kiss my ass, and then walk away, but every time I decided to do just that, she called and wanted to do something fun, or expressed concern about me, or brought something to the house to make me feel better. When that happened, I just let the rest go. I fell back into the gutter of codependency every single time. The thought of living without her was unbearable.

During our long conversations, she told me about the tragedies in her life that had led to a case of depression that was so bad some days that she could barely function. When she talked to me about it, she told me that she didn't need a counselor because she had me. But then, she pushed me away for days, sometimes weeks. I always felt like I was on a rollercoaster that could derail at any time and go hurtling into a pile of fire and debris.

I knew that part of her depression was about her bills, so I started giving her money. I never gave it directly to her, though, because I didn't want to hurt her pride. I just left the money in her mailbox. We called it "playing Santa Claus." Every time I played Santa, she was happy, warm, and welcoming for a few days. She asked about me and my family. She showed concern and made me feel important in her life by bringing food by the house when my back was hurting—things like that. Her attention fed me like a shot of heroin, and I was high for days. But a few days later, she turned cold and bitter again. *What am I doing wrong?* I thought. Her coldness devastated me. I sank further inside myself, became quieter and more withdrawn. The friendship began to consume me. I was obsessed with making her happy. I slept two or three hours a night, but the rest of the time, fixated on whatever I could do to help her battle her demons.

My life at home was just like everyone else's, though. Randy and I spent time together at lunch every day, and in the evenings when he wasn't calling play-by-play. We also attended as many of our grandkids' ballgames as possible, and spent time on the weekends with our family members, or the Quilters and their husbands. Randy knew that I was working feverishly on the *Misty* book, and he had complete faith in my ability and the future of the project. I was very lucky to have a husband who supported my dreams. But since he was gone most of the time, I was able to easily hide my emotions, and everything else about my slide down into the black hole of depression and obsession. I was awake most nights into the early morning hours, and he went to bed early, so I usually slept in the spare bedroom. (Plus, he snored like a truck driver, so I couldn't sleep anyway). That was how I got away with my insomnia, and the resulting despair.

I spent most of my days either traveling with Misty and Jane to give our presentations, or lying down so I could work on the *Misty* book. No matter what I did, my back hurt unbearably all the time. Because it did, I took my Hydrocodone three hours apart instead of four. Since I had terrible anxiety and couldn't sleep, I also got prescriptions for Xanax and Ambien. My depression hit the bottom of the barrel, so my doctor prescribed an antidepressant, too. Plus, I was taking medication for a blood disorder. I washed all of those down with my four beers nearly every night. I stuck with four because the fifth one made me jittery and restless. The combination of Hydrocodone and the four beers made me sleepy, but the Xanax and Ambien made me practically comatose. I had crazy, frightening hallucinations. But worse, I often quit breathing during the night. I jerked awake, gasping for air. Twice, my lungs flat-lined. I had no air in them. None. Both of those times, I bolted out of bed and ran into the living room. I tried to breathe in, but my throat was closed and created a terrible noise, like the screeching of a pinched balloon. That sound scared me to death, so I was afraid to close my eyes and go back to sleep.

The anxiety and lack of sleep began eating me alive, so I started meeting with a counselor—Bob Kohles of Blue Valley Behavioral Health in Nebraska City, Nebraska. Throughout several sessions, I told him all about the book, the pressure I was feeling, and the turmoil with My Friend. Bob said if the book was consuming me, then I needed to end the project. Period. He also said I had to find a way to end the pattern of codependency, or I would never reach my true potential. As hard as I tried, though, I couldn't envision my life without that one person whose presence made me feel alive. I had leaned on it ever since I was a little girl, whether it was a love interest or friend. I didn't want to give it up. I didn't know HOW to give it up! So instead, I obsessed about how to fix everything. I knew if My Friend would just talk to me, just tell me what was wrong, I could fix it. After all, when she was "on," we laughed hysterically the whole time we were together. When she was depressed, she confided in me. She made me feel special and needed, so on the days that she was angry or cold, I overlooked it because I wanted the good days so badly.

In meeting after meeting with Bob, he tried to convince me that the good times were not worth the bad. He didn't understand why I couldn't see that. After about a year of counseling, I finally told him that I was taking painkillers and a variety of other prescription drugs, and was drinking beer with them every night. He couldn't believe that it had taken me that long to tell him about the drug use, but he urged me to seek treatment immediately. I just tossed off his comments. The meds weren't the problem! The alcohol certainly wasn't the problem! The only problem was that My Friend said I was her best friend one day, then completely ignored me the next! I couldn't get her to understand how much it hurt me! I felt like she didn't care. Sometimes, she even told me it was my fault! Why? Was I suffocating her? Was I giving too much? What was I doing wrong? I tried in vain to get an answer, but none ever came. I was just met with silence. Then, the next time I saw her, she acted like I was God's gift to the world, and I ate it up. The rollercoaster was making me crazy. Meanwhile, Bob continued to press me about all of it—the painkillers, alcohol, the book, and My Friend. My thoughts raced. *How can I live without her? I don't want or need to live without beer! And I cannot live without painkillers!* My back pain was real. It was practically debilitating! I needed those narcotics to get through my days!

"Lori," Bob said, "I've seen a lot of people in my career, but I've never been this close to calling the authorities. If you don't get help for your addictions—ALL of your addictions—you won't be here in another year." I wouldn't be here in a year? Did he think I was going to die? Yes. He thought I was going to die. But my reaction to his declaration was a mixed "nah" and "eh." Firstly, I didn't believe it, and secondly, I was in such a bad place that I really didn't care. I had become a recluse who was puffy and bloated, obese, and obsessed. I looked twenty years older than my fifty years.

Me, fifty years old

But more importantly than the way I looked was what the medication was doing to my personality. I continued to withdraw, working feverishly on the *Misty* book for twelve to fourteen hours a day. And I continued to bend to the whims of My Friend. I talked to Bob about that once a week, but I couldn't talk to anyone else because I knew no one would understand. I didn't even understand! So, I became lethargic, bitter, and angry. Some days, when My Friend didn't answer my calls, I was even worse than angry. I was enraged. I was so lost that I didn't know what to do. I thought about turning to God, but I hadn't been to church more than a dozen times in thirty years. How could I ask God for help when I couldn't even show up for worship?

I continued to spiral out of control for another year, packing on more pounds. At that point, I had gained more than ninety. I'd gone from trim and fit in size seven jeans, to puffy and bloated in a size twenty. My thighs rubbed together so badly that they were constantly chafed. I couldn't walk up my basement steps without breathing hard and breaking a sweat. I had to stop at the top just to breathe.

Me, at my highest weight of 216 pounds.

I couldn't climb a set of bleachers without help, or sit through an entire ballgame without writhing in pain. I couldn't walk to the end of my block or tie my own shoes. I felt out of control and disgusted by my lack of willpower. And that just fueled the racing thoughts in my head. I had to find something, do something, to keep my mind busy!

When I wasn't working on the *Misty* book, I began writing query letters to literary agents for the book and screenplay about the story. With the first letter I sent out, I landed one of the top agents in New York City. He offered me a contract based on my query letter and the first chapter of the book. I was ecstatic! I couldn't wait to tell Jane and Misty! When I did, though, I was surprised by their reactions. Neither one seemed that excited. Jane acted kind of scared. I understood that because baring one's life to the world can be daunting, especially when those details affect the whole family. When I asked her if she wanted to continue the project, she said yes. Misty did, too. However, both became increasingly distant from that point on. They stopped attending the presentations that we were giving about the book. The pressure from that worry made my anxiety ten times worse. In addition, I knew that the book wasn't ready for an agent to read! Firstly, I hadn't expected to land my first choice, and secondly, I hadn't thought he would respond within days! But he had, so the tension about the book continued to build. I began spending every waking hour on it. When I wasn't doing that, I was with Randy, my family members, My Friend, or the Quilters. But I was rapidly sinking into a cold, muddy well because I was still only sleeping two or three hours a night. My mind constantly raced about the book and my codependent friendship.

And then, on September 29th, 2012, I truly hit rock bottom.

My Friend, her daughter, and a friend of her daughter's named Hope* went with me that day to the River City Rodeo in Omaha, Nebraska. I had arranged for a private backstage tour that afternoon through an acquaintance who served on the rodeo board. The tour was just for us, so I knew it would make the girls feel special.

My Friend lived in the country, so I met the three women near her house, where the highway met her country road. She parked her pickup, then she, her daughter, and Hope got in my car. I commented on their hair because they had clearly been to a salon that morning. My Friend thanked me for noticing, but didn't even look at me. I asked her a few questions and she answered, but her answers were short and curt. *Oh God, please don't let her do this today*, I thought. *Not in front of Hope.* The two-hour ride to Omaha was uncomfortable. My Friend acted like she didn't even want to be there. She answered questions when asked, but never turned to look at me, and didn't ask me anything or start a conversation.

When we got to the Quest Center in Omaha (now the CHI Health Convention Center), we were whisked away on a "mule" vehicle, for our private tour. The three girls sat in the back, which was like the bed of a short pickup, but I was too heavy and infirm to climb back there, so I rode in the double seat up front. The driver took us out behind the arena, to stables that corralled horses that were each worth hundreds of thousands of dollars. The problem was, other than a few fleeting moments, My Friend and her daughter completely ignored me. They called after Hope by name, and said things like, "Come look at this, Hope," or "Look at that over there, Hope," but left me out of the excitement and conversations. I was completely frozen out of everything. My Friend took pictures of the other two and included me once when I just happened to be standing in the frame. Other than that, I felt unwanted there, like an intruder. Hurt and uncomfortable, I just kept trying to be involved. I felt and looked desperate and pathetic.

In between the tour and the rodeo, we all went to Texas Roadhouse for a late afternoon lunch. My Friend and her daughter continued to leave me out of conversations and didn't look at me when I spoke. Both answered questions when asked, but stared straight ahead. The air was so cold that I could've hung meat. Hope squirmed in her seat across from me. She was clearly uneasy, too. I was frozen out again. Why? I didn't understand! My Friend and I had had an amazing week, and I had given her some money to help her pay some bills! What was I doing wrong? My heart raced. My thoughts buzzed in my head like a chainsaw. I became hot and angry.

When we went back to the Quest Center that night for the rodeo, My Friend acted like she hated being in the same room with me, so the air around us was stifling. I asked her privately what the problem was, and she told me that she didn't feel good, but also said that her son had called and wanted her to babysit that night.

"I had to tell him 'No' because I had to come here with you," she said. So that was why she was being so cold? She was pissed that she "had to" be at the rodeo when she could have been babysitting her granddaughter? I offered to take her home then, so she could babysit.

"I'll just drive back up to get the girls," I said.

"That's ridiculous," she said, hatefully.

While waiting for the arena to open, we all sat on chairs outside the main doors, and for the most part, the two younger girls talked to each other while My Friend stared straight ahead. I sat beside her, fuming. *You don't deserve this*, the voice in my head said. *She is ungrateful for everything you do for her. You just gave her a lot of money. You bought tickets to this event and arranged for a wonderful private tour. And she has treated you like crap.* I was seething. I felt like her behavior was totally unacceptable, but I was so deep into the relationship that I was willing to do *anything* to please her. But my self-esteem and pride were constantly ripped to shreds.

As I thought about the afternoon, anger pulsed through my veins. My chest felt heavy, like I was watching helplessly while someone beat a child. I couldn't breathe. I knew I was in trouble. I needed something to relax, so I downed a Hydrocodone. Then, as the girls took their seats in the arena, I guzzled a few beers in the concourse. I was so upset that I couldn't think straight. Thoughts from the past couple of years twirled in my head. I was dizzy with anger. I didn't know what to do about it either. I knew I needed to stand up for myself, but also knew, if I did, My Friend would cut me out of her life like she'd done twice before. The thought of that was unbearable.

Unable to think or reason clearly, I bought another eight-dollar beer at the concession stand, then walked down the steps to our seats and took my spot on the aisle. Hope was seated next to me, My Friend's daughter was on the other side of her, then My Friend sat on the other end. She obviously didn't even want to sit by me. The girls all talked to each other during the parade of horses, and Hope tried to include me, but the other two kept me out. I was enraged. I couldn't get any air into my lungs. My thoughts screamed at me. *Stand up for yourself! She is treating you like an outcast, and you're taking it! Enough is enough!* My neck throbbed unbearably. I started to panic. The arena closed in on me. I couldn't breathe! I needed help! I had to get out!

I asked Hope if she could drive my car home and told her I was "getting out." I felt like I was going to pass out. The anger was unlike anything I had ever felt before. I didn't just want to hit My Friend. I wanted to pound her face into the concrete floor until blood squirted from her head. But, in the very next second, I wanted to beg for her forgiveness for whatever I had done to upset her. I was so conflicted that I felt like I was losing my mind. It was the worst feeling I'd ever had, including the overdose in the hospital a few years prior. I was certain that I was dying. The feeling of impending doom was over-whelming. I had to get away. I got up and stomped up the steps to-ward the concourse. The incline was steep, and I struggled to breathe, so I stopped on the middle landing. My heart squeezed in my chest. Panicking and severely out of shape, I tried to take a deep breath, but couldn't. *You're going to die!* my thoughts roared. *You're having a heart attack!* If it wasn't a heart attack, then it was a nervous breakdown. I was sweating profusely. My whole body shook. In severe trouble, I turned around to see what was happening with the girls. Deep down inside, I thought My Friend would come after me to see why I was so upset. However, I watched in disbelief as she, her daughter, and Hope chattered away about my leaving, then moved over one seat, so Hope was on the aisle in my seat, and the other two were next to her. My Friend looked totally pissed, like she wanted me to stay away.

Completely distraught, I shook with broken sobs. Tears streamed down my face, and I fought even harder to catch my breath. I had nev-er cried like that before, not even when my dad had died, and he was a man I had (and still) deeply loved. I felt so broken. I stumbled out to the concourse, devastated yet seething. How could anyone be so cruel?

Suddenly, I felt like I'd been whacked in the chest with a sledge-hammer. The pain was intense and unbearable. I leaned against the rail near the escalator and felt my stomach lurch. Acid scorched my throat and anger burned my face. My heart pounded. The knife of My Friend's indifference punctured my very soul. Sweat beaded on my cheeks and forehead. I knew for sure then that I was having a heart at-tack, but if I called 911, My Friend would think I was being dramatic just to get attention. I was in such a bad place mentally and emotion-ally that her opinion mattered more to me than my own life. I stood there, hanging onto the rail, and felt like someone had buried me alive, and the perp had placed a small pipe into the shallow grave, just to make sure my terror lasted as long as possible.

I hurried down the steps near the escalator then, and through the con-vention center into the dampness of the evening air, hoping I would be able to breathe outside. I waddled to my car, sobbing, then vomited in the parking lot, near some poor sap's passenger door. I wiped my mouth off, cried uncontrollably, and raged inside. My thoughts crashed into each other like demo derby cars. What was I going to do!? I was losing it. I had never been so angry in my life. *How can she treat me this way after everything I've done for her? All the places I've taken her and her daughter? All the money I've given her?* I knew I shouldn't think that way. I had willingly helped her financially, and the only thing I had expected in return was kindness. Sometimes I got it in abundance. Other times, not at all. I couldn't calm my racing thoughts. My chest continued to tighten. The veins in my neck popped out like earthworms. I was in certain peril, but still refused to call 911. I decided I would rather die and let someone find me face down on the parking lot. Still, my anger and brokenness continued to stoke the flames of a rage I'd never felt before. And it scared me. I wanted to pull My Friend's hair out and throw her to the ground, then jump on her until she struggled to breathe, just like I was struggling. I knew I would never actually do that, but right then, I wanted to. At the very least, I wanted to leave her and her daughter there and let them find their own rides home. Yet, I knew she would never speak to me again if I did that. Besides, Hope would be stuck in the middle, and she didn't deserve that. She hadn't done anything wrong. I was sure she just felt trapped. I knew if I stayed there and waited for the girls in the parking lot, though, I would either die of a heart attack, have to confront the situation, or do what I normally did and act like none of it had ever happened. Option number three would make my pride and self-esteem plummet even further than they already had, and I didn't know if I could survive that.

I paced behind my car, and felt prickles of rage rise up on the back of my neck. The pain in my chest was excruciating then. I got in the car and tried to take a deep breath. My lungs would not expand. I got out of the car, felt my stomach lurch, then looked around to see if anyone rushing to the arena would stop to help me. No one looked my way. No one had looked my way since I'd gained nearly one hundred pounds. I felt like the poster child for the invisible fat woman.

There was a Hilton Hotel across the street, so I hoisted my puffy body that direction, where I intended to clean myself up in the restroom. I walked in the lounge door and saw people in fancy clothes sitting around on couches and chairs, drinking foofoo drinks and chatting as if none of them had a care in the world. No one looked my way. Couldn't they see that I was in distress? Couldn't they see the tears streaming down my face? *Someone please help me! Can't you see that I'm having a heart attack?* I wanted to ask for help but knew he or she would call an ambulance, and I worried that My Friend would think I was just being needy and desperate. Besides, I felt as crazy as I looked. I went to the bathroom, washed my face, scrubbed my teeth with my finger, then walked back out to the car. My head pounded and my vision blurred.

Throughout the two-hour show, I sobbed, vomited, panicked, and felt like I was dying. I couldn't take a deep breath to save my soul. Yet, no one called or came to check on me.

When the rodeo was over, Hope called and asked where I was. I told her that I had gotten sick and was by the car. She and the other two came out then, and Hope expressed concern for me, but the other two didn't. I told My Friend that I couldn't drive home, so she drove, and I rode in the passenger seat. She stopped at Taco Bell in Council Bluffs, Iowa, for a late supper, so she and the girls went into the restaurant and sat down and ate. Although I knew that Hope had to go along with anything the other two did, I felt like my condition and feelings were of no concern. I sobbed while I watched them through the restaurant windows, my heart shattered to pieces. When they were all done eating, I wiped the tears off my cheeks and tried to pull myself together. They climbed back in the car, and we headed back to Falls City. As soon as we hit the interstate, I pretended to be asleep. The car was quiet the entire two-hour trip home. I felt like I was in hell. All I wanted was for my Friend to apologize for the way she had treated me, but all I heard was silence. When we got back to her vehicle, I apologized for my OWN behavior.

My Friend said, "It was kind of a bummer of a day all the way around." That was it. No apologies for freezing me out and treating me like crap. No nothing. She did ask if I needed Hope to drive me home, though. I had to give her credit for that. But why Hope? Why couldn't she drive me home? I left her and the girls with her truck and drove

myself home, sobbing the whole way. Randy was staying the night at
the cabin we had built on our family farm, so I knew I didn't have to
worry about him seeing me. I continued to cry after taking my bedtime
medicines, which included another Hydrocodone, then Xanax, and
Ambien, just to see if any of it would help me sleep. It didn't. I paced
around my living room, seething, and was awake the whole night with
a pounding headache and racing heart.

The next day, I called My Friend and left a message on her answer-
ing machine. I told her I wanted to talk about the way she had treated
me. When she called back two days later, I hadn't slept more than four
hours, total. I was exhausted and emotionally distraught.

She said, "If I'm such a bad person, then I'm ending this. Besides,
spending time with you is getting in the way of things that I want and
need to be doing." I knew I would never forget those words, ever. They
slit me from throat to waist, then pulled my heart out and stomped on it.

I said, "How can you cut me out of your life after everything we
have been through?"

"It's easy for me," she said, coldly. I had thought that her behavior
at the rodeo would be the most painful thing that would ever happen
in our friendship, but I was wrong. Telling me—point blankly—that
it was easy to cut me out of her life was the most painful thing anyone
had ever said to me. Ever. I was devastated. I walked around the house
in a trance, sobbing uncontrollably. Because of the drugs, the pressure
from the book, my sleeplessness, and the situation with her, I was in
such a bad place that I wanted to take my own life. I knew I had bottles
of Hydrocodone, Xanax, Ambien, antidepressants, and much more in
my cupboards, and at least a case of beer in the three refrigerators in the
house. All I had to do was swallow all of the pills and drink all the beer,
and I could end this emotional hell. I would never have to feel this way
again, ever. I knew I couldn't survive this. I couldn't. It would take too
much work, and I didn't have the strength to get through it. I would
fall too many times. I would be in the pit of depression every day and
never climb out. I had chased after that soul-to-soul relationship my
entire life. I had to have it. I had to have the spark that it gave me, the

little girl giggles, and the deep connection that made me feel alive.

I got my Hydrocodone out of my purse, then walked to the bathroom and opened the cupboard. Bottles of pills stared back at me. There they were. My comfort, my peace, my final resting place. Tears streamed down my cheeks as I gathered all of the bottles and set them on the counter. I turned around and looked at myself in the mirror. My face was puffy, blotched, and bloated. My eyes were red, wet, and crazed. My blue plaid sweatpants and gray, size 2X T-shirt hid a body that I no longer recognized. I was way beyond fixable.

"I'm not worth it," I whispered. "I just want it all to stop." And I decided then to end it. I opened the Hydrocodone bottle and dumped all of the pills into my hand. I knew there were still forty pills left. That would be enough to start. Slowly, I looked back up at the mirror, and I saw Cassie's eyes in mine. I thought about her and my family. If I ended my life, my daughter would not survive it. She had a wonderful boyfriend and a beautiful future ahead of her, but my death would end all of it. She adored me. I was her rock, her confidante, her best friend. How could I do this to her? How could I do it to my wonderful husband, who had remained steadfast in his support of me and anything I pursued? How could I do it to our other two children, both of whom I loved like my own? And my grandsons? How could I do it to them? To my mother, who called me her "rock?" How could I do it to my sister? Brothers? The Quilters? My other true friends? How could I consider ending my own life because one person—one person who was even more broken than I was—had ended our friendship?

I knew *then* that I was sick. I knew then what Bob Kohles had meant when he'd said I wouldn't be here in a year. I wanted to take my own life just because things were falling apart around me, and that was frightening. I had finally hit rock bottom. I knew I had to change the pattern of my life, or I wasn't going to make it. The situation—the painkillers, relationship, book, everything I was doing to myself and allowing to be done to me—was all going to kill me. I needed help and I needed it immediately. I knew that the only place I could start was with the painkillers. They had changed my personality completely.

I had no pride anymore. I didn't know who I was, didn't have the strength to say enough was enough. I couldn't think clearly, so I didn't have the perception of reality to see what was happening, or what I was doing! I knew that My Friend's behavior was unacceptable, but she was a broken soul, too. Plus, I was culpable in our relationship, as well. I was obsessed with making her life easier, with doing whatever it took to make her happy. I was sure she just felt smothered sometimes.

In addition to that heartache, my obsession with the book consumed me. Jane, Misty and I had worked on it for three years, and had given motivational presentations all over the region, but my contact with them had lessened substantially. I was afraid they were getting cold feet. So, I knew I needed help to break those chains as well. But I couldn't do any of that until I had a clear mind, and I wouldn't have a clear mind as long as I was taking painkillers and a wide variety of other drugs and drowning them all with beer. I didn't know how to get started, though, and thought that the only answer was an inpatient detox center. I knew several people who had gone to a nearby rehab facility for alcohol and/ or drug detox and counseling, so I figured I might as well start there. The rehabilitation center (hereinafter called The Center*) had a good statistical rate of success, so I researched it online, and saw that it had a "medically monitored" detox ward, which was exactly what I needed. If I was going to go through anything like I'd gone through in the hospital, I wanted an IV in my arm, and a nurses' call button beside me. I didn't have a clue what to expect, but knew that I would probably be as sick as I'd ever been in my life. I hoped that the sickness would only last a few days, and then I would start counseling. I had no idea what the whole experience would look like, but I did know that I had a long road ahead of me. I had to walk it or I wasn't going to make it. I firmly believed that I would die if I didn't get help, but that wasn't my biggest fear. My biggest fear was that I would continue to live the way I was.

At that very moment, I made the decision. I either had to change my life or lose it. I knew if I chose to change it, I would be in for the fight of my life, and a fight FOR my life. And, when faced with the reality of my own death, I finally had the desire to live.

Chapter Two

The Wednesday after My Friend cut me out of her life, I called The Center and reserved a bed in the detox ward. Surprisingly, I was able to get in that Friday, so I knew I had to tell my family members. I told Randy first, of course. He was my husband and constant support. Telling him was very difficult, though, because I hated crying in front of people—even my own husband. I just didn't want to show any weakness. But I knew I needed help, and I wanted his support so I could get it. I was totally relieved after I told him the whole story. Randy was, too. He'd watched my health deteriorate for twelve years, and had really wanted to intervene, but he'd been afraid to do so. The few times that he had broached the subject of my painkillers, I'd completely shut him down. I didn't think I had a problem! I appreciated his support so much. He loved me beyond measure, and I just hoped that, after I finished the thirty days at The Center, I would come home with a renewed sense of self and a new purpose for my life. He deserved that. Quite frankly, I had been a pretty crappy wife since I'd hurt my back more than a decade prior. I simply never felt good anymore. But also, I hadn't opened up to him about the ordeal through which I was going. I didn't think he would understand any of it—the constant pain, the pills, alcohol, the crushing blow when My Friend cut me out of her life. He would probably understand an addiction to work because he himself was a workaholic. That was how I had hidden most of my anguish. He was simply gone all the time. Other than that "flaw," he had his life together. He was successful, confident, and assured. If he thought someone had mistreated him, he would walk away and not look back. I wished I had that kind of confidence.

After I told him, I called Cassie, Todd, Shanda, and the rest of my family. Cassie said she was proud of me, and would do whatever she could to help. Todd and Shanda, and the rest of my family members, including my mom, were equally supportive. I didn't tell them about My Friend because I knew they wouldn't understand. I just told them that I had a problem with painkillers and needed to do something about it. All of them knew about my back pain, of course, but most thought that something else was going on, as well. I'd become a distant hermit who spent most of her time in the house. When I told them that I had to battle the painkillers, all of them were happy that I was going to face my demons.

That night, I gathered the Quilters together and told them. Most had no idea that I was still taking Hydrocodone, but knew that something was "off." I wasn't myself anymore. I looked like a different person. I had gained weight to the point of popping like a balloon. My personality had been completely altered, too. The Quilters all cried and offered unconditional support. I had known that they would because they were wonderful, caring friends. In addition, our group had lost our friend Karen just two years prior, and the women didn't want to lose another friend. Karen, a vivacious, caring woman, had died in an accident, and I didn't want to die of an accidental overdose. I was gradually drinking more and sleeping less, (even though I was taking a sleeping pill), waking up in the middle of the night to take a painkiller, and overall, just becoming miserable, overweight, and out of control. I needed to make some changes before one of my abuses ultimately killed me.

The morning after I told the Quilters, I told a friend named Jerry Joy, who was running for state senator. I was helping with his campaign. I was his sounding board, one of the people with whom he shared his ideas and frustrations. I helped with his media platform, too. I knew that I would have to abandon him in his final month, and I felt guilty about it. Jerry said he understood my decision, but I could hear the disappointment in his voice. I felt like a heel, but for the first time in my life, I had to put myself first.

The last person I told that day was a friend from Omaha named Lisa Roskens. We had met through a mutual friend, Mike Kelly, who wrote feature articles for the Omaha World Herald, the state's largest newspaper. Mike had done a story about the *Misty* book, and Lisa, an equestrian, had contacted him afterward. He'd then introduced her to Jane, Misty, and me.

Lisa had become a confidante, an adored and trusted friend. Because our lives were busy, she and I only communicated via email, but that was the way both of us wanted it. However, we communicated a lot, about a wide variety of subjects, and one of them was the fact that I needed help. She told me to stick it out at The Center, and to let go of anyone who didn't support me. Her encouragement was crucial to my decision.

That night, (Thursday), I met the Quilters for a drink out at Lem's, our local hangout. We smacked on chicken wings and toasted Karen, whose birthday would've been that day. She had lived and breathed her family and the Quilter group, and I missed her terribly. The Quilters had a few drinks, and I had my four beers, then we all went outside to say our goodbyes. The weather was cold for October—fifty-three degrees—but crisp. Just the way I liked it. I was so out of shape and full of toxins that the cool air was refreshing. As we stood in the parking lot, we all cried. Everyone knew that I was headed into inevitable sickness, so saying goodbye was difficult. The big pink elephant in the center of our circle was the knowledge that one of us would enter her darkest hours the next day. We hugged each other, said "I love you," and headed off to our respective homes.

When I got home, I left a message on Jane's voicemail, telling her my plans, and that I was going to send the book to our agent before I left. Then, I prepared the *Misty* book to email. I knew it was too long, but felt like I had no other option. As the email uploaded, I organized a package to send to My Friend. It included some items that she had left at my house. I also enclosed a letter detailing where I would be and why. I didn't know if she cared or not and feared that she didn't, but I wanted her to know anyway.

Later that night, I started packing my suitcase for my voluntary trip to hell.

Chapter Three

The next day was Friday, October 5, 2012. Entering drug rehab was not at all what I wanted to do that day. On a typical Friday, I would have gotten up at 7:00 a.m., read the Omaha World Herald, and jumped in my Endless Pool to splash around for a while. Randy and I had purchased the pool in 2005, as part of my rehabilitation for my back. I was only forty-four at the time, but several doctors had told me that I would be in a wheelchair by the time I was fifty if I didn't get some exercise and therapy. All of them recommended swimming, so Randy and I had bought a pool. It was inside the house, eighteen feet long, and had a current against which I could swim. It was the best thing I'd ever had in my life. Prior to 2012, though, I had only played around in it. I hadn't seriously exercised. I'd become a victim of my back pain, and honestly a victim of victimhood. I had thought I was too infirm to work out hard. I was scared to death of reinjuring myself. So, I'd just gone through the motions.

Usually, after I got out of the pool, I worked on my book the rest of the day. When I needed breaks, I did laundry, went to lunch with someone, answered phone calls from Jerry about the campaign, answered calls from Cassie, my husband, my Quilter BFF Linda, my mom, sometimes my sister, and anybody else who needed me for some reason. But that day, I was packing a large suitcase for drug rehab.

It was black canvas, and as big as I'd ever carried. I would be staying for thirty days, though, so I packed clothes, magazines, hair products, over-the-counter medications, and even a swimming suit, in case the place had a pool for exercise.

My anxiety level as I packed was astronomical because I thought about being away from my life for a month—my husband and family, home, and friends (including My Friend). My racing thoughts just compounded my nervousness. I also became increasingly worried that I would go through the horror that I'd gone through in the hospital. I knew I would be terribly sick, but feared that I would have seizures and convulsions. While attempting to mentally prepare for that torture, I thought about my PTSD. Surely the compassionate people at a drug and alcohol rehab center would understand my claustrophobia. Surely, they would take my condition into consideration. Surely.

My husband came home for lunch at noon, and amidst my nervousness, began talking about a robbery and shooting that had happened a week prior at the Sun Mart store in Fargo, North Dakota.

A note here about my husband—Randy was (and is) a good and honorable man. He worked harder than anyone I had ever known, had an excellent business mind, and loved being a grocery man. But he was reared on a farm in the "olden days" when a man's life revolved around work and providing for his family. Occasionally, the man took time off to do things he enjoyed. Meanwhile, his wife took care of the family and household. That was how Randy's relationship with me worked. He was a good provider for our family, worked his tail off and made a very nice living. I did everything else.

Our grocery store could be very frustrating at times—like the time that Randy got paged to the customer service counter because a middle-aged man at the counter was enraged. The checker wouldn't cash the man's five-hundred-dollar personal check.

Randy looked at the records on the computer and said to the man, "You've written several bad checks here. If you want this one cashed, you'll have go to the bank."

"They know there's no money in that account!" the man shouted.

"Are you going to cash it or not?" Randy bit the insides of his cheeks and passed the check back to the guy.

"No, sir, I'm sure not," he said, trying not to laugh. The man stomped out while calling him every name in the devil's camp.

Whenever Randy came home for lunch or for the night, he shared stories like that one. He needed someone to whom he could vent. As I packed my suitcase for rehab, though, I was already having trouble focusing. However, he told me all about the robbery, and I tried hard to listen. Apparently, the store manager and an assistant were both taken into the cooler during the hold-up attempt, and were told to get down on their knees. (This helped my anxiety tremendously). When they followed the robber's demands, the manager saw the assailant's gun right above his head. He knew then that he and the assistant were about to be shot, so he swung back and clobbered the robber, but the thief shot him in the leg and arm. The distraction was enough that the robber fled, leaving the woman shaken, and the manager injured but alive.

The manager was getting married that day—the day that I had decided to change my life. He was at his wedding, in a wheelchair. Still, it had to have been the best day of his life because he was alive and able to leave the hospital long enough to get married, despite a tremendous trauma. Meanwhile, I was experiencing one of the worst days of my life. I tried to pay attention to the story, but felt like I was in a stalled elevator. I wanted to tell my husband that, "just for today, I can't listen to stories that have nothing to do with me." As usual, though, I didn't say a word. I listened politely and acted interested. But my skin was jumping.

Before Randy left to go back to the store, he loaded my suitcase into my car. Afterward, he came back in, hugged and kissed me, told me he was proud, then rode off to face customers who were ninety-nine percent honest and decent, and one percent frustrating. I didn't tell him often enough, but I was so very grateful for him.

I postponed leaving Falls City as long as I could. I emailed my agent a synopsis and the first several chapters of my second book—a novel. I wanted him to know that I was as serious about my next book as I was about the first. Then, I did laundry, washed the dishes that had piled up in the sink, and packed some more clothes in a small carry-on. I went to Shopko and picked up a few travel-size items, then said, "Yeah," when one of the clerks asked if I was going on another trip somewhere. It was true; I was.

When I couldn't postpone my departure any longer, I drove twenty miles south of town to Hiawatha, Kansas, then drove around there. A rippling canopy of rusts, browns, and reds from the oak and maple trees waved in the breeze. The scene looked like a movie set, and the irony of that moment hit me between the eyes. I was in a beautiful place where crisp leaves crunched beneath my tires, and a light warm breeze blew through the window. Yet, I was also headed toward the most traumatic battle of my life. It was as real as a story got.

I went to Walmart, where I picked up a few pairs of sweatpants, for comfort not good looks, then I downed a Quarter Pounder at McDonald's, and took off for The Center.

Forty minutes later, I realized I was lost in Lancaster, Kansas, population 291. I thought I was in the town where The Center was located, but tiny Lancaster was not that place, so I called The Center's office to get directions. The lady who answered the phone soon figured out that I was in the wrong town, so she patiently told me how to get where I needed to be, and chuckled when she told me to call back if I couldn't find my way out of Lancaster. Then, I drove as slowly as speed limits allowed, toward The Center, where I *hoped* I would find myself again.

When I pulled into the parking lot, I opened the console in my car, took a Hydrocodone out of the bottle, melted the pill in my water bottle, and downed it. (I could no longer swallow pills after I watched my dad struggle to swallow while he battled esophageal cancer.) I was postponing withdrawal symptoms as long as humanly possible. I stashed the bottle of pills back in the console. I didn't know if having the meds in my car was against the rules or not, but figured it probably was. Still, I wasn't giving up my safety net. If The Center didn't take care of me, and I went through the sheer panic and convulsions that I had experienced in the hospital, I wanted to know where my out was.

I wanted to know that I was in control of my fate.

The wave of painkiller satisfaction soothed my mind, then I looked up at The Center. It was old red brick, with a few separate buildings out back made of yellowish brick. Everything was tucked behind a few trees, back away from the street, and it just felt eerie—like a secret lab for mad scientists. I got out of the car to check things out and smelled cigarette smoke permeating the air. It was like the buildings were standing in the corner at a junior high party, stoking on cigs and yanking their pants up as Jimmy bragged about feeling up his girlfriend. I asked a smoker to point me toward the admissions office, and that was exactly what he did. As I walked over there, I looked to my left at a gathering area outside. Several smokers took drags on their cigarettes in what was apparently the smoking section. Nobody out there looked like me. Well, that wasn't true. Most looked like the younger me—like I had looked when I was in my early twenties. Back then, before I'd had Cassie, I had bounced from college to various jobs, including a bartending gig at Big Daddy's, one of the bars in my hometown. The owner, Big Daddy, was a bear of a man, but a teddy bear at heart. He actually encouraged me to drink on the job if someone wanted to buy me a beer.

"Don't ever turn down a drink," he said. "If someone buys you a beer, they'll stay and drink with you." So, when that happened, I accepted it. I just sipped on the beer, though. I worked eight-hour shifts, sometimes doubles! I had to be able to get through them standing up! However, when I got off work, I chugged, even if it was midnight. I got tipsy or downright drunk nearly every night, and nursed a hangover every morning. Even so, I left Auburn at 7:30 a.m. to drive the eleven miles to Peru State College in Peru, Nebraska, just in time for my 8:00 a.m. class.

Back at that time, I'd worn hip clothes, too, and in the throes of my daily hangovers, looked spent, disheveled, and depleted. Many of the kids in the smoking section at The Center looked the same. They were just starting (and screwing up) their lives. A few looked like they'd just come from classes at a college. Some looked like they'd been traveling with the carnival during the summer, and others looked like dead people walking. Those were the serious street-level addicts. That knowledge hit my panic button. *I will never fit in here!* I thought. I'd never even met a serious drug addict (or so I thought). The way I felt wasn't a feeling of superiority either. It was one of isolation—of being excluded, of not being accepted. It had been a long time since I'd faced the types of problems that most of my fellow rehabbers probably dealt with daily. How would I ever get along here? Nobody would accept me! Once again, my own feelings of inferiority shot up like a thermometer in a sick toddler's mouth. And I was at drug rehab!

As I walked into the office, I looked up at the ladies behind the counter. One was a tall blonde with cat-rimmed glasses, and another was a squatty lady with shoulder-length hair that was too black for her age and pale complexion. Both could tell I was nervous, so they were very nice, warm, and welcoming.

The blonde said, "So, you're the one who got lost in Lancaster?" When the black-haired lady walked over to the counter, she said the same thing. Both laughed, so I chuckled nervously. I commented that, for the next thirty days, I would be known as "the one who got lost in Lancaster." The blonde then led me back to the office of Admissions Representative, LaTonya, a beautiful black woman with a compassionate face.

"So, you're the one who got lost in Lancaster?" LaTonya asked. I nodded and smiled. She had my file in front of her, and had already filled out my name and address on the "permission to treat" form. She pointed at a chair, so I sat down. LaTonya then turned to her computer.

"How long have you been using?" she asked.

"Six years this last time," I said. "I was on the meds for six years, weaned down to one a day over several months, then hurt my back and was right back on them for another six years."

"So, actually, twelve years," she said, matter-of-factly. "Have you ever been suicidal?"

"I've thought about it, but would never do it," I said, thinking about my mental state a few days prior. I was sure she had heard that answer dozens of times. Nope, not dozens; hundreds.

"What is your drug of choice?"

"Hydrocodone."

"Opiates," she said, as she typed it into her computer. I shrugged. I guess I had never thought of it that way. Opiates were for drug addicts. Hydrocodone sounded more medicinal. And what was this "choice" bullshit? Honestly, if it was a choice, would I be here? She should've asked, "What is the drug you're chained to?"

"When was the last time that you 'used'?" she said.

"On my way down here," I replied. I didn't want her to know that I had popped a pill in the parking lot. That would make me look like a drug addict.

"What about alcohol, Lori? Do you drink?" she asked.

"I have to admit, I used to drink quite a bit," I said. "Now, I limit myself to four beers when I go out with friends. A couple nights a week." That was an outright lie, but I knew if I said I drank those four beers nearly every night, she would think I was an alcoholic, and I absolutely was not going there. "Wait a sec," I said, already feeling guilty about the lie. "I've been drinking more often lately because of some problems with a friend, but I never drink more than four in one night." She nodded, but had that "Uh huh, sure" look on her face.

I answered everything else as honestly as possible and showed little emotion other than tremendous nervousness. Before we finished, we had to move to another location because the office closed at 5:00 p.m., so LaTonya led me over to the detox building. The word "detox" scared the crap out of me. I couldn't even say it. On our way, we walked by the small group of seven or eight people in the smoking area, and I noticed again that they all looked like high school kids, hip and smoking, dressed in tight jeans and tennis shoes. Nobody looked like me.

When we entered the detox building, I discovered that it was the "everything" building. Other than the sleeping quarters for those who were going through detox, it was the gathering place. Off to the right was an area with cushioned, high-backed chairs at the perimeter of the room. There were three couches in the middle, in a U shape, and all three were pointed toward the only television set. A pool table sat off to its right. LaTonya said that the classrooms were directly behind the pool table, along with a conference room and a library. To my left was the detox ward. It started with a nurses' station where people scurried about, and friendly faces looked out over the gathering area.

I wrung my hands as I stared down the hallway to the left of the receptionist. There were several closed doors back there, marked A, B, C, and so forth. The doors frightened me because I knew there were sick people behind them, so I glanced back at the gathering room. The thing I noticed about it was that nothing was fresh or new. The carpet was stained and filthy, and reeked of cigarettes. The cushioned chairs, the same. My skin started jumping, and my panic button lit up like a tornado siren. *Run, run, run!* my mind said. I took deep breaths and tried to calm my racing heart. *Don't panic. Don't panic! The 'medically monitored' detox facility will be an actual hospital room, where you'll be hooked up to an IV, given a call button, and treated with care and compassion.* I looked again at the nurses' station, and noticed that most of the staff members were dressed unprofessionally. Some were in dress pants and nice shirts, but most wore T-shirts, sweatshirts, and jeans or sweatpants. I didn't want to be judgmental but couldn't help it. *The staff doesn't even dress professionally! Do they know what they're doing? Am I safe here?* My anxiety skyrocketed.

LaTonya took me into the detox office, where I answered the rest of her questions. Then Lacy, a nurse dressed in dark brown pants and a light brown top, came to check me in. She weighed me in at 210 pounds, another painful admission. When this whole thing with my back started, I'd weighed 120 pounds, and was trim and fit. Then, I'd packed on weight like a hog in a feed lot. At my highest weight a few weeks prior, I had reached 216 pounds. I felt like such a failure! I couldn't even bend over to pick something up off the floor, whether standing or sitting down. My stomach had multiple rolls and my T-shirt got stuck in those rolls all the time. I constantly had to pull at my shirt! And I hated it!

Lacy looked at me like I wasn't focusing, so I turned my attention back to her. She asked many of the same questions that LaTonya had just asked, and I gave the same answers, specifically about my overdose in the hospital. When we finished, she described the detox process.

"When you feel jittery or nauseous, we can't see that," she said. "You'll have to tell us. Just come down to the nurses' station and ask us to take your blood pressure. Then we can give you all sorts of meds—things like antianxiety medication, sleeping pills, Maalox. In twenty-four hours, we can give you Suboxone, which is an opiate substitute that will help with your withdrawal symptoms." Wow! That didn't sound at all like what I had expected. I had to go *to* the nurses instead of them coming to me, and I didn't really understand why, but I guess I had no choice. All I cared about anyway was that I wasn't going to go through the horrific trauma that I had experienced in the hospital. What a relief! I felt my shoulders actually loosen. Lacy said, "Don't let me kid you. You're going to be sick. But it's not going to be like it was then." *Hot damn!*

When we were done, two other nurses in dress pants and nice shirts took my personal items, which I was no longer allowed to keep—my iPad, allergy shots, over-the-counter medications, and much to my horror, car keys.

"Do you really have to take my keys?" I asked. I was fearful then because I knew it would make me feel trapped.

"Yes," Nurse Beth said. "We can't risk that you'll go driving around town during the early withdrawal stages." My shoulders tightened back up. How bad was it going to be if they were worried about me driving during the throes of withdrawal? I tried to remain calm. I didn't want to give myself away before I even started having symptoms! Beth snapped on a pair of rubber gloves, then she and the other nurse went through my things. The Transportation Security Administration (TSA) needed to take lessons from the nurses at The Center. Those women did everything but rip open the seams on my jeans. They went through every pocket in my clothes and every hidey-hole in my suitcase. I felt like a high school kid with a suspicious backpack. If I'd had anything hidden in there, I would've been sent to the principal's office for sure.

"You didn't bring any opiates onto the property with you, right?"

the other nurse said, nonchalantly. I mulled that question over in my head. Surely by "property," she meant "the buildings," right? She hadn't meant the parking lot?

I decided to claim a Bill Clinton. I thought about how former President Clinton had looked right at the camera and said, "I did not have sexual relations with that woman," when talking about his sexual relations with White House intern, Monica Lewinsky. What he'd really meant was that he had no intention of ever doing it again. Me either. I had no intention of going to my car to pop a pill, which I could access through the keypad. I was at The Center voluntarily. I was in it to win it. However, the nurses had already taken my keys. I couldn't get away if I wanted to. The pills in my console were my only remaining safety net—my only "out." I knew if anyone took that away, I would panic and rip apart anything that stood in my way. I would do *anything* to avoid that terror. Even lie.

"No," I said, lying directly to her face, as I looked her straight in the eye. I justified my reasoning in my head. My conscience knew I had lied, but my conscience was scared to death of my PTSD. My PTSD could kick the crap out of my conscience.

When the nurses finished man-handling my things, they gave me a plastic cup for a urine sample, then asked Nurse Jamie to take me back to my room. Nurse Jamie was dressed in nice clothes, all in brown. On the way, she told me that I would be sharing my room with three other people. *Say what?* She opened the door and stepped aside. I walked in. The room was dimly-lit, had cold linoleum floors, and was very creepy. Plus, it smelled like an entire community had farted and hurled in there. Actually, I couldn't pin-point the smell. It was like farts mixed with ammonia mixed with vomit mixed with feces mixed with pee. And it was overwhelming. It made me sick to my stomach. The room was also freezing, but that was O.K. with me. As a large post-meno-pausal woman, I liked the air cold. But I knew if there were any "skinny bitches" in there, they were going to be upset.

I glanced around the room then. There was a long wall on the south side, with three twin beds two feet apart, lined up like a ward. A fourth bed was along the short wall. Nothing was hanging on the walls. There were just bed numbers in small letters taped above the beds—1C, 2C, 3C, and 4C—so the surroundings were very stark. Two dressers stood near the only bathroom. I thought, *One bathroom for four women who are all going to be sick at the same time? How can that possibly work?*

I turned to Nurse Jamie and said, "So, if I have diarrhea when someone else is in the bathroom, I just have to go in the trash can?"

She shrugged and said, "I'm new here, but I 'spose.'" *Whaaaaat?* I looked back at my room. This was the detox area? Where were the hospital beds? The IVs? The call buttons for the nurses? I turned again to ask Nurse Jamie, but she had already walked out and closed the door. I knew then that I wasn't in Nebraska anymore.

As I dragged my huge suitcase toward my bed—the last one along the wall, closest to the bathroom (a good thing) but furthest from the door (a bad thing)— I heard the door open. Soft footsteps walked in, so I turned to meet one of my roommates. She was Caucasian, maybe seventeen years old, and anorexically skinny. She had two lip rings and fire-red hair that was swooped up on her head. It stuck out in all directions and was pinned in place with something that resembled a knitting needle. She was fashionably dressed in hip-hop attire—black leggings, a white wifebeater, and a black and pink one over that. Draped over the top was a matching jacket. Although the girl was chicly dressed, she looked downtrodden and pissed that she had to be there. I introduced myself. She said her name was Anna, and I asked her what she was in for.

"I don't want to be here," she said. "I got legal issues. I'm just here so it looks good to the judge. I gotta do this or jail."

"So, will you have to go to jail when you get out?" I asked.

"Fihty-fihty," she said. Not "fifty-fifty," but "fihty-fihty." Then, she pulled out her cell phone and called Pizza Hut for takeout. *You can do that?* I thought. *What if the delivery boy smuggles in drugs?* When she got off the phone, she said, unprompted, "I don't want to be here. I just want to get home to my mom." So much for first impressions and judging a book by its cover. I figured Anna hadn't talked to her mom in a decade. Maybe they lived in the same house, but talk to each other? Nope.

"So, what are you in for, if you don't mind me asking?" I said.

"I don't mind," she replied. "Crystal meth." She'd been busted. I hated to hear it. I knew people who reportedly were on meth, but I didn't know anyone who admitted it. Especially not someone so young!

"Anna, you've got too much of your life ahead of you to be doing that crap," I said. I knew by the look on her face that I had overstepped my bounds. "I'm sorry. I'm in a detox ward at drug rehab. I have no right to judge you."

"No problem," she said. "I don't want to be here. I don't know why I am here. I just want to go home to my mom." *Yeah, you said that.* She lay down on her bed then, so I took my plastic cup to the bathroom and peed in it. I felt like a prisoner starting her jail sentence. I washed my hands and delicately carried the cup down the hallway to the nurses' station, where I turned it over. One of the receptionists asked a patient named Haley to take me on a tour. The first thing I noticed about Haley was her model face. She had porcelain, pinchy skin that looked like a baby's butt—the creamiest I'd ever seen. There wasn't a blemish or freckle anywhere. She also had doe eyes with long silky lashes. Her hair was long and amber, messy chic, pulled up in random places and pinned. That must have been the style of the moment for the fashionable in rehab.

The first room on the tour was the room in which we stood. I had already seen it, of course, but she said it was where the patients gathered in the evenings, and in between classes or lectures. At that time, there was one woman watching the big-screen TV. She looked like she had spent half her life glued to a slot machine. A young buck who looked like Matthew McConnaughey was playing pool, and a few guys with red faces and scraggly beards watched him shoot. I had actually won a few pool tournaments when I was younger, but I knew the guys at The Center would never accept a fat old lady like me around the pool table. Nobody would accept me here.

Haley and I left the TV room and walked into the lecture hall, which was a big classroom with long tables and approximately seventy chairs. The room was dank and smelled like stale smoke and last night's alcohol. The first thing Haley pointed out was the "cup wall," where all of the current patients had hung their painted coffee cups. The cups were lavishly decorated with bright colors, flowers, suns, moons, stick figures, and anything else that my fellow drug abusers and the alcoholics felt like painting to express themselves. Adjacent to that wall was a separate one with nearly forty cups that were half colorful and half black.

"Those are all alumni who have died from their addictions," Haley said. The starkness of that moment took my breath away. The black meant death. Wow.

"They didn't die while they were in here, right?" I asked, only half-jokingly. She chuckled.

"No," she said. *Thank God.*

Haley then showed me two private conference rooms. The first one was as big as a living room, with chairs around the perimeter but nothing else in the room. The second one, which was called "the library," was smaller—about the size of a bedroom. The only thing that made it a library was the wallpaper border, which was designed with books. There wasn't one actual book in sight. I made a mental note to send them mine after it was published so the library had at least one book. Haley and I walked back through the main room then, past the nurses' station, and toward the steps that led to the basement. She asked me what I was in for.

"Opiates," I said. Man, that word was tough for me. I could barely squeeze it out the corner of my mouth.

"Heroin," Haley said, before I asked. I had never met anyone who openly admitted she was a heroin addict. But then I wondered—how could someone so startlingly beautiful destroy her life with heroin? That blew me away. It made me nervous. This young girl with gorgeous skin was a hard-core addict who shot up with needles! I had to say something. I had to take my mind off where I was, or I knew I would bolt.

"I did Hydrocodone for my back," I said, as if that somehow made my reasons better. It wasn't meth or alcohol or heroin. It was a pain-killer. For my back.

"Are you high now?" she asked.

"No. I'm never high. I never take more than the prescribed amount."

You stupid idiot! my mind screamed at me. *This girl's probably thinking, "Yeah, sure. You're bullshitting a heroin addict?"*

She led me downstairs and showed me the washer and dryer for the detox ward. There was also a vending machine with snacks like Snickers candy bars, bite-size cookies, and potato chips, and another machine with pop and bottled water. Then there was the painting station for the coffee cups. I was sick to my stomach as I looked at it. It was a table with blank coffee cups, just waiting for us newbies to make our statements. The thought of wasting precious time painting a stupid coffee cup made me want to hurl. I was certain there were deeper reasons for it, but the logic was lost on me. Back home, I would've been writing a book, helping Jerry with his campaign, spending time with my daughter, or doing something productive. Here, I would be painting a coffee cup? My anxiety hit the roof. I started fidgeting.

Haley took me into the cafeteria then. It was a huge area with dozens of tables, a cereal bar, and a serving table with two bowls of fruit and another bowl filled with creampuffs. Those looked like they had been there most of the day. Maybe two days.

On our way back upstairs, we stopped on the steps for a moment, and Haley looked out the window. She pointed at the separate buildings out back, where residents lived after detox. The rooms in those buildings were all part of the former motel. Looking at them made reality hit me squarely in the heart. Everything was dismal—the place, the moment, the reality, the future. Even the sky needed a fresh coat of paint.

"I feel really bad for you," Haley said.

"Why?" I asked. A heroin addict felt really bad for ME?

"I've been through detox three times—this time for the heroin, but before, for alcohol and once for opiates," she said, "and opiates are the worst. Detox from those is a walk through hell." Then she started back up the steps as if she'd just told me we were going to see Disney on Ice, not that I was going to walk through hell. I stood on the landing and looked out the window. *God?* I thought, as panic set in. *Where are you? Why did you let me sink this low? Why have you forsaken me in this dark and lonely place? How did I get to this point, where I will soon go through the worst detox there is?* I wasn't actually praying. Not REALLY praying. I didn't deserve to talk directly to God. I had abandoned Him three decades prior, so why would He be there for me? I certainly didn't expect Him to be! I knew that He knew my thoughts, though, so I hoped He would read them and take pity on me.

Haley turned around and looked down at me, so I started up the steps. Suddenly, I had a hot flash or panic attack and wanted to run outside. Sweat poured out of my pores. My mind screamed at me to run. *Escape! Escape!* it said. I wanted to bolt! I wanted a Hydrocodone! I wanted a beer! I needed something. I couldn't go through with this! I couldn't! I needed painkillers and alcohol to help me deal with my pain! With my life! I wasn't strong enough to do this! I'd made a mistake. I wanted to go home!

I took several deep breaths and tried to calm myself down. If this young, beautiful girl had done it, then surely I could get through it, too. Couldn't I? But how successful had it been for her? She was apparently back at The Center for the third time!

When we got back to the lobby, I thanked her for the tour, said hello to a few of the other patients, then hurried back to my room, where I hoped I would feel safe. Chilly air blew around the room and felt great on my flushed face. A pretty blonde, about forty-five years old, walked in then. Long and lean with highlighted golden hair, she looked like one of the Desperate Housewives of Somewhere. I introduced myself, and she said her name was Laura. Her hair was swept up like everyone else's and pinned in place. I told her I hadn't gotten the memo about the hair. She told me she loved vodka.

I said, "So, you must be in for alcohol?" *You dumbass,* the voice in my head said. *Here's your frickin' sign.*

"Oh yeah," she said. "I'm on my sixth day of detox, and my second round this year." She said it proudly, like she was a pro at this so I could ask her anything.

"Sixth day?" I asked. She looked like she had just come from the country club.

"Yeah," she said. I asked her why she was still in the detox ward after six days (thinking that it would only last a few), and she said The Center just didn't have enough beds in the regular rooms out back. She was very confident and aloof, which I liked. She was also very forthcoming with her information. I expressed concern about being sick, and she said, "Oh, they'll give you lots of things to help with that." My heart leapt with joy every time someone said that. I walked over to my bed then, and on the way, noticed that a woman around fifty years old was lying in the bed closest to the door, with covers pulled up to her chin. She waved two fingers at me.

"Donna," she said.

"Lori."

"Nice to meet you."

"Let me know if I can get anything for you while you're sick," I said.

"Oh!" she replied, as if no one in her entire life had ever made that offer before. "O.K. Thanks. That's real nice." She lay her head back down and pulled the covers up over her head.

"She's in for meth," Laura whispered. Then she winked and gave me the thumbs down as she headed to the bathroom. I looked at the time on my phone. It was after 6:00 p.m., so it was past time for my Bud Light. I squirmed on the bed and wondered how I was going to get through the next thirty days without my evening bottles of beer. I hadn't really thought about that before pledging to detox! Why did I have to go without beer anyway? I was dependent on prescription drugs, not alcohol! Ugh! Why hadn't I thought this through? I just wanted one beer! And since I couldn't have one, it was worse than a craving for brownies or ice cream or any of the things I loved to eat!

I plugged my computer into an outlet and lay down on top of my thin, blue bedspread. Above my bed was the letter and number that identified my place in rehab. Bed C4. That was how I would be identified for the next several days. Bed C4. I began to type these words. They came rapidly. I let my emotions flow. *This is a hell hole. Everything reeks. I get the feeling that no one is going to take care of me if I get sick. Where is My Friend? Why isn't she calling me? I can't live without her. I can't live without my husband either, and he's been so patient with me and my book. He doesn't know about the debilitating emotions I am feeling, but why do I always keep everything to myself? Why can't I open up to anyone except the one person I know I can't trust with my heart? Why can't I let other people know how much I'm hurting?* Nope. I couldn't go there. Everyone thought I was Superwoman. I was the rock of my family. I was Randy's reason for living. I didn't deserve him. He deserved someone so much better than me. *I don't want to be here. I want to go home.* But I knew I had to stay.

Laura walked out of the bathroom then, and over to her bed. I watched as she climbed in under the covers, fully dressed in her jeans and everything. Even her tennis shoes. I started getting tired so I walked out to the desk and asked if I could get my Hydroxyurea medication, which I took because I had too many platelets in my blood.

The woman behind the desk said, very condescendingly, like she was talking to a spoiled toddler, "Bedtime medicines are given at eight-thirty—every night." She said it like the Wicked Witch of the West, like—*you remember that, you pesky drug addict, and don't you ask me again.* I wasn't even jumpy yet, but wanted to slap her. I wasn't a little kid asking for a cookie before bed. Hydroxyurea wasn't a narcotic. It was a low-dose chemotherapy pill to control my platelets. I should've been able to take it at 5:00 p.m. if I wanted to. But I supposed, to a receptionist with all the power over drug addicts, alcoholics, and pimps and hos (which was how I felt), it was all about popping a pill. I walked away, mentally calling her all the worst names I could conjure. If I had said them out loud, I would've been in "time out" for the night, or even sent home.

Since I couldn't have a beer but desperately wanted one, I needed to keep myself busy, so I decided to find something to eat. I walked over to the steps leading down to the cafeteria, and one of the patients who had overheard my conversation with the receptionist told me that the seasoned patients called her Nurse Ratched, the whacked-out, cold and heartless nurse in the 1975 film, *One Flew Over the Cuckoo's Nest.* So, it wasn't just my imagination then. The woman really didn't belong in the people business.

I walked downstairs and made myself a bowl of Golden Grahams from the cereal bar. The creampuffs were still on the table, so I poked one. It was cold and spongy, not very appetizing. I shrugged and wondered why I'd felt the need to poke it in the first place. I was losing it. I carried my bowl of cereal back up the steps and walked back to my room. I crawled on top of my bed again, chomped on my cereal, and started typing. Donna was passed out across the room, and Anna was sleeping two feet from me. Laura had apparently gone somewhere. The smell in the room made me nauseous, but I tried to ignore it. Several minutes later, I set the empty bowl and my computer down on the floor, then I lay down and fell asleep.

At 9:00 p.m., a nurse stuck her head in the room, and woke me up.

"Roll call is at nine-thirty. Mandatory," she said. I rolled over and couldn't believe the dive I had taken in just thirty minutes. I felt like I had the flu. I had sudden chills, and aches that had no source. My whole body felt like I'd run a marathon. I was so exhausted that it took serious effort to move. I rolled over on my side and noticed that Anna was shaking beneath her covers.

She turned toward the nurse and said, "I don't feel good, and I'm so cold. Could I have a bottle of water?"

The woman said, "You'll have to get that from the vending machine," and without looking back, closed the door. I thought, *What the hell? Are you kidding me? What kind of place is this with nurses who won't even get a kid a bottle of water?*

"I'm sorry, Anna," I said. "I would get it for you, but I don't think I can. I feel like crap."

"Me, too," she said. "I don't want to be here. I want to go home and see my mom." We both lay there silently. She was a child in need, and I couldn't help her. I felt awful. I couldn't ask anyone else to help her either. I'd been completely abandoned. At least I felt that way. And I suspected that Anna felt as alone as she had ever felt in her life, too.

Twenty minutes later, Laura walked in and told us it was time for roll call, so Anna and I literally dragged ourselves out of bed. My feet felt like concrete blocks. My legs were heavy, and heart-attack bloated. I walked as slowly as humanly possible past Donna (who didn't budge), and forced my sorry ass down the hallway and into the lecture room. Some people bounced and fidgeted, others walked, and some dragged along behind me to the classroom, where our names would be called to make sure we hadn't bolted or run amok downtown, looking for alcohol or drugs. There were young freshly-tattooed people, middle-aged saggy people, and wrinkly old men and ladies who hadn't seen a dry day in decades. Nearly everyone smelled like smoke or last night's alcohol, as if a Pigpen cloud followed them everywhere.

Laura sat down beside me. I asked her where she was from and she said, "Overland Park, Kansas." Yep, country club wife. That was the ritzy area of Kansas City. She told me that, Saturday night, she had escaped from The Center and had walked three miles to the closest bar downtown. She'd gotten "completely trashed" on vodka, and when the folks from The Center picked her up, she'd had a blood alcohol level of .40. Almost dead. She wore it like a badge of honor, though. She was also slurring her words as she told me.

When I asked her if she was drunk, she said, "They gave me a really good sleeping pill."

I have to get some of that stuff. We heard our names called, raised our hands in reply, then got excused. It took all of five minutes.

On the way out, I said to Laura, "It sounds like you would be a lot of fun with my group of girls back home." I could tell by the look on her face that I had crossed the line. "Sorry," I said. "I don't know you well enough to joke like that."

"I don't mind at all," she said, actually pleased now that I had pegged her as a good partier and fun person with whom to hang. She tottered beside me down the hallway, and I asked her if everyone just went to bed now. It certainly looked like it. I felt like crap, and really wanted and needed a painkiller and a beer, so I didn't feel like being around anyone anyway. I just didn't want to fail on the social scale on my first night in drug rehab.

"I'm tired," Laura said, as she bounced from wall to wall.

"You're really feeling that sleeping pill, aren't you?" I said. She nodded.

I went to the room, plopped down on my bed and started typing these words again. Anna and Laura climbed into their beds. Anna fell asleep very quickly, and Laura started reading. Before I knew it, it was eleven o'clock, and I had finished most of my notes. Suddenly, Anna sat straight up in her bed. I didn't know what to think because she was a stranger who was going through drug withdrawals, so I laid my computer down and sat up on the side of my bed. Anna looked at me, totally forlorn. Then I felt sorry for her. If she hadn't been in rehab, her night would've just been starting. Inside rehab, she was stuck in a room with the chunky old lady in C4, the country club wife, and the old-lady meth addict.

Looking at Anna reminded me that this was just my first night of many in this desolate place. I tried to keep calm, but the harder I tried, the more agitated I became. The walls (with no windows) and the reality of thirty days in this stinky hell hole, without my husband, daughter, friends, My Friend, pills, or even a beer, started to close in on me. Then, Anna suddenly jumped from her bed. I stood up in case I had to defend myself, although the only thing I could've done was sit on her.

"What is that disgusting smell?" she said. "It's making me sick."

"Me, too," I said. "I hate to blame the defenseless, but I think Donna is farting in her sleep. I can't take it anymore. There's no way I can spend several days in here." Anna sprayed her designer perfume throughout the room while Laura got up and smoothed out her bed. "That smells a lot better," I said. I watched Laura climb back under her covers, this time with pajamas on. She looked up at me.

"You're shaking," she said. "You look really anxious."

"I'm very anxious," I said. "I'm afraid the nurses aren't going to help me when I need it."

"Oh," she said, calmly, "if they don't give you antianxiety meds, I'll have my husband bring some from home in the morning."

Instead of thinking, *why am I here if it's that easy to 'cheat'?* I said out loud, "That would be awesome. I'm very claustrophobic, and the walls are closing in on me." I didn't really want to take any drugs that I shouldn't, but I felt like I was in Afghanistan, with bombs dropping all around me. If things continued like this, I was taking any medication I could get my hands on, no matter where it came from. Laura nodded with complete understanding. She got up from her bed and opened the door for some fresh air, then she, Anna and I shimmied back underneath our sheets and bedspreads. I lay there for 1.2 seconds before the fart-vomit-pee stench overwhelmed the perfume. I wanted to puke. Then Donna, the now-suspected farter, started snoring like a sleep-deprived mother of triplets. *Sxxxxxkkkkkkkkt. Sxxxkkkkkkttttt.* I rolled over on my side, stuck my fingers in my ears, and tried to go to sleep. It was no use. The bed was so hard that the parking lot would have been softer. The room reeked, and the temperature felt like it was thirty-two degrees. Plus, the meth addict across the room was snoring loudly enough to cause a tsunami. I rolled back over on my back and exhaled loudly. Anna turned to yell at the snorer, then turned back to me.

"What's her name?" she asked.

"Donna," I said.

"Donna? Donna?" she hollered.

Sxxxxxxkkkkkkkt. Sxxxxxkkkkkkkt.

I hopped out of bed like Clint Eastwood and headed across the room toward Donna, ready for a rumble in rehab. I calmed myself down after the third step, though, because I had no idea how big Donna was. She hadn't gotten out of bed the entire time, so I didn't know if I could take her out or not. But Anna and Laura were both watching, and I had committed myself. I had to go through with it. I poked Donna on the arm.

"Donna?" I said. She rubbed her face. "Donna?" She looked up at me with cold, lifeless eyes; like a prisoner serving a life sentence. "You have to roll over, girl. You're snoring worse than my husband."

She nodded and rolled over onto her side. I tip-toed back to bed, but looked over my shoulder to make sure she wasn't following me with a sharp object. She had already passed out. I was so frickin' cold that I put my coat on and unfurled another cheap blanket that lay at the foot of my bed. As I settled in, my coat around me, the thin sheet and bedspread pulled up to my chin, and the blanket covering all, I heard, "Sxxxxkkkkkkt. Sxxxxxkkkkkkt."

Anna slapped her blankets down to her knees and yelled, "What the hell?" I closed my eyes and thought *Good God.*

Good night.

Chapter Four

I finally fell asleep, literally with my fingers in my ears. I woke up two hours later, drenched in sweat, and trust me, no one would've paid to see my wet T-shirt. I was totally gross and freezing. I felt like someone was skinning me alive, too, starting at my ankles and slicing up to my head. My mind raced. *The seizures are starting! The seizures are starting!* My heart pounded so hard that I could feel it in my temples. *The people here control everything,* the voice in my head said. *You can't get out! You can't ever get out! If you call home, no one is coming to rescue you! Your family has conspired with the staff here! You are a prisoner in this hell hole!* I was so angry. Not just a little angry either, but kill-somebody angry. Almost as mad as I had been at My Friend the week before.

"Where is my damn call light?" I said, aloud. No one answered. The teenage meth addict next to me was out cold, the farter was snoring, and the country club wife was sleeping soundly.

My bowels suddenly moved, but I couldn't even think about getting up. My body was physically spent and felt as heavy as a truck. *A truck! A truck! I'm trapped inside a truck and it's sinking in the Missouri River!* My anxiety shot to level orange. I tried to calm my racing thoughts with logic. *You're not in a truck! This is a bed. You're in a bed! Yes, a bed! In a psych ward. They're coming to get you. They're going to put you in a strait jacket! No! Not a strait jacket! I'm claustrophobic! Please don't put me in a strait jacket! I need a nurse! I need someone to take care of me! This isn't what I signed on for! Where is my call light? Doesn't anybody care that I'm about to die? Someone help me! Please, come help me!*

Now panicking, I wrapped the sheet and both blankets around my shoulders and tried to get out of bed. My bowels were going to explode, so I got up and tried to walk, but felt like I was struggling through four feet of peanut butter. I wasn't going to make it. *Oh holy gods, I am going to crap my pants.* I squeezed my cheeks together and walked as quickly as I could to the toilet, yanked my sweatpants down, and sat, with the blankets still draped around my body. The pains in my stomach were like labor pains—muscle cramps—charley horses. They were unbearable. I was suddenly burning up and threw the blankets off, then ice cold in my wet sweat, so I scooped them off the floor. I sat on the toilet for what seemed like two days, wanting to scream because the pain was so intense. I strained hard because I had to go but couldn't. Cold sweat ran down my face. Chills shook me. It was exactly like the torture I had experienced in the hospital. The nurse during the day had told me that it wouldn't be this way, but she'd said, if it was, I could get help. *Oh God, I need help. Please let me go to the bathroom so I can get help!* The cramps in my stomach bulged. I felt an overwhelming need to push a watermelon out my butt. But pushing made the stabbing pains worse. They weren't just stabbing either. They were also twisting, cutting, then gutting me like a fish.

Last night's cereal finally torpedoed out in a "floosh" after substantial groaning and straining. I wiped the tears off my cheeks and just sat there, trying to take deep breaths. When I was done, I cleaned myself up, zipped up my jacket, washed my hands, and threw my blankets on the bed while I changed into a different T-shirt. I fidgeted as I did so, not only because I was freezing, but because the anxiety was more than I could bear. I used my cell phone to light my way out of the room, then jerked and shivered down the hallway, ping-ponging from wall to wall like a ball in a pinball machine. Then I stood in front of the reception desk. Nurse Ratched had gone home, thank God, so a new nurse was there to dispense medication. She was short and chunky and, in my detox fog, looked like a frog in a sweatshirt and striped pants. She also needed to comb her hair, but then again, so did I. She sat on a rolling stool that scooted across the linoleum floor without her ever having to get up.

Off to her left was a nicely dressed, large black woman who was seated on a rolling, high-backed chair. That woman wore a cream-colored pantsuit, dangly earrings, a bunch of gold jewelry, and tinted glasses. She was more dressed up than any staff member that I'd seen during the day when people were actually awake (although several people milled about the room at that time, and two guys were playing pool). I looked at both ladies, told them that my heart felt like a race car, and asked them as calmly as possible to please help me.

"Come around and get your blood pressure taken," the med dispenser said. I wanted to leap across the chest-high counter, grab her around the throat, and choke the living crap out of her.

"O.K.," I said, trying to look like I was in control, as I had done all my life. I walked in staccato steps, very stunted, like an MS victim. I had no idea why, but I couldn't pull it together. My thoughts spun around in my head like clothes in a dryer. And I couldn't control my body. My limbs twitched uncontrollably. I sat down in the blood pressure chair and waited for the other nurse to come take my vitals. She was dressed in blue jeans, a gray college sweatshirt, and tennis shoes. Her attire did nothing to help my panic. Neither did her pace. In my heightened state, I expected her to run across that small space and wrap the blood pressure cuff around my arm like a calf roper flying out of the chute. Instead, she walked as slowly as humanly possible. I wanted to grab her long brown ponytail, spin her in a circle, and toss her through the front window. She held the blood pressure cuff close to my arm, and looked up at someone who had just walked in the door. *Do it! Do it!* my mind screamed. *Put that thing on my arm! Stop looking around, you stupid idiot! Get me some meds!* She said something to the person who had come in from the smoking section, then methodically wrapped the pressure cuff around my arm. As my heart raced, she very sloooooooooooooooooooowllllllllllly pressed the stethoscope to my skin and pumped the bubble up. She turned her head to listen. It took for-effing-ever.

"One hundred sixty-eight over ninety-eight," she said. It was usually in the one hundred-five over sixty-eight range, so the reading was very high for me. I shook with pride because I knew it would get me some meds. But then, she started asking me the required Very Important Questions.

"What is your anxiety level?" she said. I shot her a look like *Are you kidding me?* I wanted to bash her skull in with a rock. "O.K.," she said, realizing I didn't even need to answer. "Do you have any joint or bone pain?"

"Yes," I said, with my teeth gritted tightly. Of course, I had joint and bone pain. I had all-over-my-body pain. That was what had gotten me into this cesspool.

"Is your heart racing?" she asked. I glared at her. My heart was a freight train about to run her the hell over. She should've seen it coming full speed ahead. She should've heard its horn and been paralyzed by its light. I wanted to peel her nose off with a potato peeler.

"Yes," I said, without parting my teeth.

I answered the rest of her Very Important Questions, then curled my fingers into a fist.

"Go back around the desk to the med station," she said. *Whaaaaaat? Are you serious?* I thought. I was within reach right there. All she had to do was drop the pills in my hand. I wanted to drop her in her tracks and bash her head into the floor until blood spurted from her nose. I stumbled back around the nurses' station to face her across the counter. "I can't give you anything yet," she said. I thought my head would pop up and spin around on my neck.

"Why not?" I asked.

"Well, you haven't seen the doctor yet. He'll be here Sunday morning." *Sunday morning? I will die of a heart attack before then!*

"That isn't my fault," I said. "I wanted to see the doctor when I got here but was never given the option."

"Well, until you do, I can recommend that you drink this

Chamomile tea. It's very calming." She passed a tea bag across the counter and smiled at me like I had just won a car on "The Price is Right." *ARE YOU FRICKIN' KIDDING ME?* I thought, surely loud enough for her to hear. *I'm going through detox and have the heebie- jeebies like the local electric company is testing live wires through my nerves, and you want me to drink tea?* My brows furrowed, my eyes darkened, and my jaw clenched. At that point, I would've been afraid of me.

"I'm not doing this," I said. "You call the doctor, and tell him to prescribe me something, or I'm walking home." I knew I couldn't do that. Hell, I couldn't even walk a block without stopping to stretch out my back or catch my breath. I couldn't even tie my own shoes without huffing and puffing, so I had to wear tennis shoes with Velcro strips. However, if this woman didn't give me some meds, I was setting out on the highway. She reached into her drawer of salvation then and pulled out a little white pill.

"This is for blood pressure," she said, placing it in a white paper cup as big as a quarter. "Yours is high, so I can give this to you. It should also take away some of the anxiety." The last sentence was the only one I heard because it was the only one that mattered.

"O.K., thank you," I said. I downed the pill right there and glared at her as I emphatically scrunched that stupid paper cup like a beer can. Then I walked back down the hallway. I raced the last few steps because my bowels went charging ahead of me. I headed for the bathroom, hoping none of my roommates were in there. Spinning around the bathroom corner, I quietly shut the door, then ran to the toilet. I barely got my pants down before my body let out a huge, loose stream of body waste. I shook at the thought of nearly crapping my jammies. What if, one of these times, I didn't make it? How embarrassing would that be? I continued to shake. It became uncontrollable. I was so cold! *Why can't they turn the heat up in here!?* I thought.

I cleaned myself up, then walked quietly back to my bed and lay down, still in my jacket. Within minutes, I felt the medication calm me. I quickly fell asleep.

I jolted awake at 2:30 a.m., and felt my bowels move again. I was afraid I wouldn't make it to the bathroom, though, because I absolutely could not get up. I was a corpse. It took every ounce of energy that I had to roll over and put my feet on the floor. I wrapped my blankets around me, then put one foot in front of the other like Frankenstein, and literally thought about every step while stomach cramps stabbed me in the place where my ovaries had stabbed me monthly for thirty years. I had gotten revenge on those suckers a few years prior, though, and had had them yanked out because I'd been diagnosed with stage one endometrial cancer. I wanted to yank my bowels out, too, and in my confused state, wondered if it was a possibility.

I walked all bent over, reached the bathroom, and closed the door after me. I was still wrapped in blankets, but sat on the toilet, and wanted to scream as my body punished me for twenty years of horrible choices, and twelve more years of worse ones. The pain was intense and excruciating. I was also suddenly burning up like I was sitting too close to a fire, so I tossed the blankets on the floor, and threw my jacket on top of them. Balls of sweat gathered on every inch of my body, but the ones that bothered me most were on my forehead and the back of my neck. The sweat sopped my T-shirt again in a matter of minutes. I strained, pushed, and worried that someone else in the same condition would need the bathroom. I got so cold from the drenching of my body that I picked the jacket and blankets up and wrapped them around me again. Then, my body released its hold, and immediately stunk up the already-wretched bathroom. I couldn't stand the stench of my sweaty, disgusting body, the bathroom, and the detox room. I felt like I was going to vomit.

After cleaning myself up, I walked to the sink and glanced up at the mirror. I looked like I had just finished a two-night drinking binge. My hair was matted against my head and was damp with sweat. Yesterday's makeup had smeared around my eyes and was running down my chipmunk cheeks. My heart raced. My head pounded, and my nose was stuffed up, yet mucus suddenly ran down into my mouth. *Yuck! Oooh! Yuck!* I grabbed some toilet paper and wiped my nose, then rubbed the toilet paper across my tongue. Little pieces stuck to it, so I picked them off. My sinuses drained down the back of my throat and gagged me. It was the worst hangover I'd ever had in my life, and it was just starting!

I left the bathroom and turned my phone's flashlight on so I could change my T-shirt again. I shook with unbearable chills, so I donned another T-shirt and a coat, then wrapped the blankets around me. I tip-toed past the other sleeping beauties, and ran right into the door. *Why can't I focus?* I thought. *Everything looks like it's under water!* I quietly pulled the door open, "zombie walked" down the hall, and asked for another blood pressure pill. The med dispenser took my blood pressure again, to prove that I needed medicine. I sat there totally pissed. *Why can't they just believe me? Who would make this crap up?* I couldn't gather my thoughts. The room was moving around like a spinning carnival ride. Suddenly, I saw something scurry across the floor, out of the corner of my eye. *Was that a bug? Was that a huge beetle or cockroach that just ran across the floor in this disgusting, smelly place?* I glared at the area where it had just been. Was it real? Or was I losing it?

The med dispenser cleared her throat, then made me walk around the desk again. She gave me the blood pressure medicine because my reading was 140 over something. I didn't know what. I didn't care. I just cared that she gave me the pill.

I stumbled back down the hallway to my room, freezing my butt off, then climbed into bed again—still in my coat—with the blankets draped around me. My skin buzzed like a vibrator. I felt like I'd had fourteen cups of coffee and a six-pack of Red Bull. I turned onto my right side, then tossed my huge body onto my left. I flipped onto my back. My arms and hands and legs literally shook. *Oh God, take away this electricity! Please take it away. Please. Please. I can deal with the rest. Hell, I deserve the rest for what I have done to myself and my life. But I can't take the anxiety. I don't deserve the anxiety. Please take it away.* I kicked my legs out, hoping that would help. I rolled over onto my stomach and pulled my right leg up as far as I could, just to try to hold it still. It shook worse, so I turned over onto my side then back onto my back, like a flopping fish. I flip-flopped that way for an hour, exhausted, and physically and emotionally spent. I whimpered, but wanted to wail, yet I knew if I wailed, someone would be rudely awakened. God forbid that I wake someone up or let them know I wasn't in control. Finally, I felt the pill calm me. Then I must've fallen asleep. I suffered the night away, shivering half the time and sweating the other half.

In the morning, I and my roommates were awakened by a loud voice.

"Staff!" a woman yelled. I turned over to see her opening the door. She walked in, carrying her Very Important Clipboard. Her grayish blonde hair was pinned behind her head, and she had yellow and black teeth. She wore a tattered top and blue jeans, and looked like she should've been in the bed next to me.

"Breakfast is going on now, ladies. Are you going?" she asked. I couldn't believe it was morning already. I was surprised that I had lived to see it, too, because I'd figured I would die in the night. I rolled over on my back and sighed, then lifted my head and noticed the light on in the bathroom. Laura was in there, and I could see her in front of the mirror, putting her makeup on. She hollered that she'd just finished working out, then said she would eat cereal later. *Working out? How in the world could anyone work out during detox?*

I told the lady with the clipboard that I was nauseous and didn't want anything, but I barely got the words out. My mouth was as dry as a parched pasture. Anna said she didn't "want nothing," and Donna had passed out entirely, but wasn't snoring anymore. The nurse left without asking if we needed anything, and without touching Donna, to make sure she was actually still alive. My skin started jumping again, and my thoughts bounced off the walls. *They're controlling my way out. I can't escape because they have my car keys. If I try to walk away, will they come after me? Restrain me? Hold me down? Oh my God, they're going to hold me down, aren't they? They're going to hold me down! What if they put me in a strait jacket? A strait jacket! I'll die of a heart attack when they put me in a strait jacket! I have to get out!* Again, the sensible part of my mind tried to overcome the panic, but it was futile. A battle was raging inside my head, and the bad voice was winning. I sat up in bed. Was I really being held captive, or was it just my racing imagination? *Why can't I pull it together?* My concrete body was so heavy, but I yanked it out of bed, then felt like

I was drunk. And I was freezing! And so mad about it that I had trouble taking a deep breath. *Why can't they turn up the damn heat?*

I walked out to the front desk in my coat, and told the nurse/receptionist/person-sitting-there that I needed some meds, and I wanted to go home. I wanted my car keys back, so I at least had the option.

"We can't let you have your car keys for liability reasons," she said. This very nice person named Stacy, who was a bitch in my detox-induced fog, thought I was a drug addict who couldn't even drive her own car!

I said, "Listen, I know how that must sound to you. I have no intention of using the car keys. I just need to know I can if I want to."

"But you can't," Stacy said.

"That's my entire problem!" I said, trying to hide my panic. "I am NOT going to drive away from here! I am smart enough and aware enough to know that it would be dangerous right now! I just need the ability to do so if I want to!"

"But you can't," she said, calmly. I wanted to shove two pieces of bread in her mouth, wrap duct tape around her head, and hog-tie her to the chair.

"I want to go home," I said. "I want to go home now."

"Well, you need to talk to a counselor before you can go home, and she's not here," Stacy said. I felt sheer terror—the fight or flight—rise from the ashes that were left from the fire that had burned up my life. I couldn't have gotten away if I wanted to, which I did, but now I couldn't. I was trapped. I had no way out. For me, there was nothing worse.

"Come let me take your blood pressure," Stacy said. That stupid blood pressure cuff. Maybe I could wrap the cord around my neck and jump off the medicine counter. I tried to focus so I wouldn't run into the counter as I walked around it, then I sat in the designated blood-pressure-only chair. Stacy took my blood pressure, but it was only one hundred twenty-eight over sixty-two, so I didn't qualify for meds at that point. How, I had no idea. There was no way to describe the anxiety and inner panic, coupled with my PTSD. I felt like everybody in the place was staring at me. They could all read my thoughts. They were all in on it. All of them. They were holding me captive. If I ran, they would all chase me down, tackle me, and tie my hands and legs together like a perp on one of those true-crime reality shows.

"The doctor will be here at 9:30," the other nurse/receptionist said.

"Really?" I exclaimed. I had been told that the doctor wouldn't be on campus until Sunday. That was my first moment of total relief. "I want to see him, please," I said, "and I want to talk to the counselor about going home." I looked at the clock then. It was moving around on the wall, but when I focused really hard, it read 9:12 a.m. I walked over to a chair by the window, sat down, and pulled out my cell phone. I squirmed from one position to another as I texted my fellow Quilter, Linda, to tell her that I wasn't staying, that I'd had enough, and that the place was a complete dive.

"No one takes care of us at all," I typed, "and it smells like every person here has crapped their pants." When I was done texting, I dialed my grocery store. Suddenly, the chair where I was sitting zapped me like I was on death row. I jumped up and spun around, ready for a fight. There was no one there. I twirled around the other way, sure that someone was messing with me. But again, nobody. I backed away from the chair, utterly certain that I was losing my mind. My body shook, so I paced and jiggled and tried to get the anxiety to go away! My arms flung in the air uncontrollably. *Go away! Go away! Please go away!* If any sane people had been there, they would have thought I was crazy, but I didn't have much fear of that.

On the phone, one of our employees at the store answered, so I tried to settle down so I could talk.

"Amber, I need to talk to Randy right away," I said. She called Randy over the intercom. He picked up immediately. I told him how wretched the place was, and how high my anxiety level was.

"If I call you back and tell you to come get me, you'd better be in the truck before I hang up," I said.

"I will," he said. God bless him. He was so loyal to me. It was one of his most endearing qualities. If I wanted something and he knew I really needed it, he would tear down walls to get it for me. I hung up, then sat back down and squirmed in the chair as I waited for the doctor. The hands on the clock tick-tick-ticked slowly, and they pissed me off. Why couldn't they tick faster? Laura came out of the classroom and walked by my jittery body, which was bouncing around uncontrollably while two guys racked the balls on the pool table.

"Are you going home?" Laura asked.

"I don't know yet," I said, "but what the hell kind of place is this? I thought I was going to be in a hospital, where I would push a call button, and a nurse would come, and I would tell her that my anxiety level was through the roof, so she would get me some antianxiety medication. These 'nurses' aren't even in uniform, and they don't do one damn thing except occasionally take our blood pressure, then push pills across the counter in tiny paper cups! And that's after we have proven that we need them!"

"I know," Laura said. "I think you should go home."

"Me, too," I said, thankful that someone understood. She walked away, and I tried to sit still, but tweaked like a drug addict for another half hour. It seemed like three days. The doctor finally came in then. He was handsome and young, and looked like that guy who starred on the ABC drama, *Castle*. I would've spent a few moments with him any day, if I hadn't been married. And fifteen years older than him. And overweight. And, oh yeah, a patient in his detox ward. He and I went into the only examination room in the building, and he checked my blood pressure (again), took my temp, listened to my lungs, then asked what my concerns were.

I said, "I don't belong here, Doc. I'm not your bottom-of-the-barrel drunk or street addict who can't get through an evening without a bottle of wine or a drag from a meth cigarette." He smiled. Yeah, I was naïve. I had no idea how they smoked it. "I'm just a housewife with back pain, and the pain and pills both got out of control," I said. "I just got into a problem with painkillers because I've been taking them for so long. I've never taken more than the prescribed amount, and never taken them to get high. I'm here of my own accord, not because my family wants me to be here. I *want* to kick this. But this isn't the place

for me." I looked down at the floor. I knew how all of that sounded. I
didn't mean for it to sound that way. I just wanted the doctor to know
that, if he gave me my car keys, I wasn't going to drive downtown and
wait for a guy in a trench coat to show me his lineup of pills. I just felt
like no one was taking care of me or any of the other people. We were
all sick and deserved to be cared for like patients! I turned to the doctor
again and explained my claustrophobia, need for control, and my need
to "get out." I had to be in control of my escape, I told him. He said
he understood, and that he worked at The Center because he strongly
believed in its program.

"But," he said, "this place isn't for everyone. Some people get sicker
than others and need more care." I nodded. He understood. I was one
of those.

By the time I left the exam room, I knew I was going home; back to
Falls City, Nebraska, and back to my life. I would initiate Plan B, where
I would be in control. I would start on Monday morning with the doctor
I had recently begun seeing; Sandy Catlin, APRN, and we would wean
off the pills slowly—half a pill a week or so.

I quickly called my husband and told him to get in his truck. He
said he would notify our daughter and that he and she would head out
on a rescue mission. I felt victorious, so there was only one thing that
mattered. Since I was going home, I could do whatever I had to do to
get rid of the nausea, unbelievable heebie-jeebies, and inhumane stomach cramps and diarrhea. I threw caution to the wind, and decided to
disobey the rule of never going to our vehicles alone. I walked out to
my car, punched my keycode into the panel, got a Hydrocodone out of
my console, and washed it down with a day-old bottle of water. I even
risked choking. I wasn't going to wait for the sucker to melt because
someone might have caught me first. I walked back into The Center
then, feeling slightly guilty but mostly just smug. I was in control once
again. I went back to my bed and lay down. The electricity pumped
through my veins, so I tossed from one side to the other, then onto my
back, onto my side again, then back to my back. Forty minutes of that
fish-flopping exhausted me, but then the soothing, receptor-attaching,

mood-altering feeling overtook me, and I finally relaxed enough to drift off to sleep.

At 12:00 p.m., I woke up, and saw the weekend on-call counselor walking back toward my bed. Simona was a stout black woman with short coal-colored hair. She wore a gray sweatshirt and matching sweatpants. When she got to my bed, she squatted down beside me, so she was down on my level, which I appreciated. In my less-agitated state, she was approachable, relaxed, and calm. Since Donna was still sleeping (or maybe was dead), Simona and I talked quietly in the dark. She told me that my husband and daughter had been there for about forty minutes, had taken a tour of the place, and had talked with her about my predicament. She said they were ready to take me away, if I was ready to go, but that she strongly advised against it. By that time, because of the Hydrocodone, I had settled down, so I told her I wanted to talk to my family, to make sure I was making the right decision. Simona tried to talk me out of leaving.

She said, "Lori, you know you are not thinking clearly right now, right? I know that you want to be in control of your environment, but you haven't been in control for twelve years. You know that, right?" I nodded. At times, yes, I knew that.

And yet I said, "You don't understand, Simona. I don't have to *be* in control of it. I just have to *think* I am. I can't even sit in the center of a section at a concert. I have to sit on the aisle. I need to know that I can get out. I can't get out of here on my own."

"Yes, you can," she said. "You can walk away from here anytime you want to." *What good would that do me? They'll just hunt me down like a deer during bow season. And besides, the only place I want to go is home, not downtown to the bar to see how trashed I can get.* I knew she was irritated with me, but I didn't care. At that point, I just wanted to talk to my family.

I walked out to the gathering room, where two young bucks talked trash while playing pool. Classes had just dismissed, and some fifty people milled around the room, talking to visitors, watching TV, perching on one of the three couches, or lining up for antianxiety meds. Most were dressed in T-shirts and jeans, and smelled like ashtrays when I passed them. Amidst all of that chaos, a cute little girl about seven or eight, who was dressed in leggings, a jean jacket and a darling little baseball cap, talked to Anna. The girl's mom, a gorgeous blonde in leggings and boots, knelt on the floor beside her. *Good for Anna*, I thought. *She finally gets to see her mom.* Her mom didn't look like a mom, though. She looked like a preppy college kid.

My husband and daughter stood at the counter, waiting for me. They were as out of place in The Center as Anna's mom was. Randy wore pressed dress pants, a long-sleeved blue dress shirt, and a tie. My daughter, too, had just come from work because she'd had an event at the college, so she was dressed very professionally. She wore a bright blue pair of pants, a black sweater, and a professional pea-length coat. Her blonde hair was pulled back into a long, flowing ponytail. Her makeup was flawless. She stood out against the gray backdrop like Carrie Underwood in a cattle feedlot. I, on the other hand, was completely disheveled. I knew that I looked as bad as I had ever looked. I wore my gray Walmart sweatpants, a Nebraska Cornhuskers T-shirt, and no shoes. My makeup had all worn off, and my hair hadn't been combed since sunrise the day before. It stuck out in all directions.

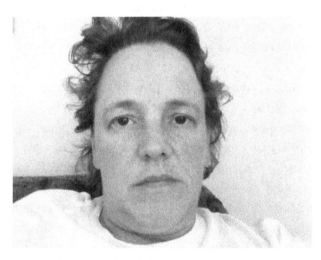

Me, on the second day of detox

I tried to find a private place where I could talk to my family, which wasn't that easy, but finally decided on the library.

As soon as I closed the door, Cassie said, "Mom, you are *not* staying here. This place is wretched. I don't even feel like you're safe here. And it's massively chaotic. That has to add to your anxiety!" Thank God it wasn't just my imagination.

"Do you feel safe here?" Randy asked.

"Well, I don't think any of the people would hurt me," I said. And really, I didn't. All of them—staff and patients—were very nice (except Nurse Ratched). But the staff wasn't taking care of us like I'd expected! As far as the patients went, I didn't know any of them, didn't know their backgrounds or what they were capable of in their altered states of drug withdrawal. Hell, I didn't even know what *I* was capable of! Plus, we were all in tight spaces. Two meth addicts slept just feet from me. There was no privacy, no place to lock up my belongings within my own power. The professionals didn't look professional either. "I don't feel like my *health* is safe here," I said. "No one comes to check on us. My anxiety was so bad last night that I could've had a heart attack, and no one would've known until this morning, when a woman came around to see if we were going to breakfast. I want to be in a place where someone brings my breakfast to me when I'm too chilled or sick to get out of bed." I knew that I sounded like a spoiled brat, but I also knew that my family understood. I was going through the most humiliating thing I would ever endure in my life, and I was already sicker than I had ever thought I would be. I wanted to detox with a shred of dignity—and I firmly believed that Anna, Laura, Donna, and every person registered at The Center deserved the same. I didn't want a roommate in the shower when I had diarrhea so badly that I couldn't hold it in. I didn't want to have to pull a Melissa McCarthy, like in *Bridesmaids*, and roll up my skirt so that I could crap in the sink if the pretty blonde in the nice dress was puking in the toilet.

"Mom, you are not staying here," Cassie said. "This place is filthy, and it's filled with hard-core street addicts. You don't belong here. The library is a room with books on the wallpaper. That makes it a library?

The counselor is wearing sweatpants! This place has no professional-looking people!" I knew I had won the battle because The Center hadn't loaded its gun.

"I want to go home," I said.

"Well," Randy said, "we've decided that you're not going home either." Apparently, I hadn't won the war. *What the hell?* I thought. *Are you kidding me? More control? Who do you people think you are? I've been taking care of your lives for twenty-seven years! Now, you want to control ME?*

"We've been talking to Simona for about forty minutes," Randy said, "and she thinks it's a bad idea to even stop at home. She thinks you might have pills stashed there." *Oh yeah? Conspiring behind my back with Simona!?* I thought. *What a dumbass Simona is. I have pills stashed in my car, and I've already taken one. Nah nah nah nah nah nah. Who's winning now, Simona?* "We've called the hospital in Falls City, and they don't do detox," Randy said, "so, we think it's better to take you to a hospital that does. How about Bryan Health West in Lincoln? At the detox center?" Bryan West was two hours north of Falls City, but I didn't care. It was a hospital. I would have a call button, and nurses who would bring water and meds to me, not make me walk down the hall when I could barely get out of bed. Most importantly, I could leave any time I wanted.

"O.K.," I said. Randy brought Simona into the room then. She, of course, tried to talk me into staying. She said I was making a big mistake, that The Center had the most successful program out there, and that I needed to be in a rehab facility.

I said, "Simona, no offense, but the doctor even said that The Center isn't right for everyone. I need to be in a place where I can push my call button, and the nurse will come around with my meds because she believes me when I say that my anxiety is excruciating. I don't want to be in a facility where, no matter how sick I am, I have to crawl down the hallway and beg for meds in front of all the other drug addicts and alcoholics." She said she understood that the place wasn't right for everyone, but that the staff's job was to make everyone comfortable, not cater to them. *Comfortable? At what point did this nightmare become comfortable?* I was sleeping in a room where an ice-sculpting contest could've been held, and I was in there with three strangers. The twin-size beds were very hard, with thin sheets and thinner blankets. The staff only came around when it was time for breakfast, or lecture class, or roll call. If we needed something, they did not get it for us. It was our responsibility to get it for ourselves. I hadn't seen one nurse offer basic medical care to anyone! Not one. I was getting out at all costs. But Simona wasn't done.

She said, "Lori, you are a drug addict. I want you to know that you are leaving against my clinical advice." *It's hard to take someone seriously when she says that in her sweatpants. And I am not a drug addict.*

"I understand," I said, knowing that I had to agree so she would sign me out.

"You need to go straight to the detox center at Bryan. And you need to give up your control," she said. "Give yourself a chance. If you insist on doing this yourself—your way—you will fail." I thought, *Then you don't know me very well, Simona. When I make up my mind to do something, it's a done deal.*

Randy said, "I've been married to this woman for twenty-five years, and the only way she'll win is if she's in control." Swish! Two points for my husband. No, no. That was a three-pointer.

I was pissed because I wasn't going home, but happy that I wasn't staying there. Cassie wouldn't have let me anyway. I stood up to face off against Simona, who had actually just sweetened the pot. She had issued a challenge. I knew, at that point, there was no way I was going to fail, and I wanted to arch my back and tell her so. However, I couldn't take her on because the room suddenly started spinning. I leaned against the wall to regain my bearings, and tried to fake my way through the dizziness. I couldn't let my family know that I had no control over the physical symptoms of withdrawal! I never let anyone know when I felt weak. Or when I felt anything else for that matter. I had built a moat around myself and my emotions and had filled it with alligators. I hadn't let anyone but My Friend cross the moat in a long time. And I wasn't about to start now. I headed toward the door.

"I know you aren't staying here, Lori," Simona said. "I know why you've chosen to leave, but give Bryan the chance to help you. You haven't been in control for more than a decade. Twelve years, actually. You are not in control now. Give yourself a chance."

"I have to have control," I said.

"Then you will fail," she countered. *Not me. I always have control, and I always win. Look, I just did.*

I signed all of the discharge papers, then packed my suitcase and dragged it down the hall. The nurses behind the nurses' station gave back everything that I had brought with me. I walked shakily behind my husband as we headed out to our vehicles, and I climbed in the passenger seat of my car. Cassie and I followed Randy's pickup out of the parking lot. When we hit the main highway in town, we stopped at McDonald's, and I ordered a Filet-o-Fish with cheese, the first "real" food I'd had in twenty-four hours. My head was spinning, and my vision was out of control, as if I was drunk. The spinning made me sick to my stomach, so I only ate half of the sandwich. But it still tasted good.

Cassie put the pedal to the metal, and I leaned back against the headrest. She and her dad had no idea that I had taken a Hydrocodone that morning, or that the pills were in the console right beside me, but I was committed to seeing this through. I wasn't going to take a pill again unless I was in a situation where I couldn't stand the anxiety anymore, and no one would help me. Then, the Hydrocodone was my safety net.

"I hope I didn't come off as a total bitch who thought she was too good for the place," I said to Cassie.

"Everyone is too good for the way they apparently took care of you," she said, "and you're certainly not a bitch. You're the most accepting person I know. You just don't have the same issues that most people there have. You're a housewife and writer. You didn't come from a broken home, have no emotional issues, and are in control of your life." *Yeah. If she only knew. She would be so ashamed of me.* "You take care of everyone else," Cassie said, "but you just have a problem managing your back pain." I nodded. Yes. Those statements were true.

We drove toward Falls City and discussed my need for control part of the way. Cassie did not understand, and I was bugging out of my skin, so I told her she would have to let it go. The anxiety was just too much for me. Fortunately, she knew that and stopped talking about it.

When she and I pulled up to the house, Randy had been home for several minutes, and had already packed his duffel bag in case he needed to stay somewhere close to the hospital or Independence Center. He was standing outside the house before I even got out of the car.

"Let's go," he said. "I'm ready to go."

"Relax," I said. "I'm not going in the house so I can crush a Hydrocodone and snort it. The pills are in the console of my car. I could've taken one any time I wanted to. Get them out, please, and put them in the truck somewhere, while I go to the bathroom."

"Simona said we should throw those away," he said.

"If you do, it'll be the last thing you do," I said, "because I'll panic." I didn't intend to take another pill. I just had to have them with me, emotionally and psychologically. "I'm the one who is voluntarily turning them over to you," I said. "If I had wanted to 'use' like a drug addict, I would've stashed them in my purse. I'm giving control of them to you! But if I'm sweating like a pig and panicking, or if I get convulsions like I did in the hospital, you'd better give them to me."

"I will," he said. He knew he'd better because I was the type of wife who went with the flow. I very rarely complained about anything he did. And I didn't issue marital threats, so he knew I was serious. I was very headstrong and had a memory like an elephant's with those who had wronged me. However, I was also very forgiving. If someone wronged me and apologized, it was over and immediately forgotten. Well, it was usually over and forgotten whether the person apologized or not. But if he or she didn't, it just took a little more time for me to let it go.

Randy and I got into the truck, and talked a little bit about how it had only taken Simona forty minutes to convince him that I was a drug addict. I'd been married to him for a quarter century and knew that he loved and respected me. He thought I was a leader, not only in our family, but in our community, so when he had believed her over me, it had stung like a wasp.

"I am not an addict," I told him. "Dependent? Yes. Addict? No."

He also said that Simona had warned him about the things for which he should watch, like the fact that my irritability level would be higher than it had ever been. Well, duh! No one would listen to me! I knew that my thoughts were racing. I was aware enough to know that I was completely out of control. But I was still a human being, and no one would listen to me!

Simona had also convinced Randy that I would do anything to 'use.' But I stood my ground on that point. I wouldn't do *anything* to use. I had never done anything except call my doctor and ask him to refill the prescription. I had never crushed the drug and snorted it, never stolen pills or money from anyone, never bought them on the street. I never had and never would. However, I understood at that point why some people did. It wasn't because they wanted to get high. It was because of the withdrawals. None of the people who sought help at The Center (or anywhere else for that matter) *wanted* to use drugs anymore. None of us were going to do "anything we could" to take our drugs of choice. But I'd heard one rehabber say that he would walk over his own mother's body to avoid the anxiety. And that, I understood. It was unbearable and indescribable, and made me feel like I was going to die every second. Any staff member in that facility—any person on the face of the earth—would have done whatever he or she had to do to avoid the anxiety and accompanying sickness. All we wanted was help. And no one was giving it to us because they didn't want to "coddle" us.

Randy and I passed Nebraska City, which was about an hour north of Falls City. I fell asleep then, due to the inevitable crash from sheer exhaustion. As soon as we reached 70th Street in Lincoln, though, I awoke with a start. I felt the withdrawal symptoms again. It was way past time for another Hydrocodone, and my body was still reeling from the shock that I had administered over the previous twenty-four hours.

My bowels went into overdrive. I needed a bathroom quickly. Randy pulled up to a gas station, and I ran through the door like a mad woman. I knew I looked like one, too. I had wild, frantic eyes. My hair still hadn't been washed or combed and was a grease ball matted against my head. I wasn't wearing a stitch of makeup, either. I still wore my Walmart sweatpants and a Nebraska shirt. I looked like a staff member at The Center.

I barely made it to the bathroom, and there were few feelings worse than that. As soon as I hit the stool, a loose gush of sewage spilled out of my body. The smell made me gag. I thought I might vomit, and looked around for a trash can. There was one in the corner, but I couldn't reach it. If I threw up, it was going on the floor. I leaned my head against the wall and cried. I was 200+ pounds of blubber, sitting on a toilet in a gas station bathroom, feeling as sick as I'd ever felt in my life, on my way to an emergency room so I could check into a rehab facility. Life rarely got much darker. I pulled myself together so I could face Randy, then I washed up and walked past the attendant without looking at him. I was too embarrassed. I jumped in the truck and headed on to my controlled fate at Bryan West. Ten minutes later, Randy pulled into the ER parking lot, and I walked slowly and dejectedly toward the window-encased desk that said *Triage*. The young woman at the desk, who had cascading brown hair and was dressed professionally, asked me the problem.

I said, "I'm twenty-four hours into detox from Hydrocodone. I just came from The Center, and I need help." She didn't ask a single question. She buzzed me in, took me to a scale, and weighed me in at 209 pounds, which was surprising, given the number of times that I had been to the bathroom. I figured I had dropped at least ten pounds. She then led me down the hallway to a cubicle with a bed. She made me give a urine sample, so once again, I peed in a cup like a drug addict. My urine was dark yellow, but I shrugged. I just plain didn't care. I walked back to my cubicle, handed the cup over and lay down on the examination bed. It was cold, but the only thing that mattered was that I was safe, in a hospital, where people would care for me.

A nurse named Bonnie appeared then, wearing actual nurses' attire. She assessed the situation.

"There's your call button," she said, pointing at it. "And here's a warm blanket that should help you feel better." She draped the cover around me and tucked me in. I wanted to kiss her. If my mouth hadn't been so foul from drug detox, I would have. "Do you mind if I start an IV?" she asked. "Your urine sample shows that you're extremely dehydrated." Dehydrated? After just twenty-four hours?

I said, "Honey, you can do whatever you want because I'm safe now." I told her I was still cold, so she gave me another warm blanket, then began searching for viable veins to poke. She couldn't find one because no one could ever find one. She tried once, and jabbed the needle four different directions, while a lab technician stood and watched. I knew he needed a blood sample, too, but he was apparently going to be lucky to get one.

The doctor came in and examined me, looked in my eyes and asked me when I had last "used." I told him the day before, at 3:30 p.m. I knew he knew I was lying. I would've told him the truth, but my husband was sitting in a chair two feet from me, and I didn't want him to know that I had caved under the tremendous anxiety. I knew he wouldn't understand. I didn't want to add fuel to his Simona-infused bonfire. The doctor felt around on my stomach, pressed on my innards, looked in my eyes, listened to my chest, then leaned directly over my face.

"When did you say you last 'used?'" he asked. I hated that word. It made me sound like a drug addict who couldn't control the pills. I started crying.

"I took one this morning at ten o'clock," I said, rolling into the fetal position—well, as much as I could—and covering my face in shame. "I needed help, and they wouldn't help me! I thought I was going to die!" He didn't say anything, so I took my hands away from my eyes. The doctor thought about it for a moment, nodded like I was lying, then walked out. I felt like such a failure. A loser. A street punk. A drug addict. I covered my head with my arms, and continued to cry as my husband consoled me.

"You have to tell us the truth," he said.

"I know," I said, "but you don't understand. No one was helping me, or any of the other patients. I felt like I had been abandoned back there in that detox room. If I had died in the middle of the night, no one would have known it. I am not a drug addict. I'm a business owner, a mom and wife, a volunteer and a writer. I just have a back problem. I just wanted the pain to go away!"

"I know, honey," he said. "We know. But you have to be honest with us."

"I will," I said, "but they wouldn't help me."

The nurse came back in, and she and the lab technician worked together to try to find a vein. They took turns and poked me four times in four different places. Another lab tech came in then, and snapped on his rubber gloves. It appeared that there was now a competition in the lab department.

"I heard there's a blood sucker in here. It's my turn to try," he said. So, he poked a vein, too, to no avail. Then, another nurse pulled the curtain back.

"Nurse Connie is here," she said. "Let me at that vein." She snapped her gloves on and saw a viable vein from across the room. She kept her eyes peeled on it and swooped in like Dracula. She patted my hand, poked the needle in, and had an IV running within minutes. I felt cold water pumping through my veins. *Thank God.* Then I must've fallen asleep.

When the nurses felt like I'd been sufficiently rehydrated, Randy woke me up, and the doctor came back in, followed by a beautiful nurse named Jan. She had angelic skin, hazel eyes that burst from her face, and gorgeous auburn-colored hair that was long around her face, and shorter in back. She stood beside the doctor as he gave my prognosis. He said that, despite the fact that I'd been dehydrated and had a urinary tract infection (*say what?*), I had taken a pill that morning, so I wasn't "bad enough" to be admitted to their emergency detox ward. I would have to wait until the Independence Center opened on Monday. He said there wasn't anything he could do, but that he would give me some pills for the anxiety and a prescription for an antidiarrheal. He told me to take one Hydrocodone a day until I was admitted to the detox program, so I didn't go through extreme withdrawals without medical intervention.

"It's hell," he said. Then, he left. Jan bent down to check on my IV. She told Randy and me that her husband had just gone through "this problem," exactly like mine, so, if I couldn't get into the Bryan program, she recommended a doctor in Lincoln named Ross Smith*.

"Bryan's program is second-to-none," she said, "and you need to call them on Monday. However, if you can't get in right away, then Dr. Smith will get you through detox as an outpatient until you can. He's really good, and is exactly what some people need." She explained more about his program, and said that he used a new medication called Suboxone, which was a replacement for opiates. Someone at The Center had mentioned Suboxone, too, and I was really interested in the information, so I asked her to make an appointment for me with Dr. Smith. She left, and when she came back, she said she had scheduled an appointment for Monday, October 22nd. I wanted to scream. How could I possibly wait that long? That was two weeks away! But I couldn't say anything because I started getting droopy. Unbeknownst to me, Nurse Connie was behind me, injecting some kind of antianxiety medicine into my IV line.

"This should make you feel better," she said. I loved Nurse Connie.

Everyone but Jan left then. She told me not to go cold turkey on the meds, and to do what the doctor had instructed, no matter where I went.

"Don't do this on your own," she said. "It's hell on earth. You need medical help." *Yeah, I've been trying to find that,* I thought.

I was there for another hour or more, but then my IV was removed and I was dismissed. Randy and I went out to the truck, and I didn't even want to "use." The antianxiety medicine had helped, so I was going to wait until that wore off. I told Randy that I wanted to be close to the hospital in case I needed emergency care, so we went to the New Victorian Inn in Lincoln, which was neither new nor Victorian. We had stayed there often, and it was much closer to the hospital than Falls City was.

When we got there, he checked us in, then hauled my huge suitcase into the elevator while I took the stairs. I met him at our room, then he went back out to the car to get his duffel bag. I literally fell onto one of the queen-size beds. I didn't even pull back the covers. I didn't have the energy or desire. When Randy got back up to the room, he pulled my shoes off because I couldn't. I was so lethargic from the withdrawals and the antianxiety meds that I felt like I'd just completed a triathlon. I could barely move! Lifting my legs was impossible. Randy helped me get under the covers, and I quickly fell asleep.

A few hours later, I jolted awake. I felt like the bad guy in the movie, *Taken,* where Liam Neeson tied the perp's hands behind the guy's back, shoved a wad of cloth in his mouth, and zapped electricity through his veins using wiring from a dinghy light. The bad guy's toes curled, his eyes rolled back, and the electricity pumped through his body as Liam walked out of the dimly-lit room. My body felt like the bad guy's. My skin was vibrating like I'd never experienced before, and I was so thirsty that my throat felt closed off. My head was ruthlessly pounding. I also had to run to the bathroom. I dashed in there, flipped the light on, and barely got my sweatpants down before the withdrawals grabbed my bowels and twisted them like dish rags. The pain was so sharp that I did Lamaze breathing just to get through it. I bore the pain for fifteen minutes while sweat drained out of every pore of my body. I honestly wanted to go to the hospital, but since I had just been there, I didn't think they would keep me. However, the pain was horror-movie excruciating. I wiped my brow with the hem of my T-shirt, lifted each roll of my stomach and swiped at the sweat that had pooled there. The withdrawal wanted out of my body so badly that it was kicking my ass on the way out. Then, my bowels exploded. I heard the mess fill the water, and felt the pain release my body. It had taken so much out of me that I leaned against the wall for a few minutes, and gasped for air. My puffy body felt like an inflatable clown suit.

When I was done, I dried the rest of the sweat off with a hand towel, and washed my hands in the sink outside the bathroom. I tried to find my way to the desk in the little living room. I shook uncontrollably, like I had a temperature of 103 degrees. This "flu" was the worst of my life. My head throbbed with every beat of my heart, and every slow step I took. My nose was completely plugged up, yet ran. I wondered how long the symptoms would last. If I had to endure the pressure-filled headaches for more than a few hours, I knew I would never make it through detox, let alone stay clean for good.

My purse sat on the desk in the living room. My Hydrocodone was inside. I took the bottle out and held it in my shaky hands, then opened the curtain on the window just a pinch so I could look outside. The lights in the parking lot shone over the guests' cars. The glare was furry. The light looked hairy. I shook like a Parkinson's victim as I looked down at my bottle of pills. I hadn't had a painkiller since that morning, and the anxiety was torturous. My teeth literally rattled. My heart raced. I couldn't get my bearings. My mind was as foggy and fuzzy as the light outside. I walked back to the sink, filled a glass with warm water, dropped a pill in it, and watched while the oblong pill became tinier, and the water became chalkier. I didn't even wait until the whole thing melted. I downed it like a shot. I swished the tiny remains around, then held the pill to the roof of my mouth with my tongue. I wanted to feel it. I wanted the habitual part of my brain to calm down so I could get rid of the sweats, the flu-like aches and pains, runny diarrhea, stuffy nose, headache, and burning sensation in my stomach.

The very action of drinking the pill-infused water soothed my brain within seconds. But I knew it would take a while for the physical withdrawals to calm down. I paced in front of the window, lay down, convulsed, got back up, looked outside, and repeated it all, like a wind-up toy. Finally, after about forty minutes of that torture, I felt the calming sensation cover my body. Then, I got sleepy, so I crawled into bed. The room was just the right temperature, and smelled like fresh, clean air. I had a big fluffy comforter over me, and the only person with whom I had to share the bathroom was my husband. It was so much better than the place where I had been. And I was in complete control.

Chapter Five

All night long, I was in and out, up and down, hot then cold, flipped then flopped, then passed out from sheer exhaustion. The anxiety woke me up repeatedly. I was awake for thirty minutes or more each time, fell asleep, woke up thirty minutes later. And when the anxiety didn't wake me, the diarrhea did. I had taken one of the anti-diarrhea medications, but it hadn't touched the diarrhea. The kind that I battled was on a different level than normal flu-like trots. But it wasn't nearly as bad as the anxiety. No matter how hard I tried, I couldn't out-sleep, outrun, or out-think the heebie-jeebies. They were constant and relentless. I wanted so badly to cry, but I didn't want Randy to hear me.

The next morning, I awoke from one of my cat naps to hear a low-grade buzzing near me. *Bzzzzzzztt. Bzzzzzztt.* I lay still for a moment, wondering if a fly or sweat bee was hanging around my ear, or if the anxiety had already started messing with my mind. I opened one eye, and saw Randy standing in front of the mirror, shaving with his electric razor. Bzzzzzzzzttt. When I opened my other eye, the room started spinning. Well, not so much spinning as it was beating, like thump thump thump thump. The ache right above my eyes radiated clear through to the back of my head. I couldn't see straight. The whole room had been slimed with

Vaseline. I closed my eyes again, and just lay there, wishing I could die without hurting my loved ones.

Randy finished shaving, then went into the bathroom to take a shower. I opened my eyes again, and the room still looked swimmy, so I slowly rolled over and glared at the pill bottle over on the desk. There those pills were, those damn little pills, just sitting in that bottle. There were sixteen left. I always had to know how many there were to make sure I could get through the weekend. But this count-down was different. This was all I would have. My relationship with the pills was love/hate. I hated that I *had to* know how many there were, but loved knowing they were there. I knew if I had to, I could take one at any time and feel a little better. But there was no way I was going to take one unless I absolutely couldn't stand the with-drawals anymore.

My mouth tasted like I imagined cat pee would taste, so I got up to brush my teeth, and had to consciously direct my feet toward the sink. My legs and feet were puffed up like marshmallows, all the way from my hips to my toes. My knees felt locked like the Tin Man's. Once I reached the sink, I took the Lorazepam, or whatever the stuff was that the doctor had given me for anxiety. Then I asked Randy to go downstairs to get something for me to eat. He got dressed and left. After he ate his own breakfast, he brought back a chocolate muffin and a bottle of Gatorade. I hated Gatorade. It was too sweet. I didn't drink pop either, for the same reason. Randy had tried to find some bottled water, but none of the vending machines had had any. I ate the muffin, and turned my nose up at the Gatorade. Randy took a picture of me then, so I could chronicle my spiral into the world of drug addiction and detox.

Me, at the New Victorian Inn, Lincoln, NE

I didn't even want to look at it because it was proof that my life had become a ten-car pileup. I couldn't help but look, though. When I did, I thought I would hurl. I had gotten so old and heavy, and my face was blotchy and bloated. My eyes were completely lifeless. I hadn't combed my hair and didn't care if I ever did again. I didn't care whether I lived through the day or not. I hated the photo. I hated being where I was, and I despised what I had done to my life. I hoped that I would feel differently after the drugs left my body, but I couldn't see the silver lining because the cloud covered my entire sky. I hoped that someday, if I ever looked and felt like a human being again, I could use the photo as a "before" picture to help others. But I really didn't think that day would ever come. I firmly believed that I would die during detox. And I didn't care. I *wanted* to care for the sake of my kids and grandkids, husband, mom, family, and friends. But I didn't. The drugs and my chronic codependent relationships had murdered my ability to care. They had wielded knives and sliced my self-preservation to death. I would rather die than live like I was, and I didn't see any way out. Ever.

After Randy showed me the picture, I walked to the sink and looked in the mirror, hoping I would see a different person than the one I had just seen. Unfortunately, the old woman in the motel room really was me. Devastated, I shuffled to the bathroom. It took every ounce of energy I had, but I took a shower so I could at least feel a little more human. When the stream of water hit my fingertips, it felt like millions of tiny needles. It hurt like hell. I didn't like it. I put my hands down, and just let the water hit my face. When I washed my hair, my scalp burned at the touch. But I didn't care. I didn't care, didn't care didn't didn't care. I did not care! I washed my face and got out of the shower, dried off and put on fresh pajamas. I had no intention of joining life. Getting dressed and drying my hair was overwhelming enough. There was no way I had enough gumption to put makeup on. I had no energy, desire, or emotions, other than complete and utter despair. Washing The Center off of me had made me feel a little better, though, so I lay down on my bed, typed these words, and actually fell asleep for a while.

When I woke up, Randy was gone. The room was spinning. I started to feel nauseous, and wondered if I would feel like total crap for the rest of my life. *Is it time for a pill?* I thought. Every time I woke up, the first things on my mind were where the pills were, and whether or not it was time to take one. I looked over at the table, and the pills were still there. Randy hadn't taken them with him. *I'm not going to take one*, I thought. *I'm not! I either have to get bad enough for Bryan Health to admit me, or I have to hold things together so Ross Smith can start on me. I can't decide which. If I do the latter, then I can take one of those pills. What am I going to do?*

Randy walked in with bottled water. Someone must've refilled the vending machine. It was time for me to rehydrate. I took one of the antianxiety meds to help me get through the day, swigged as much water as I could, then lay back down and fell asleep. When I woke up, I had immediate, race-to-the-bathroom, stream-like, water-filled diarrhea. The smells coming from my own body made me gag. My body was literally draining out the toxins, and the bathroom smelled worse than a hog confinement.

The exhaustion after my diarrhea was mind-boggling. I had never felt anything like it. Just thinking about walking from the toilet to the bed made me want to sob. I couldn't get there! How would I ever get through this when I couldn't walk to the bed fifteen feet away? I forced myself to do it because I couldn't let Randy know what I was going through. I watched my feet as one foot moved ahead, then the other. I felt like I was in deep water. I couldn't hear anything either. It was like I had earplugs in. No, it was worse than that. It was like I was on an airplane, and the air pressure was unbearable, yet my ears wouldn't pop.

When I lay back down, I could barely move my legs. I could feel them on the cool sheets, so I knew they were there, but they were as heavy as logs. I pulled the covers up over my head because I didn't even want to feel the sunlight or know it was there. That was too much of a reminder that the world was going on without me—that My Friend was moving on without me.

Within minutes, I fell asleep again.

I woke up at 2:00 p.m. and didn't care whether I ever got out of bed again. I couldn't even lift my head off the pillow. If I had to run to the bathroom, I was going to have to go in my pants instead. There was no way I could get up. I was under the covers somewhere, but my body wouldn't move. I fell back to sleep, wondering if I would ever feel human again.

When I woke up at 4:30 p.m., Randy was taking a nap, but my skin was bugging out! *Oh my God! How is anyone supposed to endure this?* I quickly rolled onto my back and felt my body shake. I could still see the pills from my bed, over on the desk in the other room. But I was not taking one unless I absolutely couldn't stand the withdrawals. I had gone all day without one, even when Randy had stepped out of the room. I was trying to kick the emotional habit of taking them. Four-thirty was feeding time, and my body and soul were screaming for their food. It was also Miller time! Or Busch Light time! Or Bud Light time! Yes, it was Bud Light time! When I had first started drinking, I had drunk Pabst Blue Ribbon, with occasional shots of Wild Turkey. Then,

I'd switched to rum and Coke, Miller Lite, Busch Light, and then to Bud Light. But honestly, now, during my detox at New Victorian Inn, I didn't care. I would've downed anything available. Bud Light was just the drink I preferred. And man, I wanted one so badly!

As I lay there, looking at the pills on the desk, and coveting a Bud Light, I suddenly felt ants crawling under my skin. Crawling! Crawling! Marching, marching, marching! I scratched my arms, but that didn't stop the ants, so I pulled the sheet off and jumped out of bed, then thrashed through the room, trying to force them out. *Get out! Get out! Get out!* Oh my God, I wanted a pill so badly! Or a beer! Just one beer! Would that kill me? No. It would make me feel better. No, never mind. I wanted a pill. I had to take a pill! The cravings were worse than sweet cravings and beer cravings and cigarette cravings combined. I had to have one! I had to!

No! my sane voice said. *"You're not going to take one! You're NOT going to take one. YOU'RE NOT GOING TO TAKE ONE! YOU'RE NOT GOING TO TAKE EVEN ONE!* But my bad voice yelled back. *But I want to. I really want to. Oh God, I have to. I have to!* My head rang like clanging cymbals. All I wanted to do was take one pill. Just one. All of this would go away then—all of it. My skin would stop jumping. The ants would stop crawling. My eyes would quit hurting all the way into the sockets. My nose would stop dripping like a broken faucet. It would unplug so I could breathe. I would feel fine if I just took *one.*

My bowels started to run, so I lumbered to the bathroom again. I sat on the toilet and leaned against the wall. My head pounded, and the pressure above my eyes felt like a boiling pot of water about to blow its lid. Sweat beaded above my eyes and ran down my cheeks. Tears joined them. I had to face it. I wasn't going to make it. The police would find my body on the toilet, my fat butt hanging over both sides, pants down around my ankles, head against the wall, wretched smell filling the room. But I was not going to take a Hydrocodone, and I also wasn't going to take any more of the Imodium-type stuff that the doctor had given me for diarrhea. It hadn't worked anyway, but I wanted to feel badly enough on Tuesday for the Bryan Independence Center to admit me. Never in my life had I tried to stay sick so someone would help me. But on the other hand, I wanted more than anything to take one of my pills so that some of the withdrawal symptoms would go away. Just one.

My back was killing me, even though I'd been in bed all day, or maybe *because* I'd been in bed all day. But at least I was at a nice hotel, and not in that dive of a pigsty where I had started my hike through hell. I filled the toilet then, and the bathroom smelled like sewage gas and vomit. But it was better than the smell that filled The Center. I didn't want to even think about that smell, but I knew I would never forget it.

After I cleaned up, I took an antianxiety pill, lay back down, closed my eyes, and bounced and tossed in the bed for an hour. Randy finally woke up, so he drove a few blocks to the Cheddars restaurant and brought back a grilled salmon dinner for me, and something for him. He ate at the little table in the side room, and I lay on my bed to eat. The salmon and rice tasted so good. I hated that both would just pass through my body, but I hoped they would leave behind some kind of nutrients. After I finished eating, I lay down again and fell asleep. I slept most of the evening, but when I was awake, I was in the bathroom. I even fell asleep on the toilet a couple of times. I leaned up against the wall because I was too spent to walk back to bed, but I woke up when I started to fall. Each time, I was disgusted with myself, so I pulled myself up, stretched out my aching back, yanked my pants up, and slogged back to the bed.

I awoke again at 10:00 p.m. when the anxiety started in on me. My blood felt like it was on fire. I jumped out of bed and tried to shake the fire out. I didn't give a rat's ass whether Randy saw me or not. But my jerking around just fueled the anxiety flames! The antianxiety meds weren't working, and neither was the shaking. *Oh God, it's not working! Nothing is working!*

Randy was in the other bed, snoring loudly, so I headed toward the table in the little room. After my second step, my head hammered so badly that I had to stop and think about the next step. Pound. Pound.

Pound. I pressed my fingers against my temples and pushed in. *Oh God, my head! It is killing me! Please make it go away! Please! Am I having an aneurism? A migraine?* I fished one of the pills out of the bottle and held it, just touching it as I stared at it anxiously. My arms flailed. I squirmed and writhed, like a boxer in the corner waiting to pound the crap out of his opponent. The squirming made my head hurt worse. The vice grip around my temples squeezed harder. Mucus trickled from my nose down into my mouth. *Aggghhh!* I wiped it out with the hem of my T-shirt, disgusted at my disgusting self. If anyone had seen me at that moment, they would've rushed me to a psych ward.

I couldn't take it anymore. I couldn't! The ants were marching! My nose was running, my head hammering! I couldn't do it anymore! I crumpled to the floor in a heap and sobbed into my hands. Unable to get up, I crawled to the bed, pulled myself up, then raced to the sink and ran the water into a cup, as hot as I could stand it. I dropped the pill in it, swished it around and stared at it while it melted. Then, I drank it. As I lay back down, I knew that the action of simply swallowing the water would calm me down a little, because my brain would know that relief was coming. So, I let the pill slowly relax me over the next thirty minutes. The pounding in my head became a snare drum instead of a bass drum. My sinuses opened up a little.

I had made it through the entire day without touching the pills that were right within my reach. And I hadn't had any alcohol. I had to admit that I was proud. When I closed my eyes, I saw myself strutting down to The Center to broadcast it to Simona. And for thirty seconds, I smiled. An hour later, my body and eyes were both heavy. I completely passed out.

Chapter Six

When the sun came up, it was Monday, and Randy needed to head back to work, but said he would stay if I wanted him to. *Yeah, right.* The nervousness caused by Randy pacing the floor on a Monday would've been worse than the anxiety from drug withdrawal. He had already been away from the store for two days!

Randy's personality was a solid Type A. He had to have something to do all the time. He had been in the grocery business his entire adult life, and had worked twelve-hour days for most of that time. He had even toured grocery stores one time when we were on vacation in Mexico. We were on a trip with two-dozen other grocery store owners, and he'd been the only one who'd spent an entire afternoon checking out the prices of Pork and Beans at Gigante. Now, as I lay in my own personal detox ward at the New Victorian Inn, listening as Randy told me that he would stay if I needed him, and watching as he simultaneously packed his duffel bag, I silently chuckled. I knew that he was already worried about the store, and I understood that. We had fifty-plus employees who depended on him!

"Go home," I said. "I could've taken those pills three times already. I'll take my one pill allotment when I can't stand the anxiety anymore, but that's all I'm going to take." He said he believed me, but he still refused to leave me at the hotel alone, so I called my mom and asked if she could come spend a few days with me while I detoxed from drugs.

Mom said, "Sure."

When she arrived, I imagined her and my husband doing a tag-team slap, then Randy set out for home. Shortly after he left, I ran to the bathroom and released the first watery diarrhea of the day.

"Don't go in there," I said to Mom, as I walked out and washed my hands. "You won't be able to stand it." She nodded, and looked at me with sympathy. I couldn't let that sink in. Nobody could feel sorry for me, or I wouldn't make it.

While Mom piddled around the room and worked on her Word Find puzzles, I called the Bryan Health Independence Center to see what they needed to admit me. I couldn't believe the overwhelming rush of anxiety as I did that, because the person on the phone wanted everything but my birth certificate. She needed records from Blue Valley Behavioral Health, where I had been in counseling, records from The Center, where I had gone through one night of detox, copies of my medical insurance card to pay for an inpatient stay, and something else that I couldn't remember by the time I hung up.

Are you kidding me? I thought! *I can barely focus enough to get to the bathroom when my lunch races around the track of my bowels. And you want releases and information and insurance cards signed and scanned, and faxed back-and-forth?* Hell, I was in a detox-induced fog. I could barely remember my own birthday! I had trouble working up the energy or will to get my own drink of water. There was no way I could do four or five different things! I didn't want to do anything—anything! And they expected me to do all of that? I didn't even want to open my eyes to watch TV or read, let alone do a checklist of things that I *had* to do before I could be admitted into a drug rehab program! I didn't want to eat, drink, breathe, or live! Where would I find the energy or desire to do everything that the lady at The Independence Center required!? It was no wonder most people gave up and went back to their drugs! It was no wonder most could not get through the sheer terror of detox. And mine was just beginning! I wanted to cry, but held it back because I didn't want my mom to see me sobbing like a child.

CHAPTER SIX

I knew, however, that I had to find some way to comply with the things that the Independence Center required. If I didn't, the disease of addiction and the rejection from My Friend would kill me. So, I summoned all my strength and called The Center. A very nice person in the business office said she would fax a release for me to sign, so I walked down the hotel steps in my T-shirt, pajama bottoms and bare feet, and asked the girl at the front desk if I had received a fax. Yes, the release from The Center had come. I signed it, leaned against the counter, and asked her to fax it back. Then, I found one ounce of energy and dialed Blue Valley Behavioral Health. As luck would have it, the office was closed for Columbus Day, or Drug Addict Day, or some other kind of holiday, so I couldn't get information from them. I signed up to spend another day and night in detox at the New Victorian Inn, and forced my body back up the steps. Just getting upstairs took everything I had.

When I got to my room, I was completely despondent. I wanted to lie on the bed and die. But again, I couldn't let my mom know that, or she would worry about me. I had to look occupied, so I opened my computer and told her I was working on the *Misty* book. But I wasn't. I had decided that I wasn't going to worry about the book until I heard back from my agent. I had to focus on myself and getting well. I didn't know how I was going to do that, though, when My Friend didn't care. I needed her. I needed her to know what I was going through, to show even a small amount of concern. I had no idea why I wanted her to care! I knew that all of my other friends loved me. All I had to do was tell them I needed them, and they would come right away. My Friend probably wouldn't. Or would she? Maybe she would! *Of course she'll come*, the voice in my head said. *Just tell her and she'll come!*

I opened my email then, and typed a message to her that simply said, "I need you." I knew if one of my best friends sent that to me, I would be at her doorstep in record time.

But as soon as I pushed "send" I felt needy, desperate, and downright pathetic. I had just humiliated myself again. Why? Why did I send notes that made me look as crazy as she thought I was? I tried to forget about it, but my thoughts just kept beating me up. I thought about past conversations with My Friend. The note that I had just sent her. The rodeo in Omaha. Then I thought about the other pressures in my life, including the fact that the *Misty* book was too long, and that the subjects acted like they were losing interest and hope. In addition, I felt guilty for keeping Randy and everyone else at bay emotionally, and guilty because I hadn't fulfilled my commitment to Jerry's senatorial campaign when he needed me most. And on and on and on. The thoughts bolted through my head with crushing speed. I felt like I was losing my mind. Sweat poured out of me then, and I rushed to the bathroom for another bout of diarrhea. *How in the world?* I thought. *How can there be anything left? How long is this going to last?*

After I finished and washed up, I changed my sweaty T-shirt and took a Lorazepam. I needed something, anything, to help with the anxiety. I stared at the bottle of painkillers, and wished for normalcy. But I held off on my fix. I had decided during the night that I needed to take the pill at the same time every night to help me sleep. I knew if I couldn't make it to that time, I would never make it through the horror of detox for good. I thought about taking the pills every second, every minute, all day long. I just had to hope that the Lorazepam would help. However, instead of getting better after I took it, my heebie-jeebies got worse. My mind raced about my ridiculous email to My Friend, and my need for that codependent relationship. I walked, paced, jolted around the room, and did everything I could to keep my body and mind busy, so I wouldn't notice the electricity crashing through my bloodstream. Nothing helped. The anxiety buzzed me. It confused me. It made me crazy and desperate and suicidal.

While Mom watched TV, I tried to work on my computer. She fell asleep, so I wrote an angry, froth-at-the-mouth, hate-filled note to My Friend. When I finished, I deleted it without sending it, then pounded my fist on the bed again and again. I wanted to hit her for not caring about me, for not checking on me. I wanted to hit *something*, hit someone. *How can she not care after everything we've been through? How can she cut me out of her life so easily after all the fun we've had? After all the money I have given her?* I was so pissed that I couldn't breathe. I tried to watch a movie, but couldn't focus, so I tried to read a magazine. I bounced up and down on the bed. The anxiety was grabbing me, shaking me, spinning me around, bouncing me. When I just couldn't take it anymore, I called Sandy back home and asked for help. I was serious about getting through detox, but knew I couldn't do it on my own.

I adored Sandy. She was a straight shooter and told it like it was, but she did so with compassion. That was the main reason that I had decided to have her guide my plan B, instead of Terry, (who usually addressed my back pain). Terry was an MD, and Sandy was a PA. They were both great at what they did, but I appreciated Sandy's bedside manner a little more. Terry was an excellent doctor, but his bedside manner was no nonsense. He had saved my life in the ER during my big medical crisis a few years prior, but he had done so with steely resolve, and with arched eyebrows above his reading glasses. I remembered it very clearly. He had swooped in when I had thought I was going to die. At the time, I had needed his steely demeanor and matter-of-fact responses. But now, a few years later, as I faced the battle of my life, I needed someone with a little more compassion. So, I'd called Sandy instead. She had the precise level of kindness and concern that I needed, coupled with Terry's no-nonsense bullshit repellent.

When she called me back, I told her I needed something for my anxiety—something nonnarcotic. She prescribed Gabapentin, which was actually for nerve pain, but apparently also helped with anxiety. My back pain was out of control, but I didn't really care about that because the anxiety was so much worse than any pain I had ever experienced. Instead of taking the Lorazepam, I took the pill that Sandy had prescribed. It made me even more hyper, so I called her back, and she said to cut it in half and try that before bedtime.

The rest of the day, I was either in a super-anxious state or comatose. There was no in-between. While I was awake, I wrote these words, and listened to my precious mother baby me about taking a nap. She and I ate wonderful grapes and apples that my husband had bought, so I was at least eating well. However, I quickly figured out that I couldn't eat fruit all day because I was already having more diarrhea than I'd ever had in my life. Plus, I drank a lot of water because I didn't want to get dehydrated again. That just made it all worse! Everything I ate or drank came out in nonstop races to the bathroom. But that wasn't the worst part. The Superman anxiety continued to kick my ass. There was no relief in sight. And I wondered how long I could take it. Any one of the symptoms would have broken me under normal circumstances. All of them together? It was inhumane.

I took my Hydrocodone at 8:00 that night and settled down shortly after. The diarrhea died down for a while, and I was so grateful. My butt had begun bleeding, and the rawness just got worse with every watery stream. I hoped to God that the diarrhea would stop soon.

When I went to bed, I took half of the Gabapentin, and I begged God to please please please let it help with the jitters that shot through my body with relentless determination. But my pleas were all in vain. Why had I expected God to help me anyway? I had cut Him out of my life decades prior, just as cruelly as My Friend had cut me out of hers! *Is my distance from God hurting Him as badly as My Friend's distance is hurting me?* I wondered. *Does God cry?* I couldn't think about that. I already felt guilty about falling away from God and the church. How could I ever ask Him to take me back? *Aggggh! Stop it!* I thought. *Stop thinking about things like that!* I could barely muck my way through the things with which I was already dealing! I couldn't add something that deep and philosophical to my plate! It was too much!

I spent most of the night either on the toilet or in the little room, quietly dancing around like a crazy woman. I worked really hard to be silent so I wouldn't wake my precious mother. I couldn't let her see me tweaking like a drug addict who didn't have any money for her next fix. Finally, about 4:00 a.m., I was so physically exhausted that I was able to fall asleep.

Chapter Seven

Tuesday morning, I woke up about 7:00 a.m., and my anxiety was at least tolerable. I had only had three hours of sleep, but I was awake, so after I ate breakfast, I tried to put the steps in place to be admitted to the Independence Center. I had signed a release for The Center and faxed it back to them the day before, so when Blue Valley opened, I called and asked the receptionist to fax a release to the hotel. I hated to even request my information. Admitting that I needed help with prescription drugs (and my life) wasn't easy for someone like me. I had worn the mask that made me appear all together my entire life. I wanted everyone to think I was still in control, on top of the world, in charge, like my life was a series of Facebook posts. Admitting that it wasn't any of those things cut me to the bone.

Blue Valley sent the release. I signed it and sent it back. An hour later, I called the Bryan Independence Center and talked to a woman named Mary. She said that The Center had faxed my records, but that Blue Valley had not yet done so. But then she said that The Center's records indicated that I was an alcoholic, as well as an opiate addict. *What the hell?* I thought. *Are you kidding me? I haven't been drunk in ten years!* Barb, the bartender at Lem's, even cut me off after four beers, if I tried to venture beyond that, because I had told her how jittery I would get if I had five. Besides, I rarely tried to drink more than four anymore.

"I am not an alcoholic," I said to Mary.

"It says here that you are," she said. "It says that you drink three to four beers every night, and that you've been drinking more lately because of a problem with a friend."

"I drink three or four beers when I go out with my friends, which is probably twice a week," I said, lying out my ass. "That doesn't make me an alcoholic." I wasn't even going to talk about the mess with My Friend. Mary didn't need to know about that. Nobody needed to know about that other than my counselor, especially if it was going to make me an alcoholic.

"Well, it says here that you are an alcoholic," Mary said. Ugh. I had never worked so hard in my life to convince people to help me! What a huge mistake I had made. I could've gone through detox at home, slowly, under Sandy's guidance. But noooooo. I had to make a big dramatic statement and "get clean" from prescription painkillers. I hated myself for what I had done to my body and my life.

"Will you take my car keys if I come there, or will I be able to leave the campus?" I asked.

"Yes, we will take your keys," she said, "and no, you won't be able to leave the campus." In other words, if I tried to leave, they would restrain me? Panic panic panic! *Warning! Do not cross!*

"Your place isn't for me," I said. Why couldn't I find a treatment program for people like me—people who had never abused the drugs, but had USED the drugs for the intended purpose? I had never doctor-shopped or pharmacy-hopped. I had gone from seven pills a day on Friday down to one pill per day overnight, and had only taken one a day since Saturday. I had done it under the guidance of a physician, but mostly I had just gutted it out on my own. Truly, it had already been hell on earth, but I was doing it! Where was the program for people like me?

I called Blue Valley and asked to speak to my counselor, Bob. I was in an anxiety-induced fog, and was also mad as hell. I knew that I sounded like a raving drug addict in the throes of withdrawal, but I told Bob that I hoped he would straighten out the "alcoholic" label when he sent my records to detox facilities, because I didn't like being labeled an alcoholic when I did not have a problem with alcohol.

He said, "Lori, you are an alcoholic. You have been drinking heavily since you were nineteen! Maybe you don't drink like that now, but you have four beers every night! And you have been drinking more lately because of the situation with Your Friend. A person who is not an alcoholic can go six months without drinking. Can you do that?"

"Absolutely," I said. "But I don't WANT to because I am not an alcoholic! I love going out with my friends! I have four beers, and I'm home by 7:00 or 8:00 p.m. Does that sound like an alcoholic to you?"

"Lori, your life is a mess. You need inpatient treatment," he said. *Ugh*, I thought. "I am not sending your records to the Independence Center," he said.

I replied, "Good, because I've already decided I'm not going there. But please don't send my records *anywhere*." I hung up and felt the hopelessness close in on me like prison walls.

I wanted to take all of the pills and end my nightmare for good. However, I limited myself to one because I couldn't do that to my mother. I hid my despondency from her the rest of the night by burying my head in my computer. Most of the time, however, I had to run to the bathroom. I either felt like I had to throw up, or I had to have diarrhea. Every time I did the latter, the watery crap pricked the cuts in my butt so badly that they bled and stung, and I cried. My body became drenched with sweat. All night long. But even worse was the sense of hopelessness. I had no idea where I was going to go from there.

Chapter Eight

On Wednesday, although I was exhausted from fighting the sickness, I was feeling caged and needed some fresh air, so Mom and I walked across the road to the Hy-Vee store, ate lunch, and bought some more food. Then we waddled another fifty yards to the Barnes and Noble on the corner. Mom perched in the café, where she stared at the brownies until she finally broke down and bought one. Meanwhile, I perused reference books about the ocean. The next book that I planned to write would largely take place in the Caribbean, so I needed to study it extensively. I bought three books, and watched Mom eat a brownie while she ogled the rest of the goodies in the dessert case. Then my anxiety kicked into fourth gear. Instead of ants crawling through my bones, there were cockroaches and spiders. *I have to get out! I have to get away!* And then, suddenly, I had to cross my legs to avoid crapping my pants. I didn't want to foul the restroom in Barnes and Noble, so I told Mom I needed to get back to the hotel as quickly as possible. She took my arm so we could prop each other up while we walked back together. I squeezed my cheeks and did my Lamaze breathing so I could make it to our room without exploding and then dribbling loose poop down my legs. When we got to the hotel, I took a chance on the elevator because I knew I couldn't walk up the steps without stopping to gasp for air, and I didn't have time for that. I was almost certainly going to soil myself.

When we finally got to the room, I nearly ran Mom over trying to get to the bathroom. I sat on the toilet and let the toxins release. *Oh God, how did I get here?* I thought. I hated it. I hated my life, and everything about it. It all stunk like withdrawal rot. I felt like I could sob for days and never run out of tears. I leaned against the wall and just sat there, my pants around my ankles, my soul diving so low that it had to be dangerously close to hell. The despondency was unimaginable. I couldn't bear the thought of getting up. I didn't have the energy to even pull up my pants. But Mom was right outside the door, so I knew I had to. But I couldn't. Maybe that was why my husband had insisted that my mom stay with me. He knew if I had stayed alone, I wouldn't have had the energy or drive to even get off the toilet. He was right. I wanted to give up. I was never going to make it. I wasn't.

"Lori, are you alright?" Mom said, from the other side of the door.

"Yeah, I'll be right out," I said. "Just cleaning myself up." I did just that, and pulled my pants back on. Then I put my mask back on. My imaginary, "everything's O.K., I'm just fine," mask. After a deep breath, I walked out of the bathroom and washed my hands. I could tell by the look on Mom's face that she was really worried. And I knew why. If my daughter had looked as badly as I looked, as despondent as I looked, I would've been worried to death. Mom hugged me without saying a word, and I struggled to hold the tears in. I had to, though. I couldn't cry in front of her, or I would fold.

Mom and I spent the rest of the day eating, watching TV, and sleeping. I ran to the bathroom every twenty minutes, and spent the next five sobbing quietly as my poor bottom burned like it was on fire. Then I summoned every ounce of will I had so I could get up, wash my hands, and make it back to bed. Mentally, I tried unsuccessfully to chase the gray clouds of my life away. I told myself that going back to my former life was not an option because the pills and alcohol and missing My Friend would kill me physically, mentally, and emotionally, and had already killed me spiritually. I couldn't bear to live the way I was living any longer. Dying from drug withdrawal seemed like the better option. I didn't see any hope of ever getting better, but had to believe that going back was worse than any future that was waiting for me.

As I continued to convince myself of those things minute by minute, I looked through my books and nervously watched the clock for my feeding time. At 8:00 p.m., I took my Hydrocodone, and by 9:00 p.m., I was a little calmed down, so I was able to fall asleep. However, I woke up an hour later, tossed and turned with relentless anxiety, flailed my arms in the air, and whimpered for relief until I went back to sleep. I woke up every hour, and just begged God for help.

The next morning, I decided to go home, where I would be more comfortable, and (hopefully) sleep while I searched for inpatient programs. I was able to haul Mom's light suitcase out to the van, then the guy at the front desk lifted my big suitcase and stuffed it into the rear space. I took my one pill allotment before she and I even left Lincoln. I hoped that it would help me make it home without having to stop at restrooms all along the way. Besides, I usually drove when Mom and I went places, and I didn't want her to know that I was out of control. I felt fairly lucid the entire way, though, wondering silently about the alcoholic and drug addict labels that had literally rained down on me. Or had they? Was I blaming other people for things that were entirely my fault? I wondered if I would ever stop demolishing my own dreams!

I did have to stop a few times on the way home, but one time was at Mom's house in Auburn, so that didn't count. Mom then drove me the rest of the way, which I really appreciated. I felt like crap, so I didn't feel good enough to drive anyway. My head rang like a gong, and pounded with unbearable pain. My nose was completely plugged up.

When we got to my house, Randy came home from the store and carried all of my stuff in the house. Mom asked if I needed her to stay, but I really just wanted to be alone in my misery, so she left. I opened my computer and lay down on the couch. I started doing research into intensive outpatient programs (IOPs) in the area, but kept in the back of my mind that The Center had a tremendous success rate (according to them), so I knew that the counseling program had to be the reason why. I didn't want to go back there—couldn't IMAGINE going back there—but I had announced to my entire support system that I was going to see detox through. I had to do it somewhere. Didn't I? Confused about what to do, I wrote an email to a friend who had gone through the thirty-day inpatient treatment program at The Center, for alcohol abuse. When he replied, he said that he "hoped to God" I found somewhere else to go for help. He said his situation and mine were much different because he'd had no choice but to get help. He knew that I had used prescription painkillers to treat pain, but he had used alcohol to get smashed. His family had intervened and had taken him first to a hospital, and then to The Center. He hadn't had a choice but to stay. He'd been in the hospital for three days, and then in the detox ward at The Center for four days before he moved to the regular patient rooms out back, and it had all been hell on earth. He said the counseling program had saved his life, though, and he couldn't say enough about it.

"But the place is a hell hole," he said. "It's not the type of place for a woman like you."

After I hung up, I thought about the previous several days. I remembered that I had talked to my counselor at Blue Valley, and with Mary at the Bryan Independence Center, but I couldn't remember either conversation entirely. I looked back through my notes, and realized that I had said some pretty angry things to Bob. I made a mental note to apologize to him when I felt better, and to explain that detox-induced anger was something that had to be experienced to be understood. It was kind of like labor when having a baby. I could tell him all about labor, but he would never understand it because he was a man. He would never comprehend detox either, unless he could find a way to have both types of flu simultaneously, and pump electricity through his veins while his body shot fire out his butt. However, I knew that he understood as much as he was able. I was sure that I wasn't the first drug-dependent person with whom he had dealt.

That night, I was just glad to be back in my own bed. Amidst my relief, however, I was also scared. In my own environment, my body demanded its regular routine. I normally got up in the middle of the night and took a Hydrocodone, then downed another one as soon as

I got out of bed in the morning. My body not only wanted the pill throughout the night, but when I got up on Friday, my mind wanted one, too. My head swirled. I walked with jolts out to the kitchen, and looked at the bottle of painkillers on the counter. I knew I could rid myself of the fog and jilted steps just by taking one of those little pills. I hated them. But I wanted one so badly that I would have paid a thousand dollars if it just promised not to ruin my life. I picked the bottle up and shook it. I started to twist the cap open. But then I heard Simona's voice say, "If you leave here, you will fail." It boomed out like Mufasa's did when he talked to Simba in *The Lion King*—only Simona's voice wasn't as uplifting or encouraging.

I set the bottle down, then walked back down the hallway and fell into bed. I denied both my mind and body their drug, but it wasn't just because I wanted to beat this rap, and prove that I could. It was also because the exhaustion that I felt was incredible. Every time I had to run to the bathroom, I waited until the absolute last minute because I could not force myself to get up. Most of the morning, I lay face down on my pillow, or face up and pulled the comforter up over my head. I couldn't breathe under there, but I didn't care. The seconds were as long as days.

By noon, I didn't have the energy to walk to the kitchen again, where my meds sat on the counter. I had never felt such extreme exhaustion, not even with a bad flu or champagne hangover. The hopelessness made gravity heavy. It felt like my body was made of monstrous magnets, and gravity was pulling me down with all of its might. My legs were steel columns, and my feet were concrete blocks. I could not get out of bed. I had to force myself to power walk to the bathroom just to have diarrhea. The only reason I got up was because, if I crapped my pjs, I would have to clean myself up. And I feared that I wouldn't care enough to do so.

For the next five hours, I fought to breathe, open my eyes, close my eyes, calm down, stop tweaking, stop crawling inside myself, marching marching marching. My nose was plugged up but running. My head pounded when I rolled onto my side. I couldn't move, didn't want to move, didn't want to breathe, live, be. I hid under the covers and hoped they would suffocate me. For about twenty minutes, I fell asleep, and when I woke up, I was sweating buckets under the blankets. Then I was cold. So cold I was probably dead. *Oh God, please don't let me die. No, I don't mean it, God. Please let me die. Please take me. Please, God, take me home.*

"What makes you think you're going 'home'?" Satan hissed. "Your home is with me. You don't worship God. You worship me. I'll give you those pills. Wait right here and I'll go get them for you. Just take one. One will help you feel better. Hell, don't take one! Take them all!" I hated Satan. But he was right. I hadn't been to church in such a long time. Why in the world did I think God would do anything for me when I had forsaken Him?

Overload! Overload! My mind screamed. *This is too much! It's too heavy! Stop! Stop!*

"Listen to me," the devil whispered. "Do what I say. At this point God considers you nothing but a giant wad of garbage, but I care. I'll take care of you!"

While Satan tempted me in the desert of my own making, the muscles in my stomach spasmed, and my bowels twisted. I ran to the bathroom as quickly as possible. My butt was raw and on fire. I saw no end to it either. I knew I would feel like this for the rest of my life. I would spend the rest of my days on this earth wincing from the sting of continuous trots.

For the rest of the afternoon, I did just that. Every fifteen to twenty minutes. I was drained out, thirsty, exhausted, hungry, bloated, sweaty, freezing, filthy, tired, humiliated, angry, hateful, hateful, hateful. I hated My Friend, drugs, and alcohol, but I needed all three so badly. If I had all three, I would feel normal again!

By 5:00 p.m., I could nearly smell my body rotting, so I forced myself to get up so I could take a shower. First, though, I stood in front of the wide mirror above my bathroom sink. My body looked like Homer Simpson's face.

I shook my head and said, "Doh! Lori, you have to do something about this!" And then I felt as crazy as I looked. I slowly got undressed and ran the water in the shower as hot as I could stand it, then I climbed in and stood under the stream, letting the water hit me. It still stung my fingertips, but at that point, I didn't even care if it scalded me. I finally worked up enough energy to turn around and let it hit my back, but I couldn't scrub myself or wash my hair. I didn't have the energy to open the shampoo bottle. The thought of doing that one simple thing was too daunting.

When the bathroom was completely steamed up, and the water started getting cold, I knew I had to get out. Just stepping over the tub felt like climbing a mountain. Once out, I dried off, and lay back down with wet hair. My head was on the pillow and it was cold, but I didn't care. I couldn't summon the desire or energy to get up and dry my hair. The only energy anywhere near me was the anxiety that raced through my nerves. I turned over and tried to shake it out. I would have run away if I could have, but I knew the anxiety would hunt me down like a pack of ravenous wolves.

I pulled the cover up over my head, and wondered what My Friend was doing right at that moment. It was obvious what she wasn't doing! She wasn't caring about ME, and that was for sure. Maybe she didn't even know I was home from rehab. Or maybe she did know and was laughing because she had known I wouldn't make it. Or maybe she wasn't thinking about me at all. Or *maybe, maybe, maybe.* My thoughts were devouring me!

I tossed and turned in my bed all evening, angry at My Friend one second and grieving the loss of our friendship the next. I missed her. I missed her laugh and the way she made me roar. My body buzzed. The anxiety zapped me. *Ugh! How am I ever going to get well when I can't get rid of this racing heart and creeping veins, or the persistent thoughts in my head?*

I was still awake under the covers at 1:00 a.m. because my anxiety medication hadn't touched the heebie-jeebies. At 2:00 a.m., I finally took a painkiller, just to get rid of the electrical current that pulsated under my skin. I was able to fall asleep an hour later. However, I was up at 4:00, and again at 5:30 to go to the bathroom. Each time, my heart filled with sadness, and my mind filled with obsession. I had no idea how to get the thoughts about My Friend or my book, the detox, or my guilt over my demons out of my head. I was wide awake and my mind was screaming.

Saturday, I decided to take the Imodium-type stuff that the doctor had given me, then I stayed in bed between bouts of watery diarrhea because the pills still didn't work. Detox trots were much different than any other kind I had ever had. Nothing stopped them. Nothing.

I tried to talk myself into getting up for other things, like swimming or showering or even walking out to the mailbox, but I couldn't. I just didn't have any desire whatsoever. Normally on a Saturday, I would've had a few beers while watching a Nebraska football game with the Quilters and their spouses, but there was no game that day, and I wasn't drinking anyway. Besides, I didn't want to stink up someone else's bathroom with my disgusting toxic smells. I didn't have anything else that I cared about doing either. I just wrote these words, and sent text messages and emails to friends. The rest of the time, I drowned in the quicksand of my own making. I imagined that My Friend and her daughter were out having fun with Anastasia, and that made my blood boil. *This is stupid!* my thoughts shouted. *You have no idea what she is doing! And why does it matter?* Aggggh! The voices! The voices in my head were making me crazy! They were paralyzing me! It was the same story, different day. I had given up my own identity to be someone that someone else needed or wanted me to be. I had become obsessed with My Friend's painful depression, with making her happy, with changing her life. What about my own life? My life was the one that needed changing. Why did I always treat the object of my codependency better than I treated myself?

Saturday night, I decided to take my daily pill allotment at 8:00 p.m. again, to see if it would help me sleep. It didn't. I slept from 1:00 a.m. to 4:00 a.m. The rest of the time, I writhed with anxiety and flew to the bathroom. When I was able to lie down, I lay on one side, and worked on my computer for a little while, then turned over and tried to catch the elusive Zs. As I stared morosely out the window at the streetlamp that split the darkness, I thought about cutting my skin open so the electricity could escape like steam from a coffee pot, but I was aware enough to know that that would create more problems than it solved. I stood up, fidgeted, jittered, lay back down, turned over, turned back over again.

When I heard the newspaper hit the front porch at 4:30 a.m., I got up and walked out to get it. Normally on a Sunday, I would've read the Omaha World Herald, then worked on my book, or done something with someone—Jane and Misty, Mom, Cassie or Randy, or My Friend. I would've gone with Randy to one of our grandsons' football games, or gone shopping with my mom or Cassie. But I lay in bed all day, working on this book, running to the bathroom to drain the toxins out of my stinking, rotten body, or staring at the ceiling, wishing I could die. I didn't have the energy or desire to do anything. And

the cloud of hopelessness that covered my room told me that I never would again. I took a selfie just so I could chronicle the devastation that reeked from my soul. I wanted to see what it looked like, to stare it in the eye.

It was even worse than I had suspected. My eyes were completely lifeless. If the eyes truly were the mirror to the soul, then my soul was barren. There was no light in them. And I knew I had to face the sad truth. I didn't have to hope to die. I already had.

Me, at home in my bed

Chapter Nine

Sunday evening, I decided to further throw my body into turmoil by taking half of a pill instead of a whole one. I wanted to wean myself down because I had to be drug free for forty-eight hours prior to my appointment with Dr. Ross Smith. That appointment was scheduled for Monday, October 22, 2012—eight days away. It seemed like a century. I wanted to surrender rather than fight for eight MINUTES. How would I fight through eight more days?

That night, I slept from 1:00 a.m. to 3:00 a.m. The rest of the time, I had the heebie-jeebies so badly that I paced around my living room, into the pool room and dining room, then back. Over and over and over again. I knew I was losing my mind, but I had to get through detox somehow. If I didn't, my life would continue to be a wreck. I had to have hope that there was a better life on the other side. If I made it that far.

On Monday, October fifteenth, ten days after I had entered The Center, I counted the pills left in my bottle. Ten. Even though I'd had very little sleep the night before, I was so proud of my ten pills that I bounced into the shower, and actually got ready to face the day. Bob at Blue Valley had set up an appointment for me with a licensed drug and alcohol counselor there, because I wanted to see what my next step should be. I planned to drive to Nebraska City after I bought a few groceries at the store and unloaded them at home.

When I got to the store, most of our employees acted surprised to see me. I hoped they didn't think I had "failed" and had just come back to Falls City to resume life as it had been. Eager to find out what people were saying, I walked up the steps to Randy's office. He said no one was talking about it, and he hadn't told anyone anything. He didn't even think people knew I had gone to rehab! I was surprised by that, but told him, if he heard anyone say that I had failed, I wanted him to set them straight. Otherwise, I just preferred to fly under the radar for as long as possible. Of course, I knew he would have my back anyway, but wanted to make sure we were on the same page.

I walked back down the steps to buy my groceries, and hit the produce aisle to pick out some asparagus. As I did, a wave of anxiety struck me. I couldn't focus or think straight. The apples and bananas were breathing. The bread rack was writhing. I felt like someone was knocking on my forehead, right above my eyes. My nose ran, but I couldn't breathe through it. My bowels raced. My mind spun! *I need to get out of here! I need out! I have to get out!*

I took my groceries to the checkout counter, and longtime checker Judy Harmon started ringing up my purchases. I tried some small talk as she scanned my items, but I couldn't concentrate. She finished my order, but realized she had made an error on my charge account number, so she started over. Visibly, I remained as calm as possible, but on the inside, I was screaming, *No! No! No! I can't do this again! It's too much! Please don't start over!* My insides were jumping around like kids in a birthday party bounce house. The time was 10:30, and I needed to drive the hour to Nebraska City for my 1:00 p.m. appointment, but first, I had to go home and put away my groceries. Plus, there was major construction on the highway between Falls City and Nebraska City. Normally, none of that would have bothered me at all. But under my detox conditions, my head pounded, and my heart raced. Sweat dripped down my face. I panicked. Judy ran the items across the scanner again and apologized for the error. I told her it was O.K., and it was. But I wasn't. I had to get out! Sweat ran down my back then as I listened to the beep beep beep of the scanner. When Judy finished the last item, I thanked her, grabbed my sacks, and bolted for the door.

As I drove home, I looked at the gorgeous fall colors. Crisp yellows, burnt oranges and reds, the browns of oncoming winter. But the landscape heaved in and out as if it was breathing, just like the produce had done. I knew there was no one in my support circle who could take me to Nebraska City during the day, so I went home and took half of a painkiller. My surroundings continued to squish me, but I had to get on the road, so I drove north out of town, endured the construction delays, and headed on toward Nebraska City. By the time I got to Peru, which was about three-quarters of the way, the half-pill had calmed me down just enough to make the landscape stop breathing. Damn that effing white pill!

When I got to Blue Valley, the receptionist checked me in, then the drug and alcohol counselor, Brad, walked out to welcome me into his fold. He was a husky balding man with kind, inquisitive eyes. He was built a little like my favorite animated character, Shrek, and I hoped his personality was just like Shrek's, too. I loved Shrek. He was so kind, vulnerable, and hilarious. I wasn't sure what to think of Brad at first, though, because I was somewhat leery of people who wanted to listen to other people's problems all day (including my other counselor, Bob). But I hoped that Brad would understand what was happening to my mind and body, and could lead me on the pathway back to sanity.

He and I sat in the corner of his office, my cushy gray chair facing his, and a lamp on an end table off to my right. We were away from his desk, so I felt like I was just talking to a friend. He told me to tell my story as it related to my drug dependency, so I talked for forty minutes or so about my back pain, the subsequent weight gain, the painkillers, all of my other medications, and my schedule of ingestion. Then I told him about the emotional turmoil from the *Misty* book, my fears that it wasn't good enough and that the girls would back out, and my relationship with My Friend. I told him all about her warm and welcoming personality, sudden mood swings, the rodeo in Omaha, then her abrupt cut-off. He listened intently, and occasionally interjected a question, which I openly answered.

When I finished, Brad said the following, as I interpreted it: "So, let me see if I have this straight. You're an upstanding citizen, with no arrest warrants or drug charges. You took painkillers for twelve years for a chronic back condition that has been verified by thirteen specialists. You never once took more than the prescribed amount. You drank with the pills to take the pain away, but rarely more than four beers, except recently. One time, you took two pills by accident, but never did it on purpose to get high. Some people in your closest support system didn't even know you were still taking the medication. You are detoxing on your own, under the guidance of a physician. You went from seven pills a day down to one overnight, and you stuck it out despite tremendous sickness and unthinkable anxiety. You have the pills in your house, and you can go the whole day without taking any, despite the anxiety, and you only take ONE when that gets so bad that you can't stand it." I nodded. "I still recommend inpatient treatment," he said, "because of the long-term effects and unfortunate reoffending rate, coupled with the alcohol, but if you are unable to do that because of the constraints, I believe I can help you on an outpatient basis." I smiled for the first time in days. Did someone finally get it? "You are *dependent* on the painkillers, there's no doubt about that," he said, "but you have never abused them. You never stole money to buy the pills on the street. You weren't doctor-shopping or pharmacy-hopping." I nodded excitedly. "You took the pills for a legitimate reason, but just got caught in the trap where you had to eventually take them to avoid the withdrawal symptoms. If you want an intensive outpatient program, we offer one in Auburn three nights a week. You could drive there in thirty-five minutes from Falls City, attend the three-hour sessions, and drive home. But you've already done everything that we would cover in the first two weeks. You have a support system in place, you've *told* your support system and have asked them to hold you accountable. You are detoxing under the supervision of a doctor, and even called your pharmacy to make them aware." Yeah, I HAD done that! "So, you know that the pharmacist is not going to give you any more pills.

You are doing everything you can to kick this. You just need some help getting through it, and help understanding what is happening to your body and brain." I could hear the Hallelujah chorus in my head, but I restrained myself from bursting out in song.

"I can help you with those things," Brad said, "and with your codependent relationships." More choral singing. "What you are going through is similar to a patient with a head injury. You have probably experienced a lack of focus and significant memory loss, including entire conversations. Physically, I'm sure you've had diarrhea, anxiety, maybe even some vomiting, and headaches above your eyes. You will continue to experience those things every day for up to eight weeks."

Eight weeks? Are you effing kidding me? I thought. I felt like Janice on Friends. *Oh. My. God.* My head dropped into my hands.

"I'll never make it eight weeks," I said, despondently. "I won't. I don't know how I'm going to make it through the next eight MINUTES!"

"It *will* get better," Brad said. "Every individual is different, so it may not take that long. But on average, it does. The withdrawal symptoms should start to taper off after eight weeks. Until then, you will also feel emotional for no reason. You'll feel like you're crazy or losing it. You'll be angry out of the blue, and will say things that don't make sense, and can even be hurtful." I had already done that with my husband and probably my daughter, and even my mom. I knew that they understood because I didn't normally do that. But sitting there listening to Brad, I went from devastation to elation—not because I'd been angry or cruel, but because someone understood. Brad was telling me that it wasn't really ME doing those things. It was all of the substances that I'd been using to abuse myself. The bottom line was, Brad knew his stuff, and had been able to communicate in a way that related to me.

"I do want you to do one thing for me, though," he said. "You need to avoid alcohol, too."

"For how long?" I asked.

"It's in your best interest to avoid it for good, but for now, at least a year."

"I'll tell you right now, that's not going to happen," I said. If he was going to be my counselor, he might as well know my boundaries from the very beginning. I was not going to quit drinking. "I am not an alcoholic. When this detox is over and I get those painkillers out of my system, I'm celebrating with my friends."

"Six months for starters," he said.

"No," I said. I was so disappointed. I was going to have to look for someone else.

"Then let's finish these first thirty days," he countered. "We'll revisit the discussion when your thirty days are up." First thirty days? That meant twenty more. The last ten had nearly killed me. When I hadn't thought I could get through thirty *seconds*, I'd thought about the day that I would feel better and could party with my friends. But if he wanted twenty more days in exchange for helping me, then twenty more days I would do.

"O.K.," I said, "we'll revisit it at the end of my first thirty days." I had finally found the help that I needed.

When I left Blue Valley, I drove twenty miles south to Auburn, and had a late lunch with my mom at a barbecue place. I was so hyped up after finding help that I almost felt high. It wasn't the Hydrocodone either. The pills hadn't made me feel that way in nearly a decade. They had just calmed me, made me feel less anxious. I was feeling so much better that I ate half of a grilled chicken salad and a warm breadstick. Mom was so happy to see that. When people around her ate well, she was comforted.

My mother was (and is) the sweetest woman on the face of this earth. Everybody in our small town who knew her loved her. Everybody. Plus, her entire life centered around my siblings and me. Her love was truly unconditional. She deserved my time and attention, even when I was going through drug detox. As we sat there and talked, however, I started feeling very sluggish. My head started twirling again, and everything in the tavern got fuzzy. I had to run to the bathroom, too, (and I do mean RUN). After I finished cleaning up, I rushed back out to the booth where Mom was waiting.

"I need to go home," I said. Mom didn't ask any questions, which was adorably atypical. I quickly paid, then Mom picked up her purse and followed me out. I dropped her off at home, and headed back to Falls City, worried that I would have to go to the bathroom again on the way. I was especially concerned because of the construction delays. I didn't want to have to dash out of my car into the brush and trees while construction workers watched. I did have to stop for the delays but didn't have to run into the weeds. Thank God. Once I got home, however, things took a dramatic turn for the worse. I was *really* sick the rest of the day. My nose was plugged up again yet ran. I had sneezing fits that lasted five minutes and left me unable to breathe. A vise squeezed my brain, and my eyes felt like they protruded like a frog's. I had massive stomach cramps and diarrhea, and *severe* aches and pains all over my body. I dashed to the bathroom at least twenty times between 3:00 p.m. and 8:00 p.m., and the watery stools felt like razor blades. I was so drained and deathly ill by 9:00 p.m. that I seriously considered going to the emergency room. And the anxiety was like I had ingested multiple Red Bulls. No matter where I went or what I did, I couldn't get it to settle down. It pulsated through my body. It jabbed me. It poked me—my stomach, my head. It held me under water; drowning me, drowning me, drowning me. I couldn't stand it anymore. I was so sick that I took a whole Hydrocodone, then continued to run around the house, waiting for the pill to calm me down. I switched channels on my bedroom TV manically, and lay down on the bed. But suddenly, I felt like I was getting zapped, so I waddled downstairs, went to the bathroom, huffed back upstairs, sat down on the couch in the living room, turned on the big-screen TV, and changed the channels. I tried to get away from the surging electricity! But I couldn't. I couldn't couldn't couldn't get away!

Finally, after about thirty minutes, my anxiety started to calm down. The pounding in my head became a dull roar. And my nose stopped dripping. I drew a deep breath. The aches and pains were cut in half, the diarrhea was better. Damn that little white pill, and curses on me for taking it for so long.

Chapter Ten

Tuesday morning, I slept until nearly 11:00 a.m. My body was totally drained from the experience the day and night before. I'd gone from a euphoric high to an incredible crash in an hour. It was like a very short drunk followed by the worst hangover I'd ever had. And I'd had some stinkers.

While I was sleeping, I had one of the most vivid dreams I'd ever had in my life. It was grand and sweeping, and the colors were exceptionally vibrant. And it was about My Friend. In the dream, I had to deliver a package to her. Although I didn't know what was in it, the gift was in a beautiful white box, elegantly wrapped in crystal-studded white ribbon. I took the present out to her house, which in the dream was a big, sprawling plantation, with a wrap-around porch—kind of like the house in the 1994 movie, *Forrest Gump*. I knocked on the front door, but My Friend didn't answer, so I went in to just leave the package. She came in the back door, from the garden, covered in dirt, with her hair up.

She said, "You look like crap."

I said, "That's what happens when you're sick for a month. But you wouldn't know anything about that, would you?" I started to walk out, pissed as hell at her for disappearing in my time of need. She started crying from all the pressure she was under. I arched my back. I wasn't going to break or let her back in, so I walked out and hustled down the steps, determined to leave her behind for good. But I heard her crying. I stopped at the end of the steps and knew I couldn't go. I ran back into the house, and she stood up, opened her arms and let me in. I hugged her tightly and told her I would never leave.

Then, though, my dream switched to a field of grass as green as the pastures in Kentucky. My Friend and her daughter were sleeping on a blanket while I tended to two racehorses that the three of us owned together. The thoroughbreds were gorgeous—muscular mares with beautiful brown coats. They were restless, though, and I couldn't get them to settle down, so I gave each a shot of some type of sedative. Both horses lay down then. Their legs jerked violently, and both died. When I woke My Friend up and told her, she was furious.

The next scene was a sweeping funeral procession for the horses. I walked up to My Friend's house with a covered dish of lasagna as her entire family left in limos, to go somewhere on her land for the funeral. (The land must have been miles wide). I didn't go because I felt so guilty, and didn't think she would want me there, even though the horses were mine, too. When she came back, I was still at the house, full of grief and guilt. But she wrapped her arms around me and told me it wasn't my fault. Her daughter did, too, and both meant it. But the guilt was overwhelming. Then, they had a party to celebrate the lives of the horses. Hundreds of people showed up. My Friend's kids cooked several different kinds of meat, and all of the guests brought side dishes. Five country western dancers—men in jeans, boots, and cowboy hats—did a dance on a platform that the family had erected on their land. It was huge and grandiose. Everybody was happy. I had no idea what it all meant, but I hoped it meant that My Friend would someday have that house, arena, life, and land, probably in heaven, because her life on earth had been hell.

When I woke up, I was so mad at myself for caring about her still. She hadn't even tried to contact me, had shown no concern whatsoever. I was going through the worst thing I would ever endure unless stricken with a terminal illness, and she couldn't even call to check on me? I hated her. But I wanted her to call so badly that I looked at my cell phone and willed it to ring. It didn't. I hated her. I hated my cell phone. I hated the blinds in my room, the gray lifeless sky outside the window, the leaves on the trees, every living thing that dared to breathe while I was inside dying a slow and painful death. I hated her.

That afternoon, I decided to go see Sandy. I thought that there had to be a better antianxiety medication that I could take—one that would help me get through my days without wanting to shank every living, breathing thing in sight. I had already killed all of the mums behind my house by denying them water, and I had honestly done it on purpose. I couldn't bear the thought of bending over to turn on the hose, plus I wanted to hurt something. I seriously considered destroying the flower bed in my front yard, too. My Friend had built it for me during that summer when I'd paid her to help me with a few projects around my house. I wanted to toss the bricks out into the street and break them into a million pieces, but I knew that it would make me look even crazier than I was. Why destroy my own environment? Slowly killing my flowers was as destructive as I could get without actually looking like a psycho.

When it was time to go see Sandy, I summoned every ounce of energy I had just to put my clothes on. I drove out to the clinic, about three blocks as the crow flies, but six blocks on the actual street. That made me angry, too. *Build a damn road straight through!* I thought. *Geez, how tough would that be?* Everything made me angry. The street, the drive, the air, the sunlight. Everything. I hated all of it. I got to the clinic, checked in, then sat in the waiting room and bounced my legs nervously as I waited for the nurse to call my name. Whitney*, a cute thirty-something nurse with coal-black hair, brown eyes, and studious glasses walked out.

"Lori?" she said, while she looked right at me. It was a small town. I was the only person in the waiting room, and besides, I was probably the only Lori that she would see the entire day.

Whitney walked down the hall ahead of me, made me step on the scale (210 again, ugh), then led me into a room, took my temperature and blood pressure (134 over something, which was very high for me), and turned to look at me.

"What can we help you with today?" she said. Help me with? Couldn't she see what was going on? Didn't she already know? Didn't the whole town know?

"I'm in withdrawal from prescription painkillers," I said, "and the anxiety is killing me. I need some help." The nurse reached over and put her hand on my arm.

"I went through this myself a few months ago," she said. "I couldn't get out of bed for three weeks. It was the hardest thing I've ever done." Instantly, I felt like we were comrades in a foxhole, and she had just thrown herself over me to save my life.

"Really?" I asked.

"The anxiety was incredible," she said, "and nobody understands. It's hard to describe to anyone who hasn't experienced it." She was right! Oh man, it was so nice to talk to someone who understood! At that moment, I had an epiphany.

"It's like someone has just told you that your child is missing," I said. Whitney looked up suddenly but didn't smile. Neither one of us did. We knew that this was one of those moments where two people connected and both understood, yet the meaning of the moment was so terrible that neither one of us felt like celebrating the win.

"Yeah," she said, "that's about the only thing that comes close to describing it."

We were both parents. Neither one of us had ever had a missing child, so we didn't want to lessen that horror for those who had. But we were able to imagine what it would feel like for *us*. The anxiety from the withdrawal was just as bad. We nodded at each other in understanding.

She proceeded to tell me all about the withdrawal symptoms she'd experienced. Everything she described was similar to what I was going through. The unbearable heebie- jeebies, the incredible exhaustion, the speeding heart and racing mind, the physical illnesses that sometimes shot projectiles out of both ends at the same time, the all-over-our-bodies aches down to our bones, the constant allergy-like symptoms, from compulsive sneezing and hacking coughs to dripping noses and throats filled with gunk. Somebody finally understood, and it wasn't an expert who had never been through it, or someone who thought he knew but really didn't. It was a medical professional who could put it into words because she'd experienced it herself. We talked for several minutes, and by the time she left the room, I already felt safer. If Sandy didn't understand, at least her nurse did. I could call and talk to her about it.

I only waited a few minutes, then Sandy walked in. Sandy was a beautiful woman. Long and lean with that natural sleek body type that made her look even taller than her six-foot frame. She was trim and fit, had a tiny doe face and spindly fingers. And she had smoky gray eyes that glowed with compassion. I told her everything that had been happening the last few days, and begged for her help. I needed something to take the edge off the anxiety, something to make me feel human again.

"I don't think anything is going to do that until you get through this," she said. I nodded. I knew I was looking for the impossible, but felt like I was losing my mind. I had always been the person in control. Why could I not control my galloping thoughts or my jumpity-jumpity-jumpity nerves? She prescribed another antianxiety medication, then hugged me tightly and told me I could contact her anytime, and she would do whatever she could to help me get through the inhumane battle.

I left there with a sense of hope, filled the prescription at Shopko, went home and immediately took one. It didn't touch the anxiety. I felt like the Gabapentin had done a better job, so I stacked the new medicine up on my kitchen counter, next to the other eight pill bottles, and headed back to my bedroom. I lay down for the rest of the day, trying to control something that was uncontrollable. When I couldn't stand the heebie-jeebies anymore, I bolted out to the living room and paced in a circle.

I heard Randy's truck pull up about 6:10 p.m., so I raced back to the bedroom and lay down. He peeked in and asked what I wanted for supper. I asked for a chocolate malt from Frosty Queen. The local business had great sandwiches, but no one could touch the chocolate malts! If I hadn't been so big on personal responsibility, I would've blamed the people there for my inability to lose weight.

After I slurped my malt down, I lay in my cave with the covers up over my head. It was dark outside, but I knew that trying to sleep would be futile. I could hear Randy clearing his throat. He opened the door.

"Can I get anything for you before I go to bed?" he asked. His tone was one of concerned pity. He loved me unconditionally and I knew it. But I couldn't let him feel sorry for me. If I did, I knew I would lose my strength. The minute anyone showed any type of sympathy, I would fold. That was one of the reasons I'd kept everyone at bay: my mom, sister, daughter, friends, everyone. I knew I had to fight this battle alone or I wouldn't make it. Any show of emotion would send me to the pill bottle, or at the very least to the mini bar in my living room. *Oh God, a beer would be perfect right now! It would help me relax! Maybe even take the anxiety away! I think I'll have a beer! Oh God, a beer would taste so good!*

"I just need something for the anxiety," I said to Randy, trying to let him in a little bit.

"I know you don't like Gatorade," he said, "but the counselor told me that it helps. She recommended Pedialyte, too." At that point, because the anxiety was worse than terror, I was willing to try anything. If the counselor had told him that drinking my own urine would help with the anxiety, I would've peed in a cup and downed it like a shot.

"O.K.," I said. "Please get me some of each so I can see which one I like best."

He took off for the store and I tried to stop thinking about the beer in the mini bar. Ice cold beer. Probably some Busch Light and Bud Light. I loved both. Hell, I didn't really care at that point. I would've settled for homemade wine. I walked out to the living room and opened the door of the mini fridge. Yep. Busch Light and Bud Light. Man, did I want one. Maybe I could just open one and smell it. Maybe just one drink would be O.K. I heard Brad's voice then, telling me that alcohol would significantly increase my chances of relapsing.

"Shut up!" I said, out loud. "I just want one drink! Just one beer! Just one!" I wanted one so badly! I had wanted one for two weeks, had dreamt about drinking one, had fought off drinking one! But I knew I could not go through detox again. That thought was worse than my desire for a beer, so I shut the door. Darn that counselor and his advice!

Randy returned fifteen minutes later with bottles of orange and red Gatorade, and grape Pedialyte. I tried the red Gatorade first, chugging eight ounces. It didn't taste anything like my beer would have! I shook from the taste. It was sweet and dry like red wine, which dried my mouth out terribly. And I didn't believe it would help me with the panic either. What a farce! Why had he believed Simona when she'd told him about the Gatorade anyway? She was my imaginary nemesis.

I set the bottle in the refrigerator and slogged back to the bedroom. I plopped down on the bed, pulled the blanket up to my chin, and laid the pillow over my face, pulling down on it until I couldn't breathe. Maybe I could suffocate myself in my sleep. Angst consumed me. I was at the bottom of the barrel—in the pit. If the anxiety didn't kill me, then the depression would. I lifted the pillow off my face, moaned again and tried not to cry because I knew the minute that I did, the battle would be lost. But I couldn't help it. I was exhausted and couldn't fight anymore. I knew Randy couldn't hear me because he had taken out his hearing aids and had probably fallen asleep, so I let the tears flow. My body shook with the sobs of a broken life.

God, why did I ruin my life like this, with alcohol and painkillers and toxic relationships? Why aren't the people who love me ever enough? Why do I have to have that one relationship that makes me feel so alive when things are good, then makes me wish I was dead three days later? I wanted to die. I wanted to die during the night in my sleep. It had been at least ten days since I had talked to My Friend, ten days since I'd taken a full schedule of my painkillers, eleven days since I had guzzled a beer. In essence, I was detoxing from alcohol, painkillers, other medications, and my codependent relationship all at the same time. I didn't want to do it anymore. It was too hard. I wanted a Hydrocodone, a beer, an Ambien, and a call from My Friend. I felt so effing pathetic!

No! The voice in my head said. *You are not pathetic. And none of those things deserve your time and attention anymore. Or your life.* I lay there for several minutes, just breathing deeply, and suddenly noticed that my anxiety level had quietly dropped from level red to orange. I rolled over on my side and peeked out from under the covers. It was nearly 10:00 p.m., but the light in my room was still on because I hadn't been able to walk two feet to turn it off. Maybe I could even get up and do that! There had been a few nights when I hadn't been able to, so the light had stayed on all night. Was my anxiety really a little better? Had the frequency of the lightning bolts slowed down? I pulled the covers down and looked at the ceiling. Well, I felt like I was slightly closer to being human. Had the Gatorade helped? Really?

I got up to turn the lights off, but actually felt like I could walk into the bathroom and maybe even take a shower! I knew I would sleep better if I did, so I got undressed and stood in the shower, staring at the water that rushed from the showerhead. I just stood there, letting the water pound me, and letting the steam fill the bathroom until I could barely breathe.

Cleaning up made me feel a little better, so I dried off, donned a clean pair of pajamas, then slid back into bed. My anxiety, though still pulsating, wasn't clawing at my very soul, and for that, I was grateful. I watched TV until about 2:30 a.m. and fell asleep from complete exhaustion. Like every other night, though, I woke up an hour later, and tossed and turned the rest of the night.

Chapter Eleven

Wednesday, I stayed in bed all day, except for the two dozen or so necessary trips to the bathroom. The antidiarrheal had no effect on me whatsoever. Plus, the exhaustion was on the opposite end of the scale from the anxiety. I still had the latter, too, though. I could not drag my body out of the bed and could barely open my eyes. My head pounded from sinus pressure, but I couldn't even get up to find the bottle of Motrin. When I lay still, the anxiety crawled like quiet creepy-crawly spiders inside me. Spiders crawling inside me, tippity tippity tippity crawling! My arms shot into the air. Aaaagh! I couldn't stand the crawling anymore! I rushed out to the fridge and poured a large glass of Gatorade, downed it quickly, then went back to bed and pulled the comforter up over my head. I knew I would completely waste the day again, but I didn't care. *Oh God, please let me care about something!* Lying under the comforter, I begged for mercy. The anxiety slowly tapered off to a level that was tolerable. But that was it. The rest of the symptoms remained steady and strong. I had never felt that level of mental, emotional, and physical heaviness.

When the mailman stopped later that afternoon, I looked out the window and knew that there was no way I could walk to the mailbox. I was sinking inside myself, and had neither the desire nor ability to do anything about it. The cloud of depression was as thick as fog. I could not even walk out to my own mailbox!

Suddenly, I was enraged about the cruel way that I was being ig-nored by My Friend during my time of need. Sure, my husband was there, my mom called every day, and so did Cassie. Linda checked in periodically, and no-doubt kept the Quilters updated. A few other friends called once in a while, too. But when they did, I pulled myself together as much as possible, just long enough to talk. I couldn't tell any of them what I was really going through. How could they possibly understand? I couldn't explain it. I didn't know any words that came close to describing it. Being buried alive came close. Drowning in the Missouri River came close. But still, nothing fully described the con-stant terror-filled anxiety, the flu-like sickness, or the black hole of de-pression. I was glad that some people checked on me, though. It made me feel like they cared. But My Friend continued to widen the chasm with her cruel silence. I was so mad at her that I flipped my computer open and wrote a long rambling email about her indifference, and how angry I was that I'd had no say-so whatsoever about the demise of our friendship. But I was even more upset that it was so easy for her to cut me out of her life!

As soon as I hit send, I regretted it. *Why do I always do this?* I thought. *Why do I let my emotions run away with me, especially now, when I have no control over them? Why do I care about someone who has proven that she doesn't care about me? And why do I chase after people who find it easy to end our friendship when I have so many friends who would do anything to fix something that was broken?* I knew I wouldn't be able to answer those questions without a lot of work, and I wasn't sure I had it in me. I certainly didn't that night, so I did nothing but watch TV in my bedroom—when I could keep my eyes open. When I couldn't, I pulled the covers up over my head, and wished for the world to go away. Even though my eyes were heavy, it wasn't like I could sleep. Closing them just made my racing thoughts circle even faster. It made the heebie-jeebies worse, My Friend's deafening silence louder, the de-pression as deep and hopeless as a dark, dank well. I was so tired, and could barely keep my eyes open, but I fought to do so, so I wouldn't experience the things that happened when I closed them.

The night dragged on like a monotone preacher. I was awake and staring at my comforter most of the night, when I wasn't dashing to the bathroom.

The next morning, I felt a little better, and was so stir-crazy from being cooped up that I actually wanted to get out for a while! Jerry was hosting a meet-and-greet that night at the Grand Weaver Hotel in Falls City, and I knew that his wife and campaign manager were decorating the venue that morning. I thought I could at least hang some signs or set out chairs. It took me two hours to talk myself into going because of my withdrawal symptoms, but at 10:00 a.m., I got in the shower to get cleaned up. By 10:45, I was down at the Grand Weaver. However, the women had already decorated the room. It had taken me so long to get ready that I was too late to help. I talked to the girls for a while, and told them I was proud of the campaign they were running. But as we stood in the beautifully-renovated room, the place started spinning. I felt fuzzy all over. I leaned against a wall so I could talk to my friends without appearing drunk.

Jerry showed up about 11:15 and wanted to go to lunch at a local hangout called One Stop. I started to feel a little better, so we all jumped in our cars and headed out.

One Stop was a diner straight out of the '60s. Actually, I didn't think it had been updated since then. The restaurant was sometimes used in wedding shoots because of its old-fashioned décor, which mainly featured Coke memorabilia. There were eleven booths and about ten swivel chairs at the counter, which resembled an old-time soda fountain. The food was home-cooked good, and there was plenty of it. My favorite meal of the day there was breakfast. The pancakes covered an entire platter, and the omelets were made-to-order. The hash browns were the best I'd ever had, anywhere. Crisp on the outside, soft and flavorful on the inside. Lunch was pretty great, too, and included everything from the hot beef sandwich (which was heaped on a meat platter) to fried chicken with real mashed potatoes and gravy. The food wasn't just plentiful, it was richly sinful.

Jerry, Chris, Vicki, and I sat squished into a small booth. Jerry and I had the fried chicken special, Chris ate a salad with strips of fried chicken on top, and Vic had half of a hot beef sandwich. We were all stuffed within thirty minutes, when the former (now, the late) Falls City mayor, Rod Vandeberg, came in. Rod and Jerry were both movers and shakers, so they got along well and supported each other. Rod's late wife's family owned one of the banks in town, and had for decades. He'd run the bank for most of those years. He had retired when he was in his early seventies, and could have rested on his laurels and traveled freely. Instead, he ran for mayor as a write-in candidate and won. Some people didn't care for his philosophies, and he often gave introductions that were longer than the speeches, but everybody in town knew that, if they wanted something done, they gave the job to Rod. He then collaborated on the projects with people like Jerry and me. Rod and I were both big supporters of Jerry's campaign. We served as confidantes and advisors.

Rod waltzed over to our table but seemed surprised to see me. I was sure he'd been told that I had gone to rehab, but may not have been told that I had come home. At least that was the impression I got. He was very warm, like usual, and didn't ask any questions. We just talked about the campaign. When he was done talking, he walked away from our table to go say hello to the local newspaper publisher in the back booth, and the room, for me, started to swirl. Just then, Ron Ebel, husband of my late friend, Karen, walked in and sat down at the counter. My detox fog started in again, and he looked like he had peach fuzz all over him. I told Vic, Jerry, and Chris that I had to get out of the restaurant quickly. I got up and ran into a swivel chair because the room was tipping sideways, so I tried to calm myself down. Then I wrapped my arms around Ron from behind, basically to hold myself up, and gave him a big squeeze.

"Where are you watching the Nebraska game Saturday?" Ron asked.

"Probably at home," I said.

"How are you feeling?" he asked.

"Not the best, but I'm winning," I said. He nodded, and I left. I knew the subject was hard for him to talk about. It was hard for everyone to talk about. I wasn't ever the person who needed help. I was the person who helped people.

All the way home, I felt like my car was standing still, but the road was moving, like one of those video games with the steering wheel on the column of the machine, and the racetrack on the screen. I had felt that way once before, about a year prior, when My Friend, her daughter and I had spent the morning together, and had gone to a restaurant in town for lunch. My Friend was angry about something, but wouldn't tell me what, so I got the cold shoulder throughout the meal.

On our way back to my house where her truck was parked, we made uncomfortable small talk. I asked her if her ham and bean soup had been good, and she said, "Not as good as my own." Then she asked if my husband liked ham and beans.

"I don't know," I said, nonchalantly. Immediately, her demeanor changed. It was like rage ignited inside her. She laughed a dry, annoyed laugh and sat up straight in her seat, then turned toward me.

"You don't know if your husband likes ham and beans?" she yelled. "Your marriage is a farce. How can you not know if your husband likes ham and beans?" I was completely taken aback by her tone of voice. Sweat beaded on my hairline and dripped down my back. My face was hot and flushed.

"I don't know," I said, meekly. "I guess because I don't make ham and beans."

I slowed down at the next corner, and she thrust herself toward the dash, in an apparent exaggerated slam against my driving.

"And there's another thing," she said. "I'm gonna hook a trailer up to this car and teach you how to drive. You start and stop, start and stop, start and stop. It's making me sick to my stomach. She does that, doesn't she, honey?" I looked in the back seat, and her daughter's face was as red as mine. The poor girl held her hands up like she didn't know what to say. "And besides that," My Friend continued, obviously now on a rant, "all day today, you've raced around and changed directions like a squirrel being chased by a dog. It's like you're on drugs. Are you high right now?"

"No, I'm not high!" I said. She shook her head like I was the dumbest ass she had ever met in her life. I wanted to take her apart, but I just froze. I didn't know what to do. I was so afraid of losing her that I just pulled into my driveway, and all three of us got out. Then it was like somebody flipped a switch on her. She thanked me for lunch, and insisted on helping me carry some of my stuff into the house. So, I let them both help. When we finished, My Friend asked me if I needed help on any projects around the house the next day. I told her I didn't think so. She acted like the previous ten minutes had never happened! Her daughter tried to do the same thing, so I did, too. I acted like my feelings hadn't just been ripped to shreds like grass with a weed whacker. My Friend held onto my arm, and said she'd see me in a few days. I watched out the window as they climbed into their truck, and then, they were gone. I stood there, frozen in my living room. However, the longer I thought about the ride home, the madder I got. I had just plain had it. I tried to call My Friend's cell phone. She didn't answer, so I called her home phone and left a message that said I would like to talk to her about the way she had treated me. She didn't call me back because she never called me back. She gave me the silent treatment for more than a week, and the anxiety that her silence produced was excruciating. The next time I saw her, though, she acted like I was God's gift to the world. So, I let it go. Again.

Now, as I was driving home from lunch with Jerry and his campaign staff, I relived the feelings I had felt that day with My Friend—feelings that had made me an irritable, overweight, lethargic recluse. And a pushover. I was definitely a pathetic pushover.

When I got home, I headed back to my sanctuary to lie down so the road would stop moving, and my thoughts would stop swirling. I rolled over onto my side, and tried to extinguish my volcanic anger about My Friend's silent treatment. An hour or so later, one of the Quilters named Sue called, and asked if she could come see me for a while. I didn't feel well at all, but was thankful that someone wanted to come. Of the Quilters, I had only seen Linda. I knew that the rest were keeping up with my progress through her, but I was anxious to catch up with Sue, and see what was going on with her and everyone else.

Sue came in at 4:00 p.m., carrying an old-fashioned picnic basket. She'd brought a homemade lasagna, garlic bread, and banana nut bread. I squeezed her hard and thanked her for her kind heart and excellent cooking. We set the lasagna out so I could bake it for my dinner. We talked for two hours then about the difficult journey upon which I'd embarked, about her unconditional support, and about my need for control of my way "out." She admitted that she'd never understood it, but after I explained the episode in the hospital, she said she "got it" completely. I was so thankful. Her kindness reminded me how blessed I was to have friends who truly cared.

When 6:00 p.m. rolled around, I was feeling so buoyed by her visit that I decided to attend the meet-and-greet for Jerry. I knew that every *body* was important, so I needed to be there. Sue said she would go with me, too. I took half of a Hydrocodone before we went, so I could feel decent and not make an idiot of myself. Sue and I then ventured out on a rainy, cold, and windy October night, and headed down to the Grand Weaver.

When we pulled into a parking space on the south side of the building, we could see a crowd of, maybe, twenty-five people. I was crushed for Jerry. I knew how important the night had been for him, and people just hadn't shown up. Sue and I went in, perused the food table that had been set up by a caterer, and listened as Jerry talked about his campaign and the things he intended to accomplish when he was elected to the state legislature. I was so proud of Jerry. A man of great dignity and integrity, he promised to focus his campaign on the issues and not on negative advertising, and he had stuck to that plan from the beginning. His political party, sadly, had not done so, and neither had several special interest groups, but HE had. As he stood and addressed the small crowd, I hoped for bigger and better things, and bigger audiences yet to come.

When he finished, I told him I was proud, then I snaked through the serving line and grabbed some delicious hors d'oeuvres. The caterer had made Swedish meatballs that were to-die-for, and popcorn that had been coated with almond bark. (I'd never met a snack that couldn't be improved with almond bark.) I ate my small plateful, then decided to mingle a little, even though I no longer worked a room like I had when I was younger. I had been like a politician back then, shaking hands with everyone, introducing myself. But I'd become much more withdrawn as I'd gotten older—not so willing to put myself out there. I knew that most of it was because of the painkillers and my weight gain. I was ferociously battling the first one, and hoped to conquer the other when the first was done.

I stood with a circle of people and talked to some of those who had been instrumental in Jerry's campaign. I knew that all of them knew why I had bailed out, but I wasn't sure that they supported my decision to do it *during* the campaign. That night, my fears were allayed. Every volunteer wished me luck, commented on my health, and said that he or she admired me for tackling a difficult problem. Their comments buoyed me, and made me even more determined to beat my demons.

I talked to Jerry then, about my disappointment with the size of the crowd, and he reminded me that both high schools in town had football games that night. Bad timing on our part! As he walked away, I polished off my munchies, but then the room began to sway. I leaned against a post and tried to calm my zooming heart. My eyes bounced around, and sweat pooled at the nape of my neck. My head started ringing and hammering. I closed my eyes and pressed against the lids. *Why is this happening?* I thought. *I took a pill before I came, to make sure this wouldn't happen.* I felt like a drug addict, but of course withdrawal was still going to happen. I had been on the painkillers and many other prescription drugs for twelve years. Why had I expected the withdrawals to only last a few days?

Sue came over about that time, and asked if I was ready to go. I didn't know if she had been watching and knew I needed saved, or if she was just ready to leave, but I was grateful for the interruption. She took hold of my arm and walked me outside. The cool air jolted me awake. We jumped in her car, and she took me home. I hugged her, and told her how much I appreciated her time, attention, and the dinner she had made. Then, I went inside, rushed to the bathroom, and wondered how long withdrawals would literally drain me.

Randy was broadcasting one of the ballgames about which I'd forgotten, so I didn't have to worry about his supper. I ate some lasagna, then spent the evening typing some of my story, and watching Grey's Anatomy. My husband came home after his ballgame and checked in on me. I held myself together just long enough to convince him that I was doing O.K. He showered, then went to bed.

At 11:00 p.m., I decided that I'd seen the *Friends* rerun enough times, and needed to go to sleep. I tossed and turned until 2:00 a.m., though. My skin didn't crawl—it was worse than that. It felt like that test for carpal tunnel, where the doctor sends a jolt of electricity into the patient's hand, and the hand flops uncontrollably. My whole body felt like that. When I tried to stay still for three or four seconds, my body began flopping, my arms shot up into the air, and my legs convulsed. I was completely tweaking. I paced into the living room, sat down in the recliner, and stared outside as my extremities continued to spasm. *Will I feel this way forever?* I thought. *Always unable to sleep? Always as if electricity is bolting through my veins?* My house seemed to answer. It was speaking to me, talking, breathing, shaking, swelling, circling; circling like a tiger ready to attack its prey. In addition, a million needles poked at my body. So, I bolted up out of the chair and dashed into the sunroom. Then I walked into the pool room and back to the living room. I circled through again. Prior to my detox, my home had been my haven, my sanctuary. But everything was moving around! It was moving! It was breathing in and out! I felt like I was in a horror movie. I worried that the phone would ring, and someone would talk to me from inside the house. Still, I was so glad that I had decided to go through this experience at home, where I knew every nook and cranny. I couldn't imagine the terror that I would have experienced in a foreign place, where I would've been trapped while experiencing the worst sickness of my life.

Thinking that the most unbearable anxiety was in the bedroom where I spent the majority of my time, on my computer, I decided to sleep on the couch for the night. I took my blanket and pillows out to the living room, and lay down on the couch. My skin still jumped, but by 3:00 a.m., I was finally able to sleep.

Chapter Twelve

I woke up two hours later, at 5:00 a.m., when Randy got up to go to work. He didn't realize I was on the couch, so he turned the light on in the kitchen. The light streamed over into the open dining room and living room.

"Don't let me scare you," I said. "I'm on the couch."

He brought a bottle of water to me, told me he was proud of me, then went into the bathroom and took a shower. I was still awake when he left for work. It was about 6:00 a.m., and I could barely move because of the exhaustion and depression, but my skin started in on me. I was so irritated and angry. I needed to sleep. I wanted to sleep. I wanted to feel better, get better, stop feeling like crap, stop jumping out of my skin. I fell to my knees on the floor and buried my head in the pillows on the couch. Suddenly enraged, I pounded the pillows. I was so mad that I had chosen to go through this hell. Why hadn't I done it slowly, over a six-month period, with Sandy? And why wasn't My Friend calling me? Why didn't she care? The answer to that question ripped my heart apart. I hated her and wanted to pound her face in. Then, I wanted to die.

My Hydrocodone was on the counter. All I had to do was take one and I could sleep. *I won't feel this way for a few hours*, I thought. My skin would calm down, my mind would stop racing. My head would stop pounding, my bowels would stop draining. I wouldn't feel like crap for a while.

Just take one! Satan teased. *Just one! No one will ever know!*

Damn it, shut up! my thoughts shouted. I had come so far, and I wasn't going back. I wasn't even taking *half* of one until that night.

I figured that I was scheduled to see Dr. Ross Smith on Monday at 1:00 p.m., and I had to be off the drug for forty-eight hours prior to my appointment so he could give me the Suboxone, which was supposedly non-addictive. So, my plan was to take half of a pill at 8:00 p.m., so I could hopefully sleep for a while, and then take the other half on Saturday about noon, to meet the two-day requirement. Besides, the Nebraska Cornhuskers played at 2:00 p.m. on Saturday, and the Quilters were watching the game at the Elks Club. Even though I couldn't drink, I could still watch the game with them for a while. I just didn't want to do it with the room spinning. And I definitely didn't want to have to run to the bathroom a dozen times.

As I battled my desire to take a pill, I pulled myself up off the floor. *Damn it!* I thought. *Damn my bugging, jumpy skin. And damn the sunrise, which threatened my peaceful sleep anyway. And damn those pills. And damn my body and my life and everybody and every moving thing.*

I decided to go downstairs to our guest bedroom, where it would be darker. The temperature was also cooler down there, so I could maybe sleep better. My legs felt like lead, but I tried to get down the steps. I was shaky and couldn't think straight, so I was afraid I would fall. I held onto the wall. When I reached the bottom step, I dragged myself through the TV room, another living room, and into the guest bedroom. I slipped beneath the gorgeous brown and rust-colored comforter on one of the two queen-size beds in the room. I sunk into the pillow-filled haven. The silky sheets felt so smooth on my skin! So much better than the sheets on my bed! *Why do my occasional guests sleep in better conditions than I do?* My own bedroom was a mess. The sheets on my bed were flannel, and periodically slipped off the corners, so I was constantly lying on layers of wrinkled sheets. My pillows were flat from years of use. I put better sheets and pillows on my guest beds than I had ever purchased for myself. *Why? Why do I always treat everyone better than I do myself?* I made a mental note to decipher that question with Brad. I didn't know the answer to the why, I just knew it was true. I hadn't made time for my own health in nearly a decade. I had worked on my *Misty* book with fierce determination, because I wanted so much for their lives to be easier. But what about me and mine? Shouldn't I have the life that I deserved, too? Was it selfish to get in the pool every day? Was it really selfish if I took thirty minutes away from the book, and lifted weights instead? Maybe if I had done that, I wouldn't be in the physical, emotional, and mental state that I was in. I forced myself to think about something else, then I finally fell asleep.

At 7:30 a.m., my cell phone rang, so I woke up quickly and tried to use my, "No, you really didn't wake me up" voice. Jerry was on the other end and wanted to talk politics. I tried to think straight, but I was soooo tired. I wanted to listen, but just couldn't stay awake. *Why can't I feel this way at eleven p.m., or even midnight?*

I finished the conversation, lifted the blanket over my head so I couldn't see the sunlight filtering through the shade, and fell back to sleep until 9:00 a.m. I finally got up then, and looked at the pile of laundry in the laundry room. That was all I could do, though—look. Then I stared at the washer. I had no energy or desire to even open the lid. I couldn't! It was too overwhelming to just reach over and lift it! So, I walked upstairs and checked my email. I started working on this book. Jerry called again then, and wanted me to go through my mail, to decipher a negative flyer that had been sent out about him. I was too embarrassed to tell him that I couldn't even walk out to the mailbox, so I slipped on a pair of flip-flops, flopped out to the mailbox, and rifled through the mail. The morning was very chilly, and my feet were cold, but I didn't care. Yep, there the pamphlet was. It was from an organization that couldn't have picked Jerry out of a lineup. The group had sent a flyer stating that Jerry would raise his constituents' taxes because he "had raised water rates as the board chairman of his tiny town of Stella, Nebraska."

"We just discussed raising the water rates," Jerry said, when I called him back. "But we didn't even take action. Besides, we haven't raised water rates in this town since the 1970s."

"Well, let's talk about the fact that the state legislature has absolutely nothing to do with water rates in Stella!" I added. It was so ridiculous. Political advertisements in this country had gotten so far out of line that something needed to be done about them. I told him so, and tried to calm him down. We decided to do damage control by running a newspaper ad to dispute everything that the group had stated, but we planned to do it right before the election so the opposition had no time to respond. Jerry was satisfied with that, so I hung up.

I didn't do another productive thing all day. I was so worn out from thinking and focusing that I could barely move. I sent a whiny-ass email message to Linda, and told her I didn't know how much longer I could take it—the draining diarrhea, accompanied by indescribable anxiety, pounding headaches, and unexpected confusion—followed by vegetative exhaustion. She sent back an encouraging message and basically told me to suck it up. Along with a smiley face. She was so awesome.

I took a shower, but didn't care enough to put makeup on. I ate some of Sue's leftover lasagna for lunch, and worked on my computer while I ran to the bathroom all afternoon. In between those dashes, I flipped through the TV channels. I couldn't find anything worth watching.

Linda stopped by about 6:00 p.m., after she and fellow Quilter, Lynne, had been out to Lem's for a few beers. I missed my Quilters, and missed joining them for drinks. I missed going places with Randy when he wasn't working. I missed my daughter, mom, family, the sunshine, feeling normal. And I missed My Friend's laughter so much.

I worked on my notes all evening, and turned the TV to *Friends* at 10:00 p.m. I didn't have the episode memorized, so I watched several episodes until midnight. Then, I turned off the light.

The next morning, Linda called at about 8:00, and wanted to go to breakfast at One Stop. I had been awake since 4:00 a.m., so I wasn't able to sleep anyway. I met her at One Stop at 9:15. The place was packed, and we couldn't get a booth, so we sat at the counter. I ordered a pancake, which was usually big and fluffy and covered the plate. A few friends were in the restaurant, but my eyes were already circling with dizziness, so I didn't get up to go chat. Besides, I didn't want to be mistaken for a pregnant woman about to give birth.

Linda and I waited nearly forty-five minutes for our breakfast (which was unusual), but when it came, it was heaping, hot, and tasty. I downed half of my pancake, which I had ordered with peanut butter on top, then had smothered in syrup. Right about that time, our friend and fellow Quilter, Gail Froeschl, came over to chat. She and her husband had been in one of the booths along the windows, but had finished eating and were heading home. By day, Gail was the librarian for the elementary schools in Falls City. She sometimes worked Saturdays after she'd been to One Stop. She waxed poetic that day about several things that were going on in town, then hugged me, asked how I was really doing, and started in on another subject. She, like most people, apparently just felt better skimming the surface of my drug detox. And that was fine with me.

After we talked, Gail and Marty left, so I waited while Linda finished eating. As we sat there, though, the room actually spun. I looked down at my plate and tried to focus, but it was no use. The bubble holes in the fluffy pancake looked like hairy eyeballs. I felt sweat at the nape of my neck, then told Linda I needed to go. We got up, paid, and headed toward the door.

Over by the window, sitting in one of the booths, was a former co-worker of My Friend's, so Linda waited by the door as I quickly said hello. Peggy Phillips* had asked if she could read my *Misty* book before it went to print, and I had forgotten about it. She asked again that morning, and I vowed to remember, even though I felt that the book was in trouble. Peggy also said that Misty was taking one of her ponies on Tuesday, to train her. The mare had been biting Peggy, and needed some discipline. I told her that Misty would instill discipline within a few days. She always did. But I tried to steer the conversation clear of the women after that. I hadn't heard back from my agent about the book, and I hadn't heard from Misty and Jane, so I didn't really want to talk about either subject.

I left the restaurant then, drove home and noticed that several yards had been decorated with Husker football decor. On fall Saturdays in Nebraska, everyplace but the bars might as well shut down. Football is the only thing that matters on game days. The Huskers were scheduled to play Ohio State that day, in Ohio. The game was supposed to start at 2:30 p.m., and all of the Quilters and most of their husbands were going to the Elks Club to watch. I had decided not to go because Cassie had called before I went to One Stop, and wanted to come down to prepare several meals for me. She didn't want me to have to cook while I was sick. I wanted to spend the afternoon with my beautiful daughter. By the time I pulled into the driveway, Cassie was already waiting. My back was killing me at that point, so I lay down on the couch, and Cass sat beside me.

My daughter was one of my heroes. She was exactly who I wanted to be when I grew up. Although I was her rock, Cassie was the one of those people whose self-confidence in nearly every area had proven un-shakeable. She had the same weight-centered fears that a lot of twenty-seven-year-olds had (although she was physically stunning), but other than that, her confidence seeped from her pores. She had once broken off a long-term relationship after buying a house with the guy because he wouldn't open up to her emotionally, and she didn't like the way he talked to her (for the record, neither did I). If Cassie was in a relationship that drained her—with a friend or otherwise—and it didn't improve after discussion, she put an end to it, walked away, and never looked back.

My daughter also had a tenacious sense of adventure. When she graduated from high school in Falls City, she went to college in Wayne, New Jersey, because she wanted to be near New York City, but not in it. After one semester, she decided that Nebraska wasn't so bad after all, plus she missed seeing the green of nature and the wide open spaces, so she moved back to Lincoln, Nebraska, and attended the University of Nebraska – Lincoln (UNL), where the Huskers played football. She was there for two years, then transferred to Peru State College so she could be closer to her then-boyfriend. She, her dad and I moved her into an apartment in Auburn, Nebraska, which was just twelve minutes southwest of Peru, and about twenty minutes northwest of Shubert, where her boyfriend lived.

Two days before classes started, I received the call that every parent dreaded. Cassie had been in a car accident, and had been thrown from the vehicle. The caller, a volunteer paramedic, said I needed to drive slowly and safely, but asked me to meet the ambulance at the hospital.

When Randy and I arrived at the emergency room, Cassie was puffed up twice her size, and her neck was in a cervical collar. She and her boyfriend had gotten into an argument at her apartment, he had left and driven twenty miles home to Shubert, and Cassie had followed him. When she was about three miles from Shubert, she had unbuckled her seat belt to reach down for her cell phone. When she did, she swerved off the road, and flipped end-over-end. Her car ended up on its wheels, but she had flown out the passenger window and landed in a harvested field.

A few hours later, a man working the night shift at the state prison in Tecumseh, Nebraska, was driving home from his shift when he saw stationary headlights in a farm field. The time was 3:30 a.m., so he knew the lights weren't from a tractor. He investigated and found an empty, destroyed car. He called 911, and the authorities quickly arrived. It took nearly forty-five minutes for the officials to find Cassie. She had been thrown 148 feet from the vehicle. She should have been a statistic in a body bag. The facts made her survival impossible. But when they found her, she woke up, and even made sense.

In the emergency room, when I first saw her, I was just thankful that she was alive. The fact that she was talking, moving her fingers and toes, and actually comforting me was a godsend. But I was worried because she was so bloated. The first thing I thought then was internal bleeding. Or her body had just puffed up to protect itself. I didn't know, but I was a basket case about it. I just had to internalize it, like I always did, because I was the one to whom everyone else in our family turned.

The long and short of the story was that she was transported by ambulance to Bryan West in Lincoln because the morning was too foggy for a helicopter. The ER doctors there evaluated her, and found that she had a shattered pelvis, several broken vertebrae, and a broken rib. She had surgery as soon as she was able, and the doctors pieced her pelvis back together and stabilized it with a fixator. That consisted of a steel plate in her back, connected to two steel rods that protruded from her pelvis.

There was no way that she could go to school that semester, so an administrator at Peru State College withdrew her from her classes. Her landlord in Auburn kindly released her from her lease, also, because Cassie's recovery would have to be spent at home, under my care, and the watchful eye of her father. Her dad took care of our livelihood, and I took care of Cassie's day-to-day needs. It was a full-time job, and I developed a new respect for around-the-clock caregivers.

Now, as Cassie stood at my stove, cooking several suppers for her detoxing mother, I thanked the good Lord for catching her in the air that fateful night on August 24, 2005, and laying her down in the field.

The rest of the afternoon, I talked with Cass while she made a Runza casserole, meatloaf, and barbecued ribs. When the dishes were done and the food was in the refrigerator, she went to Auburn, to her new boyfriend's mom's house. She and Brian ate dinner there, then went with his family to the Haunted Hollow at Indian Cave State Park, which was a camper's paradise halfway between Auburn and Falls City. The Haunted Hollow was a growing tradition where campers convened for Halloween, and decorated their campsites. It had become a very big attraction in southeast Nebraska. Spectators could view the sites on weekends throughout October. There were hayrack rides, barbecues, trail rides on horseback, and spooky goblins at every campsite. I had attended the Haunted Hollow the year prior with My Friend and her daughter, and we'd had a blast.

While Cass was out having a good time, I was sinking like a cow in mud, thinking about that time at Indian Cave. My mind was out of control. I wanted to fix the situation with My Friend, but knew she wouldn't listen. Just thinking about it made my skin prickle. My back was killing me, and I couldn't find a comfortable position anywhere. I was still lying down, of course, but I was in constant, miserable pain. The ringing in my head was overwhelming—not in my ears, in my HEAD. It sounded like a full chorus of crickets. The pounding above my eyes was inhumane. The last time I had felt like this was the first night in detox, and my blood pressure had been 168 over something high, but I couldn't remember what. I knew that a beer would make me feel so much better, and would probably lower my blood pressure, too.

I want a beer! I thought. *I want two beers! A six-pack! Twelve!* I wanted to get as drunk as I'd ever been. As I lay there worrying about blood pressure, stroke, heart attack, and nervous breakdown, I looked at the clock constantly. Evening gave over into night, and then into morning. At 2:00 a.m., sleep was still elusive! My skin started screaming, *Just go get a beer or take the damn pill!* My mind said it, my heart said it, my body said it. My mind circled the Hydrocodone track. *Just take HALF of a pill! It's only half! You're down to half!* I couldn't stand my racing mind, so I got up and walked to the living room, then around the path I had created in my house. After fifteen minutes of that, I lay back down.

By 3:00 a.m., I'd been awake for nearly twenty-four hours, and the ringing in my head was unbearable. I whimpered like a puppy. I didn't want to take the pill, but didn't see any other way. I was going to die without it. I didn't want to exist without it. I didn't know how I was going to make it through the night! Through the next five minutes! I started to panic! I called out to the emergency room at the hospital to see who was on call. The nurse who answered the phone said she couldn't give out that information, but that the doctor was someone who worked weekends, and was from Omaha. I didn't really care who it was. I just wanted to know whether it was Sandy or not. She was guiding my problem, and I didn't want to wake her up if she was on call. If it was a doctor who was staying at the hospital, that was different. The nurse said it was a PA from Omaha named Kathy and that she would ask Kathy to call me back. Five minutes later, my cell phone rang. I told Kathy that I was in detox, and was just trying to get through the night without any drugs so I could go see Dr. Smith in Lincoln on Monday. He was going to take away my withdrawal symptoms with Suboxone, and make me feel human again. I told her I was just trying to gut it out, but that I hadn't slept in days. Kathy told me to take a Benadryl, to see if that would help me sleep. If it didn't, I would have to take the pill, and just take my chances with Dr. Smith. I didn't want to take the pill; that disgusting little five milligrams that still controlled my life. I'd gutted it out for twenty-four hours. I was doing so good, and I wanted to kick those pills' butts. I was not taking a step backwards.

I scoured through the master bathroom pantry for some Benadryl, but couldn't find any anywhere. I looked in the pool bathroom, and in both bathrooms downstairs. I shoved stuff over and opened medicine cabinets. No Benadryl anywhere. *Take the pill. Take the pill!* my body screamed. I slogged back upstairs and paced around the path again.

Randy didn't have to work that morning, but he still got up at 4:30, just because he was used to doing so. I hollered at him, and told him that my heart was pounding out of my chest, the pressure above my eyes made my head feel like it was going to explode, and my skin and vision were both playing snare drums. *Rat-a-tat-tat rat-a-tat-tat.* I couldn't take it anymore.

"Don't take the pill," he said.

"I'm not going to," I said, "but the doctor said I could take some Benadryl." I knew he could drive down to the store and get some for me, but I also knew that he rarely got to sleep in. He staggered into the bathroom, barely awake, and afterward sauntered back to the bedroom and fell back to sleep. I lay in my bed then, writhing and seething because he had fallen asleep so easily. My body finally gave up the fight at 6:00 a.m. and I slept until 7:00. One hour.

I didn't take the pill.

I was wide awake when Randy got up at 8:00 a.m. He went down to the store to check on the Sunday morning crew, and at 9:00, brought home some Benadryl. I took a capsule with a big swig of water, and walked back to my bedroom, where I lay down to wait for sleep.

At noon, I was still awake and fighting through every second, every breath. Actually, it hurt to even breathe, not just physically, but mentally and emotionally, too. My breath was heavy, my chest was tight. I was so exhausted and jittery that I had trouble walking to the kitchen. When I looked out at the living room, it looked like it was covered in fog. Nothing in my brain made sense. The pistons weren't firing. Whatever had to connect for me to see clearly wasn't connecting (literally and figuratively). I needed sleep so badly that I nearly collapsed. I wasn't going to make it. I was scheduled to see Dr. Smith the following day, but my countdown was twenty-four hours, and I could barely make it through one minute! The antianxiety meds weren't even touching the anxiety. It was Sunday, so I had no medical assistance except the emergency room. Kathy would probably still be on call, but I knew if I went out to the ER, no one would understand. It wasn't that they wouldn't try because I knew they would! Kathy had been very sympathetic when I'd called at 4:00 a.m. Plus, the nurses at the Community Medical Center were some of the most compassionate and attentive that I had ever encountered. If I was going to be in the hospital somewhere, and had my choice, I would definitely pick Falls City's. But I was now in one of "those" groups—where only those who'd experienced something could understand it, like parents who'd lost a child, or children of alcoholic parents, or those left behind by suicide. Now, I was in the group of recovering "addicts." No one on staff at the Community Medical Center was an expert in drug detox, and even though all of them would try to understand, they couldn't. They were like the medicine dispenser at The Center, who thought I could calm myself down with Chamomile tea.

When my husband got up, I snapped at him for looking at me.

"You're irritable because of the drug withdrawal," he said.

In my detox-induced rage, I wanted to say, "I'm irritable because you wouldn't get me the Benadryl when I needed it at 4:00 a.m.! I'm going through the worst thing I've ever experienced in my life. If I want you to fly to Arizona to hand-pick a particular cactus in the desert, the only thing out of your mouth should be 'what time is my flight?'" That's what I *wanted* to say. I knew deep down inside that it wasn't fair to him, though. That morning, he had just awakened from a deep sleep, and had basically sleep-walked into the bathroom. He'd had no idea how much I was suffering. If he had, he would have flown to Arizona to pick the cactus for me. I knew that. But, right at that point, nothing mattered except getting relief. I didn't know what I was going to do about it either. Kathy had told me that, if the Benadryl didn't work, I would have to take the half-pill, just to get some rest. I didn't want to, but I needed help. I was delirious. I knew I couldn't make it through the day, and sleep was nowhere to be found.

I went back to my room to wait for something to happen. I just had no idea what. Meanwhile, Randy made himself some toast, then went back to the master bedroom to take a nap and watch football. He had worked all week, and had dealt with the little bit that he knew about my situation, too, so I knew he was tired. He lay back down and was asleep by the time I looked in on him fifteen minutes later. I was so perturbed about his ability to hit the pillow and snore that I wanted to rush over to the bed and scream "fire!" I didn't, of course, because I was relatively sure that it was against the law. (Or was that just in a theater or other crowded room?) Even if it hadn't been, I wouldn't have really done it. That wasn't how I rolled. I couldn't think straight, though. The room spun like a carnival ride. I couldn't remember anything, couldn't deduce what was right or wrong, or what was real and what wasn't. I walked out to the kitchen and looked into the living room at the huge clock that hung above our big-screen TV. Time ticked off slowly. I watched the second hand, and realized that my vision mimicked the tick tick tick movement. I shook the nonsense out of my head and glared at the bottle of painkillers on the counter. My appointment with Dr. Smith was nearly twenty-four hours away. The nurse in his office had told me that I needed to be "clean" for forty-eight hours, but I remembered that, at The Center, a patient only had to be clean for twenty-four hours before taking Suboxone. If Dr. Smith fudged on the forty-eight and would accept the twenty-four, it was now or never for the Hydrocodone. I knew I was justifying taking one, but the withdrawals were inhumane, and I just couldn't take it anymore. I desperately needed to sleep. I had only slept one hour in two days. I was delirious and felt like I was going to fail. I opened the pill bottle, cut one painkiller in half, and swirled half around in warm water. That simple action took my anxiety level down one whole notch. Then, I downed the pill.

Nothing happened.

At 4:00 p.m., I was completely hyped up with anxiety. I walked through the living room, around to the sunroom, through the pool room, and back to the living room. I punched the air so hard that I felt like Joe Frazier on steroids. Why hadn't the Hydrocodone helped? The receptors were supposed to be attaching to my brain cells. *Attach, you stupid receptors! Attach!* I spent the next several hours pacing around the house. When Randy finally woke up from his peaceful nap, I wanted to pop his head off like a chicken's and fry his ass up for dinner.

"Want me to get you something from Frosty Queen?" he asked.

"Yeah," I said, "I'll take a chocolate malt." If my Hydrocodone wasn't going to soothe me, then I was going to try the next best thing. Food.

Randy was back within fifteen minutes. As I slurped down the malt, I worked on this manuscript. Then, I flipped through the TV channels like a man on playoff Sunday, and finished up my worthless evening with *Friends*. At midnight, I was irrational and hallucinating. I was angry and bitter. And I hated My Friend for treating me like I didn't matter. But I knew without a doubt, if she called, I would forgive it all.

Shortly after midnight, I finally fell asleep. Other than the one hour of sleep I'd had earlier, I had been awake for forty-five hours straight.

Chapter Thirteen

I couldn't believe it when I woke up at 6:00 a.m. on Monday. I had slept six hours! Six whole hours! I'd been awake for forty-five hours before that, so I had desperately needed the sleep. I was refreshed. I felt like I might just make it after all! I had a 1:00 p.m. appointment with Dr. Smith, and if everything went according to plan, I had taken my final—ever—Hydrocodone. I hoped that, by the end of the day, I would be on the substitute called Suboxone, and would no longer be a slave to painkillers. I felt a sense of renewed hope. Maybe I really could climb over the detox mountain.

I got in the pool for an hour, showered about 8:00 a.m., and left the house at 9:00. Mom was going with me, and I had told her that I would pick her up at 11:00. She was only thirty minutes away, so I filled my gas tank, bought a few lottery tickets, and ran some other errands in town before I headed out. Mom was still at her exercise class when I arrived in Auburn, so I waited. We took off for Lincoln about quarter to eleven, and she worried about me all the way there—about my sleepless nights and jumpy skin; my whole physical condition. My mom was the sweetest, kindest woman that God had ever created. Not just the sweetest on earth, the sweetest in all of history (although Mother Teresa finished at a close second). But my mom was also a worry wart. There was no other way to put it. If she wasn't worried about one of her children, then she worried about why she wasn't worrying. We kids were her entire life, and she would have killed for any one of us, but when she got on a subject, she worried the life out of it. Although I appreciated her concern greatly, she worried about me all the way to Lincoln.

Another thing about my mother was that, if she was going out of town for any kind of appointment, she absolutely figured out another place to stop, whether she had to take back a prior purchase, pick something up for a friend, or find a shirt that she had really loved in the store the week before, but hadn't bought at the time.

When we arrived in Lincoln about quarter to twelve, Mom wanted to pick up a shirt at Kohl's that she had seen the previous week, but hadn't been able to find in her size. Since we had over an hour to kill, I told her we could stop. I pulled into the lot, we walked inside, and I asked her what color the top was. She said she didn't remember, but that she would definitely know it when she saw it. *Oh boy*, I thought. *This is going to take the entire hour.* However, she suddenly remembered that the shirt was folded on an end cap, and that it had swatches of black, gray, and white, with a little brown mixed in. It only took her ten minutes to find the right one. She held it up and asked me what I thought. It was flashier than the tops she usually wore, but I thought it would look very nice on her. She looked through the pile and couldn't find her size.

"What do you think of this one?" she asked, as she held up the same shirt in orange and rust colors. I told her I thought the colors were much better for her complexion. Then, she found the other one in her size. *Oh no. A decision.* I loved my mother with my whole heart, but she couldn't make a decision to save her soul. The previous Christmas, she had been at my house, and was helping me in the kitchen when my niece walked in the front door. Mom absentmindedly set a towel over a burning candle on my kitchen table. She looked at the flaming towel, then at Dariane, like she couldn't decide whether to put out the fire or go talk to her granddaughter. She chose my niece while I handled the fire.

"Why don't you get both shirts?" I asked, as she pondered the decision at Kohl's.

"I think I will," she said. *What?* I was so proud! She had made that decision in less than ten minutes! She bought both tops, then we decided to eat at Runza, a Nebraska-based fast-food establishment, because we didn't have time for anything but a quick bite. Mom ordered a bowl of chicken noodle soup and a cinnamon roll, and I ordered a cheeseburger. We took our food to a booth and started eating. There was one other thing about my mom that made my siblings and me laugh out loud. Mom was a swirler. She swirled her spoon or fork through her food eight or more times before every bite. If she was eating a salad, she cut the lettuce into tiny manageable pieces while the rest of us polished ours off. If she was eating a baked potato, she took half an hour to cut it, then butter and sour cream it. That day, she took the ice from her water, spooned it into her soup, then swirled it around ten times. Swirl, swirl, swirl. I hadn't had a Hydrocodone since noon the day before. I wanted to open her mouth like a bird's, and feed the soup to her through a funnel. Then I looked at her precious, trusting face, and thought about how much I loved her, and how very much I wished that my dad had been seated beside her. My heart melted. She was the most precious person I knew. I downed my cheeseburger while she swirled and sipped on her soup. Thirty minutes later, she still had a few bites left.

"Mom, my appointment is at one o'clock," I said, patiently. It was 12:45. Dr. Smith's office was just up the street about twelve blocks, so it wasn't that far away, but still, I wanted to get there a few minutes early.

"Oh!" Mom replied. "I thought it was at two o'clock!" She jumped up, and insisted on bussing the table since I had bought the lunch, so I watched while she cleaned up after us. Then, we tottered out to her van. We arrived at my new place of worship just a few minutes later. I walked into Dr. Smith's office feeling skittish, but knowing that salvation was coming. I was going to get help with the final stages of detox—the big sickness, the inevitable crash.

Forty-five minutes later, I was done with the massive quantity of paperwork. My legs bounced, and so did my eyes. I was a jittery mess. I figured everybody in Dr. Smith's waiting room understood because they were all there for the same reason that I was, but I couldn't look anyone in the eye. I couldn't even focus on anyone's face. I was sick to my stomach and fought the urge to run to the bathroom. By the time I got back to the exam room, the only thing I could do was pace the tiny space, and hope I didn't poo my undies. The nurse asked me all of the required questions as I bounced from wall to wall.

"How long have you been using?" she asked.

"Twelve years," I replied, without even looking at her.

"When was your last one?"

"I had five milligrams yesterday at noon," I said. I sat down in the chair, and bounced my legs. "But I've only taken five milligrams a day for the last week." She said that I would probably be an ideal candidate for Suboxone, then she left. I shoved my hands in my pockets, and twirled around the room. It was the only thing I could do with all of my anxious energy. Suddenly, I had to run to the bathroom. I threw the examination room door open and looked anxiously at a nurse, who pointed down the hallway. I ran down there, went, cleaned up, and rushed back.

Ten minutes later, the door opened. I was suddenly in a movie theater, watching as the movie flipped to slow motion and the good-looking Prince Charming showed up on screen for the first time, tossing his hair to-and-fro like the prince in *Shrek 2*. Bottom line—Dr. Ross Smith was hot. He walked in, introduced himself, and shook my hand. I decided not to wash it just in case he had his own reality show someday. He sat down on the doctor's stool, and I sat in the chair across the room—too far away from him, in my opinion. He asked me to tell him my issues, so I told him the whole story in the *Reader's Digest* condensed version.

He said, "Your story isn't unusual. I see so many patients like you; people who are leaders in their communities who've gotten stuck in the cycle of pain management. First of all, you have to stop beating yourself up for this. It is not your fault that you're dependent on this medication."

"I don't blame my doctor," I said. "I'm the one who took them."

"That's admirable," he said, "but it's not your fault, either. You were just trying to deal with back pain. This isn't a weakness on your part, or something that you just haven't been able to 'gut' your way through. The human body wasn't designed for long-term drug use, and it wasn't made for short-term detox. From what you described, you never took the pills to get high. You never abused them by crushing and snorting them or injecting them."

"You can do that?" I asked.

"People do that," he said. "It's not smart, though. It could kill them." I had no idea people did that. Then, he told me about the withdrawal symptoms that I was experiencing. I hung on every word. He described my jittery anxiety, confusion, inability to focus, loss of words, fuzzy vision, the pressure above my eyes, the pounding headaches, diarrhea, stomach cramps, nausea, and everything else I had felt over the past few weeks, like the loss of joy, and the hopelessness.

"We can treat all of your withdrawal symptoms with a new drug called Suboxone," he said. "It's a substitute for Hydrocodone and other opiates, and attaches the same types of receptors to the brain cells. It's just easier to withdraw from." That was the first time I'd heard that Suboxone had any type of withdrawal.

"I'm not sure I want to take another drug that I have to get off of," I said.

"It's not like that," he said. "This will be a slow taper. The human body wasn't designed to withdraw from drugs, and that's why doing it over a short period of time usually doesn't work. Statistically, over ninety percent of opiate users reoffend within the first twelve months." *Ugh.* I guaranteed him that I was not going to be one of those. But then again, I'd only been clean for a short time and I'd had to fight through every minute. I couldn't even think about doing it longer than I already had.

"While you're withdrawing from the Hydrocodone, you will

experience symptoms for months," he said, "but the Suboxone will take those away. Then, you can slowly taper off of the Suboxone. It's a film that goes underneath the tongue, and it just dissolves. Your symptoms will be gone, and you'll actually feel normal again." Normal? I would feel normal again? I hadn't felt "normal" in a long time, but definitely not since the whole withdrawal saga had started more than two weeks prior. I asked him why, if Suboxone worked so well, everyone wasn't shouting about it from the rooftops. "If you had invented the car, would you be shouting about the airplane?" he asked. That made sense. I was sure that the Suboxone people were the only ones who wanted anyone to know about Suboxone.

Dr. Smith described the procedure again and said that he preferred that I get the medication at a Lincoln pharmacy, where he could maintain control. I had no problem with that. He said that I had to pick up the prescription, then come back with it, and take the first dose in front of him.

"I've never heard of that before," I said.

"It's the law. I have to make sure you don't have a negative reaction." At that point, I didn't care what I had to do. I was nearly convulsing. And I knew how that looked to others. Dr. Smith was going to make that stop. I told him I would be back in an hour, and was looking forward to feeling human again.

Mom and I drove a few miles to the nearest Hy-Vee store, where the prescription had already been called in to the pharmacy. Dr. Smith used the business for a lot of his patients, so the cashiers knew the drill. They were kind and understanding, as I fidgeted in a pharmacy chair. I was like a little kid with a swirling chair. Spin this way. Spin that way. This way, that way, flail my arms, stand up, sit down. Mom was antsy, too, so she wandered to the deli to get a chicken dinner for my brother, Mike, who lived with her. Within fifteen minutes, the pharmacy tech gave me the film strips. Mom bought her chicken, and she and I headed back to Dr. Smith's clinic.

I only had to wait a few minutes in the office, then a nurse led me back to an exam room. While I was waiting, I felt a wave of withdrawal symptoms circulate my bowels again. I left the exam room door open and ran to the bathroom. I sat down on the toilet, and felt my entire system kick me in the stomach for being such a stupid woman and allowing the pills to get out of control. When my system was done punishing me, I washed my hands thoroughly (and not just because a sign on the mirror said I had to), then I sauntered back down the hallway and waited for Dr. Smith.

A few minutes later, I stood in front of him, waiting for my salvation. Dr. Smith and Suboxone were going to take away my withdrawal symptoms and make me feel normal again. My system wouldn't rise for battle three times an hour anymore. I wouldn't feel stomach cramps that were worse than kung fu kicks to the gut. I wouldn't run to the nearest bathroom everywhere I went. I'd be able to think clearly, and maybe even sleep. I would get through the day without counting the minutes until I could take another pill. The room in which I was sitting, lying down, or passing through wouldn't breathe in-and-out or tap rapidly. But most importantly, I wouldn't feel that God-awful electrical current that constantly ran through my nerves.

Dr. Smith unwrapped the package, pulled out several small pouches, ripped one open and slid out a small strip, which was kind of like a Crest Whitestrip. He said it was eight milligrams of help. He used a little box cutter to slice it into thirds, then handed a third to me. He said I needed to start with that one, then take another third an hour or two later, so we could determine how much I was going to need to get back to a regular day. After that, he wanted me to adjust the dose, so I only had to take the medication twice daily. I took the strip, slid it under my tongue, and waited for it to dissolve. Dr. Smith patted me on the back.

"There's no reason for you to go through these withdrawals," he said. "Suboxone will help you feel normal again." I loved it every time he said that. He said I would need to see him once a month, and that we would taper off the Suboxone in a few months. He said to enjoy my newfound normalcy. I smiled. It wasn't a little ole' smile either. It was a great big one. It had only been a few minutes, but I was already feeling very good. Very, very good. I told him thanks, and that I would see him in a month. Then I scooped up my Suboxone strips, walked out the door, out of the building, and into a bright, sunshiny day. I could almost hear the Brady Bunch singing. I looked around and noticed that the grass was greener than it had been when I pulled into the parking lot. The trees with leaves were more beautiful, the reds more vibrant. The trees that had lost their leaves were more barren. The things that were alive and breathing looked more alive. The dead things looked deader. I felt like skipping to my car. I felt like breaking into song— that one from *Beauty and the Beast*, where The Wardrobe, Mrs. Potts, Cogsworth and Lumiere sing with the dishes, "I feel human again, oh so human again." I finally felt human again.

When I got to the car, I slid into the driver's seat, turned to my mom and said, "I can't believe how much better I feel already." Nothing warms a mother's heart more than those words. Tears welled in Mom's eyes. Her baby was feeling better. I jokingly asked Mom if she had a sweater in her purse that she wanted to take back to the mall, but she laughed and said she didn't. We headed out of Lincoln and onto Highway 2. As I drove, I scanned from side to side, like I was supposed to do, and noticed that everything along the roadside was exactly where it was supposed to be. Nothing was rat-a-tat-tatting, no inanimate objects were breathing, the trees weren't singing like they were in a Disney movie. Everything was in its right place. I jabbered on and on about how normal I felt. Mom smiled and patted me on the arm, back, and nape of my neck. Right then I appreciated it, too, instead of being irritated by it. I wasn't irritated by anything!

Forty miles down the road, I stopped at the Dairy Queen in Nebraska City to celebrate. I preferred and really wanted an ice-cold beer at that point, but I still wasn't drinking yet, so I settled for a chocolate chip cookie dough Blizzard, while Mom "blew her diet" with a brownie sundae. We ate our ice cream on the way to Auburn, but when we got to her house, I felt so good that I wanted to go see her best friend, Marilyn. Marilyn was *that* person in my mom's life. She was Mom's breathing force—her constant sidekick, the Lucille

Ball to Mom's Ethel. My dad had been Mom's other half and the love of her life, but Marilyn had always been my mom's "person." I didn't remember life without her. Marilyn's family had been a constant presence in our home when I was growing up, and their family's friendship with my family had just grown closer as Marilyn and Wayne, and Mom and Dad had gotten older. So, when Mom and I got home from Lincoln, I wanted to go see Marilyn. Mom's bestie was having a few health problems of her own at the time, and hadn't been feeling well for more than a year. Everything made her dizzy. In essence, she felt the wobbliness of drug withdrawal every day, without ever having had the pleasure of the drugs. I felt sorry for her because I knew what she was going through.

We sat down in her welcoming, homey living room, and she and Mom listened as I told the story of the past several weeks of my life. Mom had heard bits and pieces, and had actually lived some of it, so I mainly talked to Marilyn. But both asked questions, so I answered. They listened, I talked. Well, I wouldn't even say I talked. I felt so good that I jabbered.

When I finished an hour later, Marilyn hugged me, kissed my cheek, and told me how proud she was that I had taken on the detox battle and was conquering the drugs. Mom and I left then, and went to her house so I could take the other one-third of the Suboxone strip. I put the film underneath my tongue and waited for it to dissolve. Ten minutes later, I was on the road toward home, feeling even better than I had before. I was almost giddy. High, even.

When I got home, Randy was sitting in the living room, watching Nebraska volleyball on the big-screen TV. He'd been home all afternoon because he had a colonoscopy scheduled for the following morning, so he had drunk the first bottle of Magnesium Citrate at 3:00 and had just polished off the second bottle at 7:00, right before I'd gotten home. He said he'd been running to the bathroom all afternoon.

"I'm really sick," he said, like a typical man.

"Try doing that for seventeen straight days, and then we'll talk about being sick," I said.

"I know," he said, grimacing. "I shouldn't have said that."

I stood by the counter in the kitchen and peered out into the dining room and living room. It was big and open—thirty-six feet by thirty feet, and I loved that space. One wall was solid windows, so I could even look out to open spaces. The view made me feel free. I thought back about how trapped I would have felt if I had stayed at The Center.

While Randy watched the volleyball game, I told him about the Suboxone, how much better it had made me feel, and how I was going to be able to resume a normal life quickly. He was really happy about that, and jumped up to hug me, then rushed back to watch the game. As I stood there, however, the TV room began to sway. The trees right outside the windows looked dark and menacing, like a Halloween scene. My stomach felt queasy. I thought I needed something to eat, so I heated up a huge slice of leftover Runza casserole, downed it quickly, then leaned against the counter to watch the volleyball game. Unfortunately, my stomach lurched.

"I think I'm going to be sick," I said.

"Are you alright?" Randy said.

"No. I think I'm going to be sick."

I ran to the master bathroom, which was disgustingly dirty because I hadn't cleaned it in two weeks, and *that* just made my situation worse. The counter was cluttered with hair products, makeup, skin softeners, and soap dispensers. Soap, shaving cream, and toothpaste had been splattered on the sink and mirror. I lifted the toilet lid and looked down into the bowl. A ring had formed around the water line. The whole thing stunk like The Center's detox ward. I heaved into the water, and tears welled in my eyes. It was different than it had ever been before. The vomit was solid, as if there was no liquid it in at all, and it seemed to explode all the way from my toes. It got stuck in my throat, and I had to force it up. I coughed and gagged and hurled. I was choking on my own vomit. I couldn't breathe. My nasal passages felt like they were collapsing. I fought through the wave of sickness, then grabbed the nearby toilet paper and pressed it to my eyelids. The pressure above my eyes was indescribable. It felt like my eyes would pop out, like that Halloween costume with eyeballs on springs. I wiped my dampened eyes, then leaned back over the bowl and did it all over again.

When I was finished, my entire body was spent. I collapsed to the floor and lay down. I stayed there for five minutes or so, but knew I had to get up because the floor was cold. I pulled myself up using the bathtub. I was so weak, though, that I couldn't walk back into the living room, so I went straight to my room right across the hall. Randy walked down the hallway then, and asked if I was O.K.

"No," I said, "I'm really sick."

"Oh, I don't have my hearing aids in, so I didn't hear you," he said. "Do you need something? Sprite or something?" God bless him, he really did try.

"No," I said, "just let me see if I can lay here and feel better."

He walked across the hallway to the master bedroom to lie down. As I lay on my bed, staring at the ceiling, the bed spun around in circles. I wished I could get up and stop it, but my stomach was revolting. Actually, my entire body was revolting against everything I had done to it and forced into it for the past twelve years. Hell, not twelve! Thirty! I had been abusing myself for thirty years! I mentally kicked myself in the butt. *Look what you've done to your life, Lori*, I thought. *You got lost in the Misty book and another codependent relationship, and in the process, you lost yourself. As a result, your book project is in jeopardy, you lost Your Friend, your pride and dignity, a large chunk of money, and God knows what else.*

Then I got up and ran to the bathroom, where I continued to lose my supper.

Chapter Fourteen

I was awake the rest of the night Monday, vomiting every time I moved my eyes from one object to another. I couldn't roll over onto my side without hurling from my toes. I couldn't even turn my head! It had been more than twenty-four hours since I had taken a Hydrocodone, and the Suboxone had made me violently ill. Since I had the Suboxone in my system, I couldn't take the Hydrocodone anymore, or it could throw me into immediate and violent withdrawals. But really, how much more violent could they be? I would rather swim through an alligator-infested swamp than go through any more sickness or withdrawals, so I had to find a way to get well.

When Randy got up at 6:00 a.m. to be at the hospital by 7:00 for his colonoscopy, I was still wide awake. I told him I wasn't going to live through the day. I'd been awake all night, was exhausted, and was as sick as I had ever been in my life. Since I knew nothing about the Suboxone, I had no idea what I could take with it. I knew that I could probably take antianxiety meds, but nothing that I swallowed stayed down. When I took a drink of water, I threw up. How could any food be left in my system? While I pondered that question and how to get some sleep, Randy shaved and took a shower, then looked in on me again.

"If you can't come get me when I'm done with the colonoscopy, I'll get somebody from the store to do it," he said. I couldn't even nod.

"O.K.," I murmured. He left to go to the hospital, and I just lay there as still as I could.

Three hours later, after I'd vomited several more times, I was lying in the same position when the house phone rang. I tried to answer without lifting my head, but I couldn't reach the phone. I had to lift my shoulders off the pillow. I pulled the phone over. My stomach swirled, and I felt acid in my throat.

"Randy is done with his colonoscopy, and ready for you to pick him up," the nurse said.

"Please tell him I'm too sick," I whispered. The nurse said "O.K.," and hung up. My stomach rebelled. I ran to the bathroom and got there just in time. I felt like a cat with a hairball stuck in its throat. I coughed and choked, forced the poison out, and waited as my stomach searched earnestly for more. My entire body lurched toward the toilet. My head beat like a war drum right above my eyes. My nose was completely plugged up. I couldn't breathe through it, which meant I couldn't breathe at all. My eyes watered, my vision blurred. I couldn't think straight.

When Randy got home fifteen minutes later, I was still on my knees, hugging the toilet. He knocked on the bathroom door, and asked if I was alright.

"No," I said, "I'm not going to make it through this."

"I feel so bad for you, honey," he said. "I wish there was something I could do."

"Me, too," I said. I stayed there until my stomach calmed down, then I brushed my teeth and walked out to the kitchen. Randy could tell by looking at me that I was in a very bad place. I'd been awake since the previous morning at 6:00 a.m. I had drunk an occasional sip of water just so I had something in my stomach to throw back up.

"I'm calling Dr. Smith's office," I said. I knew I had to do it right then, too, because, if the previous twenty-four hours had been any indication, I would soon feel inhuman again. I looked up the number on my iPhone, called, and left a message for a nurse. One of them called back within fifteen minutes. She took down the information about how much Suboxone I had taken and when, what I had eaten, and everything else she needed to know, then she said she would talk to Dr. Smith. I lay down for half an hour, ran to the bathroom and blew my stomach out again, then lay back down. No one returned my call. I called back, and was forwarded to the same nurse.

"I talked to Dr. Smith," she said, "and he said that this sometimes happens to new patients, so you'll just need to gut it out until you get used to the medication." *Are you effing kidding me?* I thought. "Just give it a couple of days," she said. I didn't even have the energy to tell her she was an idiot if she thought I was doing this for a couple of days. I was sicker than I'd ever thought a person could be. I had never had a flu or even had a hangover so bad. I couldn't sleep and was physically spent. I hung up the phone, and knew I was on my own. Whether or not I took another Suboxone, ever, was going to be entirely my decision. And my decision was no. The medication had basically poisoned me. In addition, I didn't want to work with anyone who expected me to gut it out when I was so sick. I didn't care how gorgeous he was.

I looked up and saw Randy standing over me.

"Why don't you move down to the basement?" he said. "It's dark and cool down there. Maybe you'll feel better, and be able to sleep if it's dark." At that point, I would've done anything to go to sleep—except take the Suboxone. Randy was right, though. The sun was filtering through the blinds in the bedroom. I would never get to sleep if it was light in the room.

"Can you help me get downstairs?" I asked. I was so weak that I could barely walk. He helped me down the hallway and through the kitchen, then walked down the steps ahead of me so I could hold onto his shoulders for support. Had he not been there, I would have fallen down the stairs. Every time I took a step down, my knees gave way. I felt and looked like I was in my nineties. When we got to the basement, I held onto the wall while Randy raced from room to room to turn the lights on, all the way back toward the guest bedroom suite. When he came back to help me, I told him that I was going to sleep in the middle room because there weren't any windows in that room.

"On the blow-up bed?" he asked. I hadn't yet purchased a couch for that room, so one of our grandkids usually slept there on a blow-up mattress.

"Yes," I said, "I want it as dark as possible." The guest suite at the back of the house had those two comfy queen-size beds, but it also had an egress window that allowed a little light in, despite the blinds. I needed to sleep somewhere dark.

Before I could even lie down, I had to run to the closest bathroom, which was directly off of the middle room, and right by the guest suite. I knelt down on the cream-colored tile, (which was a chore in itself for someone as big as I was), and I heaved. The force from my gut was wicked. I looked down in the water and saw dime-sized round pink chunks. Was it possible to upchuck one's stomach lining? *God, please just let me die*, I thought. *Please. I can't do this anymore. I can't!* I seriously felt like it was my last day on earth. I didn't want to leave my family and friends, but knew I couldn't survive another sleepless night, and another wave of violent twists in my gut. I had nothing left. I couldn't do it anymore. But darn it, I was *not* taking that Hydrocodone. I was willing to die first.

When I finished vomiting, I got up and tried to make it the ten feet back to the bed. My steps were labored. I had to think about each one because my head was pounding with excruciating thuds. I was certain that I was dehydrated, but couldn't do anything about it because I couldn't even keep water down. I lay down on the mattress on my side and propped my head on the pillow. I looked up at Randy.

"I'm thinking about going to the emergency room," I said. He didn't say anything. "Will you get me a trash can? I don't think I can walk to the bathroom again. I'm exhausted." He took three or four steps and was in the bathroom. I was jealous of his long legs and big steps. If I'd had his legs, I could've gotten to the bathroom much faster when I had to puke. He brought the trash can out and set it beside my bed. "I'm going to call Sandy," I said, "and if she can't help me, I'm going to the emergency room."

"Well, um, I'm really hungry," he said. "I'm starting to get sick to my stomach. Are you going to go now, or do I have about twenty minutes to go get some breakfast?"

"Are you effing kidding me?" I said. I never, ever talked that way to anyone, especially my husband. And I felt bad for doing so because I had trained him to be that way. I not only rarely said what I felt, I also wore a mask most of the time, so he never really knew what I was thinking or feeling. But right then, I was feeling like I might die. "I just told you I might need to go to the EMERGENCY ROOM, and you want to go get some breakfast?"

"Well, I didn't know if you were really serious or not," he said, "but I know you're irritable because of the withdrawals...."

"I'm irritable because I just told you I was thinking about going to the emergency room, and you asked me if you have time to go get breakfast! Just go. I'll be fine here on my own. I always am."

"No, I'm not going to leave you."

"Oh! Now you're not going to leave me? Go. I don't want you here anymore."

"No, I'm not leaving you. I'm not going to leave you when you're this irritable."

I wanted to call the police and have him removed from the house. He was a wonderful man, but I didn't want him there at that point. I usually just held my anger in and got over it, but he was just plain making me angry when I was so sick. I rolled over onto my back. I didn't want to talk to him. When I moved, however, the wave of nausea crashed against the shore. My stomach erupted. I didn't want to throw up in front of him, so I staggered to the bathroom and shut the door. I lifted the toilet seat up, and hurled from my toenails. The heave was violent and unforgiving.

"Take that!" my gut screamed. "I'll kill you for doing this to me!" I choked on a round, hard piece of vomit while trying to force it out. It wouldn't come up but wouldn't go back down! I swallowed hard, but it was stuck! I was choking! I couldn't breathe or swallow! Then I fortunately heaved again. The force of the vomit rocketed the lump out of my throat. My nasal passages had collapsed so I felt like I was suffocating. My eyes watered as if I'd been sobbing.

"I can't breathe!" I whispered. I took a short breath through my mouth, and continued to do so until I could breathe. I pulled a wad of toilet paper from the dispenser, and wiped my watery eyes and the tears that drained down my cheek. My stomach continued its unforgiveness, and I upchucked again. I had no idea how I got it out because my air passages were all closed. I thought I would suffocate or aspirate on my own vomit.

"Rrrrrrhhhhhhhhhhuuuuuuu," came out of my mouth.

"Are you O.K.?" Randy said, from outside the door. I wiped my mouth off, but the drool kept coming.

"No," I said with resignation, "just give me a minute. I'm not done." I hovered over the toilet for several minutes. I knew he was pacing right outside the door, so I couldn't think. "Just go," I said. "You're making me nervous standing there, and I'm going to be here a while."

"O.K.," he replied. "If you're sure. I'll be back in a little bit."

"I'll probably still be in here."

He left, and I was actually relieved that he wasn't waiting outside the door, listening for me to hurl. After a few minutes, I thought I could make it back to the bed, so I got up, flushed, splashed cold water on my face, rinsed my mouth out, then walked back to the mattress and lay down on my side. I didn't even have the energy to brush my teeth. And I couldn't breathe through my nose at all. It felt like it no longer functioned. I sighed as I contemplated my fate. *Should I call Sandy? Or should I just go to the emergency room?* I knew I couldn't go to the clinic. I would have to sit in the waiting area, and there was no way I could do that. I couldn't even lift my head from the pillow without throwing up!

When Randy got home, I made a few calls and was finally able to reach Sandy. She said if I was dehydrated again, I would probably need to go to the ER, but that she would call the pharmacy and prescribe an anti-nausea medication and a heavy-duty sleeping pill.

"I don't understand what's happening," I said. "The Suboxone was supposed to help me with the withdrawal symptoms, so I could avoid the big crash when I went down to none."

"Lori, that's all in your head," Sandy said. "You're down to five milligrams a day. You've already done the hardest part. There isn't going to be a big crash." *How dare she say that?* I thought. I had seen experts in the field, and every one of them had said that the biggest crash would come when there were no drugs to attach to the receptors in my brain; in other words, when I was no longer taking Hydrocodone or anything else! Those people worked with addiction and dependency every day. How could she know more than they did? I didn't argue with her. I was too sick. I thanked her for the prescriptions and told her I would call back if I decided to go to the ER.

Randy took off for the pharmacy right away. While he was gone, I got sick in the trash can. I couldn't even walk the ten feet to the bathroom anymore. He was gone for about half an hour, and when he got back, he ran a glass of water, then handed one of each of the pills to me. I took the smallest one, then the biggest. The latter got caught in my throat, and I choked on it, spitting water all over the side of the bed. If my husband hadn't been there, I would've lost it. I had no energy whatsoever. I couldn't think. I couldn't breathe. I couldn't keep anything down, or get anything down. I wanted to jump off the Missouri River bridge but had no idea how I would get there. I sat up and tried the second pill again, and then it went down.

"I hope it stays down," Randy said.

"Me, too," I said, as I plumped my pillow under my neck, and lay back down.

"Do you need anything?" he asked.

"Sleep," I said.

"Hopefully that pill will help. I'll just be upstairs. I'll have my cell phone beside me, so call if you need anything." He kissed my forehead, then told me he loved me very much, and was proud of me for gutting my way through. Gutting was the optimal word. He went back upstairs, and I lay there in complete darkness, knowing if the anti-nausea medicine didn't work, this was my last day on earth. This was how I would die.

CHAPTER FOURTEEN

Within an hour of taking the pill, I could raise my head off the bed. If Sandy had been there, I would've given her three genie wishes in gratitude. By the second hour, I could sit on the edge. The anxiety started in on me, though, so I got up and walked to the bathroom. My legs felt as big as tree stumps. They were heavy and water-logged.

In the bathroom, I looked in the mirror and saw the shell of the person that I used to be. A huge shell. My stomach looked like two stacked tires. It was less bloated than it had been before I'd gotten so sick, but I still couldn't bend over to pick anything up off the floor. My face was red and blotchy from all of the retching and heaving. My eyes were tight and pinched. I had no makeup on, wore rank blue pajama bottoms and a gray T-shirt, and looked so very old.

Anxiety bolted through my veins and nerves and sent my arms flailing. I rushed out of the bathroom and tried to shake the addiction out. I shook my arms, my legs, my head. Nothing worked! Nothing! Why wouldn't the anxiety go away? *God, how do you expect me to do this when the anxiety won't stop? No one can do this! It's inhumane!* I had to get rid of it somehow! Maybe if I walked outside! Maybe if I actually trekked to the river and jumped off the bridge! Oh geez, that was ridiculous when I couldn't even walk around the block. So instead, I climbed up the steps to my kitchen. Even that was a chore. I huffed and puffed. When I reached the top, I couldn't breathe. I stretched my back out and took a deep breath. That just made me dizzy.

Bright sunlight filtered through the windows, and it made me angry. Didn't the sun know how sick I was? How dare it shine so brightly when all I felt was hopelessness and despair. How was I ever going to make it through? The Suboxone clearly wasn't going to work. I had no choice but to go back to the Hydrocodone so I wouldn't face the huge crash when my body had nothing left to give, and I had no pills left to give it.

"That's all if your head," Sandy's voice said, in my head. Was she right? What if my efforts to avoid the inevitable crash were worse than the crash? Her opinion *did* make sense! I had only taken five milligrams of Hydrocodone each day for nearly a week. Dr. Smith had said that the human body needed to taper off of opiates, not detox quickly, and I knew that was true, but what if the lack of Hydrocodone was better than the ingestion of Suboxone, at least for me? What if the big crash, for me, had already come? But what if it hadn't? I couldn't make it through anything worse than I had already experienced. Plus, I was exhausted! I had been awake for thirty-three hours, after being awake for forty-five hours prior in the week! I couldn't take any more! I was losing my mind! Physically, I felt like I was going to die. I needed help, but I knew that no one could make it go away! I had to get through it alone! Or did I have to endure it at all? I could end it all anytime I wanted to. I had Hydrocodone sitting in a bottle right in front of me, and I still had multiple bottles of other pills in the cabinets. I could take all of them and be done with this hell forever. Or I could just take some of the Hydrocodone and feel better immediately. But that would toss me right back into the throes of addiction or dependency or whatever the hell this hell was.

I looked up at the clock on my living room wall. Tick, tick, tick, tick. If I was going to take a Hydrocodone, then feeding time was just four minutes away. I knew I would never make it to that time. I shook the bottle. My hands trembled uncontrollably. I twisted the lid off, looked down at the pills, and counted the ones still left. I had to know for sure—obsessively for sure—how many there were. One. Two. Three. Four. Five. Six. Enough to get me through twelve more days. Maybe. Aww, hell. I was just going to take all of them. I had to accept the hard truth. I was never going to stick with this for good. I never followed through with anything anymore. I started sobbing. This was it for me. I was as broken as any human being had ever been. I had to admit it. I was a drug addict, even though I had always put on a great face outside the confines of my own home. And even though I firmly believed I wasn't an alcoholic, I knew I drank too much. I also placed most of my focus on my codependent relationships when I had a family and true friends who loved me. I had even elevated those relationships way above God. Especially the one with My Friend.

To other people, I was living a life that was large and cushy. No one knew that I was broken and in despair, and going through detox for drug addiction! No one knew that I hadn't slept in days, and was physically exhausted and mentally delirious. I was sicker than I could've ever imagined, and saw no hope that it was ever going to get better. And it was all because of those stinking pills. I wasn't going to live through detox. I had tried everything, and nothing had worked for more than a few hours, if that long. I had tried several different antianxiety meds, plus Gatorade, Pedialyte, walking, pacing, swimming, talking. I had tried everything! Everything! I buried my face in my hands. Feeding time was four minutes away, and I knew I couldn't make it that long. Not this time. Not any longer. I had no hope of getting through this for good. My life was truly over. I had sunk as far as I could go. I'd done everything I could think of to beat this, and I was physically, mentally, emotionally, and spiritually drained. I couldn't do it anymore. I had done everything I could, and I was done.

But as soon as that thought left my mind, another one hit me. Had I really tried everything? I stared down at the counter. Had I? No. I hadn't. I hadn't gone to God and asked Him to help me. I hadn't prayed. And I hadn't done so because I didn't feel worthy enough to pray. How could I ask God for help when I had rejected Him for the latter half of my life? But then again, I knew from growing up as a Christian that God was always there for us, and that we didn't have to be good enough for Him to love and help us. He was my Father. He loved me more than my own dad had, and that was a lot. All I had to do was believe and ask. But on the other hand, I looked at the pill bottle and wanted so badly to take one. Just one! I was so exhausted, so tired of fighting!

"Take one," the bottle hissed. "One won't hurt you. It'll make you feel better." I held the bottle and finally let go of my emotions, letting the tears flow freely. I shook with the sobs of a life on fire. I knew that, on my own, I was never going to beat this. I wasn't. I had to accept it. I wasn't strong enough to do it long-term. I would sink so far into depression that I would never climb out. I would never be able to let go of My Friend. I would ache unbearably for the rest of my life. Every minute would be excruciating. It was all too much. I may have won a few battles, but I couldn't win the war. I knew if I didn't, though, I would continue to live the way I was, and that thought was unbearable. I had to find a way to fight. And there was no way I could do it on my own. I was at the bottom of a well that was filling with water. There was no rescue coming for me. There was no hope left if I tried to do this my way. So there, in my kitchen, I decided to do the one thing that I hadn't yet tried—the one thing that I hadn't done in a really long time. I leaned against the kitchen cabinet, and slowly slid down onto my knees. I cried so hard that I couldn't breathe and couldn't see, so I wiped my nose on my T-shirt, and swiped at the tears that ran down my face.

"God," I said, between gasping sobs, "I know I have no right to approach you right now or to even be in your presence. I have been so far away for so long. I'm asking for your forgiveness and your help, Lord. I'm not going to make it on my own. I've always believed that I could do anything I set my mind to, but this is beyond the power of any human being. I can't do it, God. I can't. Please give me the strength to make it through the next four minutes, four hours, and four days. If I don't kick this habit, it will kill me, and I don't want to do that to my family. And even though I can't see it now, I know you have big plans for me. Maybe your plans are for me to help others, I don't know. Right now, I'm just asking for help to get through detox, and let go of My Friend. If I need to let go of the book as well, help me to do so, God. My life is just in shambles right now. Please help me. I know I've done all of this to myself, and I deserve to face the consequences, but please give me the strength to fight. I've got nothing left."

I stayed there on my knees and cried so hard that my head and entire face hurt from my neck to the crown. I pressed against my temples, and continued whispering to God, begging Him to hear me.

Then I heard a quiet voice say, "I can do all things through Christ who strengthens me." I opened my eyes, turned and looked behind me. *Where had that come from?* I'd clearly heard a voice; a quiet, unassuming but very calming voice. It was like a whispering wind. Goosebumps formed on my arms. I knew that voice. I hadn't heard it in a very long time because I'd stopped listening, but that was the voice of God. Even though my head felt like it was going to explode and my eyes bulged with pressure, none of that mattered. I just started bawling my head off again. But this time, it was different. This time, my tears had a measure of hope.

"O.K., God," I said. "I hear you. I feel you. I know that I can do all things through Christ who strengthens me." As soon as I said it out loud, I felt the presence of the Holy Spirit. The electricity, instead of firing through my veins, raised on my skin. In my most desperate moment, I had finally humbled myself enough to ask for God's help. And God had shown up. There was no Superman moment, no clap of thunder, no bolt of lightning. There was just a quiet strengthening of my resolve. I had been completely drained of energy, but suddenly, felt renewed. Where I had felt defeat, I felt fight. God was there. It was me and Him, and no one was a match for that. Not My Friend. Not Satan. Not anyone.

I reached up for the countertop and pulled myself off my knees, then I stretched out my back. I could barely open my swollen eyes, and my nose ran like a sieve, but I leaned down over the bottle of pills and glared at them. I felt a fortitude that I had never felt, like David the shepherd boy must have felt before his battle with Goliath, like an Olympic gymnast must have felt on the balance beam, like every champion of every event must have felt during every practice. Tears rolled down my cheeks. I arched my back with the mind-numbing strength that welled up inside of me. I couldn't believe the power in it. It almost felt like anger, an anger that Satan was not only trying to defeat me, but was winning. And God had had enough.

He lifted me up before the prince of darkness, and said with firmness, "She is mine. And you are done here." Those words, even if they were just in my mind, reinforced my fortitude with steel. I looked back down at the bottle of pills, and felt like my defeat would be Satan's victory. And God wasn't about to let that happen. So, I turned my back to the painkillers, and…

I.

Walked.

Away.

There was no smugness in my gait. Just fortitude. Just "leave me alone, you aren't going to win" strength. And it wasn't mine. It had come from a place deep down inside—from a door that I hadn't opened in a long, long time. It had come from my soul.

I walked back downstairs, with my hands pressed against the staircase walls for security. With every step, I prayed that I wouldn't fall. But I was almost giddy about the incredible thrust of fortitude that I had just experienced. I felt, for the first time, that I just might get through this hell on earth, and find a way to fight my way back to normalcy, or even better, to a new life. I had no idea how that would happen, but I finally had a twinge of hope that it could!

I lay down on one of the fluffy beds in the guest room, and stared at the ceiling. However, I was so pumped up about feeling better that I wasn't even tired. I had been awake for a solid thirty-three hours, but at that point, I was completely refreshed and actually felt good! How could that be? How could I go from so sick that I needed an ambulance to so stoked that I wanted to open my computer and actually work on my manuscript? Was it the anti-nausea medication? Or was it God? After all I had done to ignore God for thirty years, would He really help me feel better? How could I ignore this, though? I had asked Him to show up, and He had done so. I shouldn't question how.

I worked on my book for an hour, and even though I felt a zing of anxiety, it was tolerable. I could tolerate it! I had more strength! Randy came down about an hour later, and encouraged me to just stay where I was, and try to catch some Zs.

"This room is perfect," he said. "You have a TV and your computer. It's darker down here in the mornings, so you can sleep in, if you *can* sleep. The pillows are big and fluffy, too."

He was doing everything he could to make up for leaving me to go get breakfast. I told him I would probably take his suggestion, and just try to sleep where I was. I said that I was hungry, though, and the only thing that sounded good was a chocolate malt, so he drove down to Frosty Queen and came home with a succulent malt that was just what the doctor ordered. Truly, he would've done anything for me, and I knew that. I was just in the middle of the most horrendous fight I had ever fought, so everything and everyone drove me crazy.

That evening, I continued to work on my book, and felt like I had actually accomplished something! By 11:00 p.m., I finally decided that I was tired enough to turn off the light. By that time, I had been up for forty-four hours straight, and had been violently ill for twenty-four of those. It was time to get some beauty rest, and I finally had hope that I could.

Chapter Fifteen

I would like to say that I slept like a hibernating bear, and that my anxiety and cravings were miraculously cured when I woke up. But that would be a lie. I woke up at 6:00 a.m. after seven hours of constantly interrupted sleep. All night long, I woke up, jittered, tossed, turned, wondered how My Friend was doing, wondered *what* she was doing, drank a glass of Pedialyte then Gatorade, washed off my purple or red disgustingly-dry tongue, went back to sleep, rinse, repeat. I was just grateful that I was no longer vomiting, but as high as I had been the night before, I was just as low when I got up. I knew that God was somehow going to get me through this because of the fortitude I had felt, but I figured I was still going to have to suffer along the way, just to make sure I never wanted to be back here again. I felt guilty for asking God for His help, though. I had done so in desperation, but I had no relationship with Him, so that really wasn't fair to Him. It was like ignoring a friend for thirty years, then asking for a favor. I couldn't do that again. I knew I would never forget the feeling of fortitude, though, and I vowed to carry it through the rest of my life. I just had to get through detox first. And I was determined to do it without taking any of the six pills that remained. Where they had been my weakness, I vowed to make them my strength. I knew that, if I could continue to stare them down and walk away, then I could accomplish anything.

CHAPTER FIFTEEN

I knew the anxiety was going to break me if I didn't get some help, so as soon as Family Medicine opened, I called and asked for an appointment with Sandy. Fortunately, she'd had a cancellation that morning, so I took it. I'm not sure what I expected when I walked into the office, but I guess I thought everyone would know about my situation by then, and that I would get looks of disappointment or pity or sympathy or *something*! But no one looked at me sideways or said a word about it. I was relieved, but then again somewhat disappointed. Didn't people know what I was going through? Weren't they concerned or disappointed, or dismayed, or *something*? Sandy's nurse (a different one than the first time) called me back to a patient room, and asked what I was in for. After I told her, she said, "Good for you," then nonchalantly gave me an allergy shot, since I hadn't had one in three weeks. She told me that Sandy would be in in a few moments. I played on my phone and tried to keep myself occupied while I waited, but the anxiety was eating away at my nerves. I bounced around in my chair, stood up, paced the tiny room, sat back down, jiggled my legs, shook my arms, and took deep breaths. When Sandy came in, she sat down on a stool in front of me, and told me to tell her all about what I was going through. Without mentioning names, I told her about the breakdown of my friendship with My Friend, how much I missed her, and how worried I was about my book project because I hadn't heard from my agent and really had no connection with Misty and Jane either.

"Lori, I can give you something different for the anxiety, but if you don't let the rest of this go, it's going to kill you," Sandy said. "Stress is a big factor in stroke, heart attacks, and just general well-being. You need to take care of yourself, especially right now. Your body is going through a complete upheaval. You aren't healthy enough to worry about someone else. You have to put yourself first for once." I had never done that in my life. How did one put oneself first when she was a mother/daughter/wife/sister/friend? I had dammed up my own emotions my entire life, and lately, regarding the situation with My Friend and the book, I had added logs to the dam. Now, the dam was bursting, and I was drowning.

"I don't know what to do," I said, as tears streamed down my cheeks. "I just feel like I'm not going to make it. It's too hard. I think I can get through the detox if I get this anxiety managed, and maybe I can stay away from the painkillers, but I can't imagine living my life without alcohol, without My Friend or the book, without my dreams. Life is too hard. I had such big hopes for the book and screenplay, and for what a sale would do for Misty and Jane. But I know the girls will never go through with this story. We've been working on it for nearly three years, but I don't think it will ever happen because they don't want to do the presentations with me anymore. And what about My Friend? I miss her laugh and the fun times we had sooooo much. What is wrong with me?"

"You WILL make it," Sandy said. "Look how far you've come! When you have those drugs and alcohol out of your system, you will be stronger than ever. You won't feel this way anymore. You just have to get through it. And Lori, you have to let Your Friend go. And the book? There are other stories out there. Write your own story! Think about how inspirational your story will be when you get through this!"

"I'm thinking about doing that," I said. "I'm taking notes because, if I live through this, I think I can help some people understand what it's like." Sandy smiled.

"I think you can," she said. "So, let the other book go. And let Your Friend go." How was I going to do that? I had chased after that type of relationship my entire life, and I couldn't live without it. Every time the subject of my codependency got upset with me, I felt like my life was over. "Are you getting counseling help?" Sandy asked.

"Yes. I'm seeing a counselor," I said. "I have an appointment tomorrow."

"That's good," she said. Then she told me she would call in a prescription for a heavy-duty antianxiety medication.

"Thank you," I said. When I stood up, she hugged me tightly. As I walked out, I looked at the time on my cell phone. Sandy had been with me for forty-five minutes and hadn't once looked at her watch or cell phone. I was so glad that I lived in a small town where doctors treated their patients like family.

I drove down to Shopko then, and on the way, remembered that it was my dad's birthday. October 24th. He had been gone for fourteen years, and I'd spent nearly every birthday since that time with my mom. If I couldn't be with her during the day, then I took her out for dinner at night, and we always visited the cemetery. I felt bad because she would have to do all of those things alone. I pulled into the parking lot at Shopko and called her before I went in. I had talked to her every day that I was able since my detox had started, even if it was just for a few minutes. I told her how sorry I was that I couldn't spend any time with her that day, and she said she understood. She asked how I was doing, and as I did every time I talked to her, I downplayed the sickness and suffering. Then I hung up. I missed my dad terribly, and knew that my mom missed him so much more.

When I finally worked up the gumption to go in the store, I looked around at the Christmas decorations, while I waited for my prescription. Christmas. Christmas was two months away yet, but the decorations had been out for over a month. I couldn't even think about Christmas. I couldn't even think about *Thanksgiving* yet! I knew I had to. Heck, I usually hosted twenty-two to twenty-six people. How would I entertain that many people when I couldn't even walk out to the mailbox most days? How would I make the usual turkey and ham entrees with my coveted ham gravy and less-than-perfect turkey gravy, and all of the trimmings? How would I get my house ready when I couldn't even find the energy most days to wash my hair? What if I had diarrhea all day when everyone was there? What if the room started spinning and breathing in and out like bellows? What if I still had unbearable anxiety? Oh God, the anxiety!!

After the pharmacist filled my prescription, I walked out to the car and noticed the beautiful crisp colors of the day. I hadn't even noticed while driving down the street toward Shopko. It was a sad sidebar to detox, but I had to accept the fact that the earth was revolving without me. I wasn't present, aware, or alive. So, in that moment, I took the time to stop and look. I hoped no one would come to the car and want to talk to me because I didn't feel like holding "How's your mama?" conversations. I just wanted to really see the world for once, as it went about its busy day. The sky was a brilliant sea blue, and the air smelled like burning leaves, one of my very favorite smells. Cars hurried down the streets, carrying people who had to be here or there. Everyone was in a hurry, everyone had somewhere to go.

I climbed into the car and drove back down Harlan, which was the main street. I looked at the side streets and gawked at the trees. Their leaves were still hanging, and baring bold colors of yellow, orange, and rusty red. I wanted to be like the leaves, to shine in the face of certain death. I wanted to live my life vibrantly until I dried up, and could hang on no more. I wanted to live unaware of what tomorrow would bring, completely oblivious to the fact that my dying day could come at any time. Wasn't that the right way to live? Shouldn't we all live boldly during our short time here? Fighting for every last breath? Leaves had no purpose except to be beautiful until they died, and then they became compost, spreading life to other living, breathing things that made our world gorgeous. Wasn't that the true purpose of life? To spread happiness to other things that made our world more beautiful? I had spent so much of my time for the prior three years working on the *Misty* book that I hadn't noticed life on the outside. I had spent three-fourths of my time writing, and the other fourth trying to figure out what My Friend was thinking and feeling, rather than thinking about my own life and feelings. I simply *had to* spend more time caring about what made MY life better.

I still wanted so much for Jane's and Misty's lives to be easier, and for My Friend's life to include me, but I had to find a way to let all of them go, if I had to. I had no idea what would happen to the book, either, but despite all advice to the contrary, I wasn't giving up. All of the work that the subjects and I had done would then have been in vain. If they gave up, then I would have to find a way to accept it and move on. But I wasn't giving up, no matter what.

When I got home, I took the antianxiety medication, then lay down on the couch, pulled a blanket up over my head, and tried to think about the good things in my life. I had a husband who loved and adored me. I had a beautiful daughter and two awesome stepchildren who had amazing spouses, and all were working their ways up their own ladders of success. I had three grandsons who were incredible young men. They were polite and respectful, and knew how to behave around adults. They were confident boys, amazing students, and hard-working, outstanding athletes. I loved to watch them play. My mom was still alive and at age seventy-two was vibrant. My siblings were all healthy. I had friends—true friends—who gave back as much as they took, who believed that it was inconsiderate and hurtful to stand me up, exclude me, or dump me if "someone better" called. Those friends would never expect me to just get over it if they treated me like I didn't matter. Firstly, they would never do that. And secondly, they would apologize if they did.

I had so many things going for me! When was I going to stop making My Friend a priority in my life when she didn't even make me an option in hers anymore? Could I ever do it? Could I really change my life-long pattern of codependency? Could I get through detox, give up the painkillers for good, and lose the weight I'd gained? Could I find the fortitude day-in and day-out?

I tried to take a deep breath through my nose, but couldn't. Every inch of my nasal passages was suddenly stuffed up. My nose ran. A wave of sickness overtook me. My senses were on overload once again. I ran to the bathroom by the pool room, slid my sweatpants down, and sat down on the stool. I looked up at the cinnamon-colored walls, then down at the rippling cream-colored tile. I loved my house. There were so many beautiful colors and textures in it. So many gorgeous pictures that Randy had taken of landscapes and of our family. I looked back down at my legs, and tried to concentrate as labor-style pains gripped my abdomen. A hot flash overtook me then, and was so bad that I had to take my T-shirt off. That wasn't good enough, though. I was burning up from the inside out! What were those anxiety pills doing to me? My heart raced! Sweat started dripping down my nose! As soon as I finished having diarrhea for the two-hundredth time, I ran to the kitchen, where I opened the freezer door and stuck my head inside.

My bowels wanted their turn again, though, so I slammed the freezer door and rushed to the master bathroom. After I sat down, I looked up at a painting on the wall. I had purchased it when I'd gotten one of my first "real" checks as a member of the post-college workforce. I was so proud of it! I tried to keep my attention focused on it so I wouldn't notice the pain gripping my stomach. But the cramps knotted my gut like kneaded pizza dough. There was a punch here, a twist there, a pull and a squeeze, and finally a release. It depleted me once again of the hydration my body so badly needed.

When I was done, I cleaned up, and ran an entire glass of cold tap water, then downed it. I hoped it would help replenish what I'd lost. Then, I went to the fridge and opened a bottle of Gatorade. I took it to the couch and started sipping. I lay down then, pulled the cover up over my head and tried to think about my next story. I had a great idea for a screenplay, but couldn't decide whether or not to pursue it. I lived in Nebraska. Everyone in the movie world lived in Los Angeles. Was I just wasting my time with movie scripts? I had done fairly well in the contests that I had entered, but I had never won one. Getting into the finals looked good on a resume, but never really got me anywhere. So, why should I keep going? Or should I do as Cassie had suggested, and rewrite the "tweens" book that I had written when she was about ten years old?

"Mom," the adult Cassie had once said, "I read a lot of books while I was growing up, but your book, *A Place Called Freedom,* was truly my favorite. You need to polish it up, and get it out there." I needed to polish a lot of things and get them out there. Including me. I just had to get through detox first. Or did I? What was I waiting for? On the days that I wasn't horribly sick, couldn't I try to lessen my depression and anxiety by working on something? I was waiting for my agent to respond about the *Misty* book, so why couldn't I work on a feature article for the Falls City Journal? Why couldn't I work on the book that Cassie had loved as a child? Several of my screenplays just needed polishing, too. Why did I have all of these projects that just needed some extra work to make them really good? Why was I so afraid of actually succeeding with something of my own, rather than succeeding with something for Jane and Misty? Was I always going to let my depression stand in my way? Would I forever be that person who was "working on it?" Several people, including a nationally-known producer, had told me that my work was really good, so why didn't I believe in ME? I had plenty of other stories. I could write any one of those and pursue it with the same passion with which I pursued Misty's and Jane's story. Why was I always letting a codependent relationship or some kind of obstruction stand in my way?

I hurried back to my bedroom to see if I could find the hard copy of *A Place Called Freedom*, about a teenage time traveler. I cringed when I opened the bedroom door. Clothes were strewn all about. There were 2XL T-shirts, size twenty jeans, size eighteen jeans that I hadn't been able to wear in months. There were a few huge tops, and I hated them. I never would have worn those styles if I hadn't been so heavy. They were old-lady shirts. They had bling and images on the front, like pictures of the Eiffel Tower with the word "Paris" in ruby crystals. Or the shirts were multi-colored in huge patterns. Why did the clothing companies and designers always make plus-sized clothing as flamboyant and colorful as possible? Why did they bedazzle the crap out of the back pockets of jeans? Message to those companies—when we are obese, we don't want things that attract eyes to our butts! We don't want tops in bold "look-at-me" patterns! At least I didn't! Maybe overweight celebrities did. But regular plus-sized women who didn't have a gazillion dollars didn't want clothes that screamed "I'M HUGE!" Well, I guessed I couldn't speak for the other overweight women. I, myself, didn't want clothes like that! But I couldn't really find much else!

I snatched the clothes up off the floor, folded some, and hung the others up. Then I looked through the notebooks on the closet shelf. I wanted to find *A Place Called Freedom* and work on it. But after thirty minutes of searching, I gave up. It was nowhere to be found. I sighed heavily. I had worked on that book for nearly eight months. I had saved it to an external hard drive, but one day while carrying the drive along on a trip, I'd dropped it on the cement and broken it. I had taken it to a few repair places, but it had been beyond repair. I asked several techs if they could just remove the information, but that was going to cost nearly $1500 because of the isolated conditions in which they had to tear it apart. I couldn't afford to do that. So, I lost all of the pictures I had taken for about two years, and probably Cassie's favorite book, too. I had the book in my head, so if I couldn't find the hard copy, I would just have to start over.

"Yeah, right, that'll happen," Satan hissed. I hated that voice of his, that defeated, nothing-ever-works-out, tear-me-down voice. "Your depression will slam you as soon as you start, and you'll never get it finished."

No! I thought. *Not this time! I'm going to use the fortitude that I have found—that God has provided—and I'm going to kick ass on that book!* I was not giving up; not on detox, not on my dreams, my weight or my health. If my book project with Jane and Misty was over, then I would rewrite *A Place Called Freedom*, or find some way to move on to the next one. I wasn't going to let that defeatist voice wipe the floor with me this time.

Even though I felt like crap from the detox symptoms, I walked back to the couch, turned on my computer, and thought about the books and scripts I still wanted to write. I started working on the novel that I had summarized in my letter to the agent, before I'd left for detox. I'd completed the first half, so I just had to keep going. I had to see something through!

In between bouts of diarrhea and fits of sneezing, I worked on page after page of rough narrative and dialogue. But the antianxiety medication that Sandy had given me seemed to make the symptoms worse. My heart didn't just gallop, it roared like a race car. It was like the pedal was stuck. I knew that I could calm that down by taking half of a Hydrocodone, so I hustled to the kitchen and picked the bottle up off the counter. *No!* my mind shouted. *No!* I had vowed to make that bottle my enemy; to use those pills as my strength. So, I set the bottle down, and shoved the new antianxiety pills away. I went back to the Gabapentin, which seemed to work better than anything else. I finished off the bottle of red Gatorade, and that helped, too. But all night long, I tossed and turned and turned and tossed. Would I ever be able to sleep again in this lifetime? How could the anxiety be normal? How did anyone ever live through it? I would have to ask Brad. And thank God I had an appointment with him the following day.

Chapter Sixteen

The next morning, I had to drag myself out of bed because I was so exhausted from lack of sleep, but I got in the pool and did a little bit of exercise. After I got out, I downloaded the emails I had received overnight, read through the ones that needed attention, and ignored the rest. While perusing them, I realized that I hadn't sent a note to my friend, Lisa, in a while, so I spent the rest of the morning composing one that made me sound as lucid as possible. That wasn't easy most days because I felt like I was losing my mind. The days were fuzzy, and the anxiety made me feel completely out of control. If I had a commitment of any kind, it was overwhelming, even if I just had to go to a doctor's appointment. I could only concentrate on one thing per day, and even that was unbearable. Doing two things in one day sent me over the edge. Then, I just went to bed and forgot about it all.

In my email to Lisa, I told her about the withdrawal symptoms that I had already experienced, and how Suboxone had nearly killed me. She sent me back a note that encouraged me to continue fighting because a new life was waiting for me on the other side. I loved Lisa.

After I read her email, I got ready for my appointment with Brad. At 2:00 p.m., I left the house. On my way out of town, I met My Friend coming into town. I slightly lifted my hand and waved. She stared straight ahead, and acted like she hadn't even seen me. I'd ridden with her hundreds of times. She knew what everyone in town drove, and probably knew the name of the dog sitting in the front seat or riding in the back of the truck. She waved at everyone—everyone—because she knew everyone! She was also a nice person and wanted to be friendly and cordial. But she hadn't seen ME? And this wasn't the first time she had ignored me. It was the same treatment that she'd used many times to make me feel invisible.

I knew in my head that getting upset about her gesture, or lack thereof, was ridiculous! It was just a simple wave! She probably had other things on her mind. Heck, she was probably depressed and didn't have enough of her OWN energy to wave. But no matter how hard I tried to convince myself, the anger roared inside me. *Now she can't even WAVE at me?* the voice in my head said. *She can't acknowledge me? Make me feel 'seen'?*

I told Brad about it when I got to my appointment.

"So what?" he said. "So, she didn't wave at you! So what? Is she really that important that you're going to waste your day obsessing about it because she didn't wave at you?" I had known he would say that because we already had a very frank, honest relationship after just a few appointments. But I'd had to tell him how it made me feel. After all, it had stung me badly, and my whole reason for seeing Brad was to talk about the things that stung me badly—the things that would have embarrassed me if I had told anyone else.

"I know it doesn't matter," I said. "I know it's just one little petty thing, but all of the little petty things add up, and now every slight cuts like a razorblade. How can she treat me that way, especially now?"

"The bigger issue here is why it matters so much to you," Brad said. "Lori, those are the things we have to work on. You have no control over what she does and doesn't do. You only have control over your reactions. We need to get you to the point where it doesn't matter whether she waves at you or not, or whether she acts petty or not, or whether she is in your life or not!" I nodded. I knew that was true. I just didn't know how we were ever going to get there. "You have to remember something," Brad said. "Even though the worst of your withdrawal symptoms should be tapering off soon…"

"Could you tell them that?" I asked. He laughed.

"Your brain isn't functioning normally right now," he continued. "It hasn't been for a long time! I know you've had these codependency issues for decades, much longer than you've had your drug and alcohol issues, but three-fourths of this problem could be the withdrawals from all of it. Your brain will be fighting to realign for another year. This is all part of the process, Lori, and since you were on the pills for so long, it's just going to be harder and take longer for you to get off of them. Especially because you're doing it the hard way; on your own, at home. Are you sure you don't want to try an inpatient facility? The staff is trained to deal with withdrawal symptoms, and the issues you are having! You would have daily support and full-time counseling. This would not be as hard if you were in a program away from home."

"No," I said, defiantly. "I'm a loner. I can't do this with people around me. I haven't even let my mom or most of my friends visit me! I've made it this far on my own, and with your help, I'll make it the rest of the way. Unless I lose my mind first. And from what you've just said, that's all part of it."

"It is," he said. "Your brain cells are completely different now than they were before you started using." There was that word again. *Using*. Like a drug addict. "The cells will re-learn how to survive without the medication, but right now, they are clamoring for it."

"Is that why my head rings like a gong most of the day?" I asked. "Actually, sometimes it's more like a backyard full of crickets, and they're all in my head. And is it why I have headaches right above my eyes that are worse than migraines?"

"Yes," he said. "It's not even like the pain in your foot if you stub your toe. It's like the throbbing if your foot has been cut off."

"You are so right!" I exclaimed. "How long will that last?"

"Daily for another month, but periodically for up to a year," he said. My shoulders slumped. "Maybe longer if the obsessions about Your Friend persist." I sat back in my chair and looked down at the floor.

"I can't do this for a year," I said. "I can't. I won't live through it. I don't want to live through it if it takes that long." Then I looked up into his caring, blue eyes.

"Then don't do it anymore, Lori. You've got to let go of all of this or it's going to kill you." He leaned back in his chair, and propped his legs up on the end table. "Look, it sounds to me like Your Friend is codependent, too, but not with you, with her daughter. She doesn't have room for another relationship like that. And I'm guessing that she doesn't want another one."

"She used to," I whispered.

"Maybe so. But she doesn't anymore. With codependent relationships, one person is usually the focus, and the other is the chaser. The focus is in a pit of quicksand, and the chaser wants to save her. In this case, Your Friend is the focus, and you are the chaser. She's in quicksand, so you have jumped in to help her. You've lifted her up onto your shoulders. But when you run out of air and need to breathe, she not only refuses to let you up, she actually pushes you back down. She doesn't necessarily mean to. She just doesn't know anything else. She is broken. You're both broken. Now, both of you are stuck in quicksand. Her only want or need is for you to hold her up so she can breathe. She accepts your money or anything else she needs from you, but wants nothing to do with you otherwise. How is that a friendship?"

"It never used to be that way!" I said, adamantly.

"It doesn't matter how it used to be, Lori!" he said. "That's the way it is now! My advice is to lift her off your shoulders so that you can save YOU. If she sinks, that's her problem, not yours! For her, it is not a friendship anymore, so it needs to be over for you."

I said, "How can you say she doesn't want a friendship with me when she told me over and over again that I was the best friend she had ever had?"

"She may have said those things," Brad said, "and she may have even meant them at the time! But she doesn't anymore! Besides, how has she treated you? You have to gauge this relationship by her actions, not her words." HIS words gutted me like a fish. But I knew I needed to hear them.

I left his office and thought about his advice all the way home. My Friend had told me many times that she cherished our friendship because she could be herself with me. We talked about our innermost thoughts and feelings, about our kids and our lives. We went places together and laughed until our sides hurt. She and her daughter helped me with projects around my house and cabin, and I reciprocated with cash. We shared everything. But within days of any of those things, she treated me like a stalker or froze me out of conversations, and I had no idea why. Then, I sent rambling emails to try to find out what the problem was—emails that made me look crazy. I felt crazy, too. Crazy, frustrated, confused, and angry.

Plus, in the middle of all of that heartache, I had to figure out the situation with my book. Jane and Misty had shown zero interest in it or our presentations since we'd gotten an agent. And I understood that. It had been three years since we had started interviews. But they hadn't been available more than a few times each week, so interviewing had taken nearly a year. It took me another year to write the book, then more time to edit it. Meanwhile, we were promoting it through our presentations; motivational presentations that were very well-received. But when we secured our agent, the whole situation became scary. It was scary for me, as well! Was I good enough? Was the book good enough? I thought it was too long and detailed, so I tried to cut it down before I sent it. Now, I was waiting to hear back. Maybe Jane and Misty were just waiting for our agent to respond, too. Maybe I needed to contact them and just ask if they wanted to continue the project. Brad had encouraged me to give it up because of the stress it was causing me. But how was I ever going to do that? The contract I had signed with the girls was good through October 2014. That was two more years! How could I quit in the middle of a project that we had advertised and spoken about all over southeast Nebraska? Everyone knew about it! People asked me about it everywhere I went! What would people think if I quit? I didn't want to give up. Then again, how was I going to rewrite the book again (if I had to) if Jane and Misty had lost interest in pursuing it?

When I pulled into Falls City, I rolled the window down to get some fresh air. I had to try to focus on something else. I drove to Lem's then, because the Quilters were meeting after work to celebrate our friend, Debbie Witt's, birthday. I didn't really feel good enough to go in, but knew I needed to force myself to do some things, or I would end up being even more of a hermit in my house. So, I parked and waddled in. The Quilters acted pleasantly surprised to see me. They asked how I was doing, so I smiled through the pain, and exaggerated about it all. I knew that none of them would understand anyway. Their lives were together while mine was spiraling out of control.

When the bartender came around to take our orders, I shocked everyone, including Barb the bartender, by ordering a Sprite. I wanted a Bud Light so badly, but had an agreement with Brad that I wouldn't drink for the first thirty days. That agreement was about to end, though! My thirty days would be over on November 5th, and then I was partying!

The girls and I gave birthday cards to Debbie, and laughed as she read each one out loud. The women all had a few drinks, then toasted Debbie's birthday with Slippery Nipple shots while I regrettably drank Sprite, then cranberry juice. We laughed and joked and enjoyed seeing each other again.

When 7:00 p.m. rolled around, the Quilters decided to go to a friend's house to watch the Falls City Tigers' football team play in a state playoff game, which, because of state schedules, was on a Thursday night. Linda's in-laws, Joann and Virgil Jones, had a bird's-eye view from their backyard, so whenever we wanted to watch a game, we just showed up at their house. We usually ordered pizza, drank a few beers, and watched the game over the concrete stadium wall that buffered their back yard.

I had already been out of the house for several hours by that time, and my back was killing me. It felt like it would break in half if I bent over. My head throbbed above my eyes, and I couldn't think straight. But I was determined to go watch the game. I told the girls that I would pick up the pizza we had ordered, so I stopped by Pizza Hut, grabbed the five boxes of pizza and breadsticks, stuck some napkins in a sack, and headed for Joann and Virgil's. The street in front of their house was lined with cars on both sides, and the driveway was filled with vehicles, but I pulled in and blocked the driveway. I didn't give a crap at that point. I just wanted to park as closely as possible to the house, so I didn't have to walk very far. I was dizzy and out of shape, and experiencing withdrawal symptoms. I wanted the car close by.

Linda met me outside, and carried the pizza into the house, so I lit my way to the front door with my cell phone, and walked into Joann and Virgil's beautiful home. After talking to them for a few minutes, I slid the patio door open, and ambled out into the cold night air. I wasn't usually cold, but the wind was howling, and it was chilling everything. I hoped my personal radiator (aka detox hot flashes) would keep me warm. The girls and a few of their husbands were wrapped up in heavy coats, hats, and gloves. I was wearing a jacket, no hat, no gloves. My brain cells were not receptive to the senses of heat and cold.

The girls showed quite a bit of concern about me at the game. They asked if I was doing O.K., or if I needed anything during the rest of my quarantine. I thought about what Brad had said about letting them in and telling them the truth about My Friend, about the pressure from the book, Jane and Misty, etc. etc., but I decided that the football game wasn't the place or time. I munched on a piece of pizza and a cheese stick with marinara sauce, then watched the game as the Falls City Tigers tried to whip up on the cowboys from Boys Town, Nebraska.

A friend named Carlie* then came over to talk. A member of her family had gone through inpatient detox the previous summer because of prescription painkillers, so she understood on some level what I was going through.

"How are you doing?" she asked, smiling. Carlie knew My Friend pretty well. For some reason, I wanted to tell her all about the heartache I was experiencing because I'd been suffering through this ordeal for three weeks to the day, and hadn't heard a word from My Friend. But I couldn't even talk to my circle of trust about it, so of course I didn't say anything.

"I'm doing really good," I lied. I had worn a mask for so long that I didn't even know how to take it off anymore. I couldn't tell her how I really felt—that I was on a walk through hell, and that I was devastated that My Friend hadn't even called. I didn't want to do anything that would make My Friend look bad! "This is the hardest thing I've ever done by far," I said to Carlie, "but I'm winning."

"Good," she said. Then she asked about the symptoms, so I told her. She shook her head with wonder. I thought, *maybe I CAN turn this into something good, by telling people about it so they never ever take pain-killers longer than they should. Or so they understand why family members can't seem to 'get over' their drug addictions.* Taking drugs may be a choice at first, but so many people get hooked without even knowing it. They think that, if the pills are doctor-prescribed, they can't get addicted! Wrong!

By halftime of the football game, I was experiencing sensory overload from the lights, action, chilling wind, and the high school band. All of them together made my eyes and head jackhammer. I was dizzy, and the lights were growing fuzz. I pressed my fingers into my eyelids and tried to focus on the ground. Lynne draped her arm around my shoulder.

"How are you doing?" she asked. "Are you doing O.K.?" I wanted to tell her that no, I wasn't doing O.K. I couldn't think or focus. My head hurt so badly that it beat like the high school's bass drum.

"Yeah, I'm O.K.," I said, little-white-lying again. "I'm just really tired. I think I'm going to go home." I said goodbye to my friends, and walked back through the very hot house, out to my car. I got in and just sat there. I couldn't even turn the key in the ignition. My arms felt like cooked spaghetti; my soul, like a body bag with an anchor tied around it. I felt as alone as I had felt when I was lying in the detox ward at The Center. There was no reason for me to feel that way either. Several of my friends were right behind the house! And throughout my ordeal, they had all been very available. I knew that I could have called any one of them at any time. But nobody understood what I was going through. It wasn't their fault. They *couldn't* understand. But they couldn't understand partly because I wasn't telling them. It was a vicious circle. I lay my head on the steering wheel and sobbed. My friends were only fifty feet away, but the distance seemed like one hundred miles.

My house was clear across town, which was probably just two miles, but at that moment, it may as well have been two hundred. I felt like gravity was pulling me down from the other side of the earth. Or worse yet, from hell. Oh, who was I kidding? I was IN hell. Haley from The Center had told me that detox from opiates was a literal walk through hell. And she'd been telling the truth.

I finally worked up the initiative to start the car and pull away from the house, mostly because I didn't want any of the girls to see that I was still out front. I couldn't let them see me so distraught. The trip across town was painful and exhausting. My back hurt so much, but not as badly as my soul did. When I got home, I put my pajamas on, took another Gabapentin, went back downstairs to my cave, and lay down. Randy came home from the game about two hours later, walked down to see if I needed anything, then went to bed. I'm sure he fell asleep as soon as his head hit the pillow. I, however, was awake until 3:00 a.m. because my symptoms were on overload. I ran to the bathroom time and time again, and my anxiety chased after me like a hunter. I wanted to take a Hydrocodone so badly, just so I could sleep, but walking up-stairs to get the medicine was just too daunting. I was glad that I had left them on the kitchen counter—all six pills still in the bottle—be-cause I absolutely would have taken one otherwise. But fetching them was just too difficult. I had to accept the hard truth. I was never going to live through the hell of detox.

Chapter Seventeen

Friday, I woke up at 6:00 a.m. After several minutes, I finally worked up enough energy to go to the bathroom, then I slogged upstairs into the kitchen. I melted half of a Gabapentin in water, swished it around, took it, then went back downstairs to bed. I tried to go back to sleep but my mind swirled about My Friend. I had sent several emails, and had texted a couple of times, but all I was doing was making a fool of myself. All I got back was the silent treatment. She didn't respond to anything. *I hate you*, I thought. *I hate you for not being here for me when I need you!* I turned my computer on and wrote an email to her.

"I hate you," I typed. "I will hate you until the day I die." I closed the message without saving or sending it, then turned the computer back off. I didn't hate her. I cared about her so much, and knew that she had been so wounded that she just didn't know how to let people close to her. But hadn't I at least earned a conversation about why our friendship had taken a downhill turn? I tried not to think about it. Like Brad had said, I had my own battle to fight, and needed to focus all of my energy on all of the drugs that were killing me. It was funny, though, detoxing from the other drugs was harder than anything I'd ever done in my life, but the heartache of knowing that My Friend could cut me out of her life so easily was ten times worse. She wanted to be able to pretend her way through life with EVERYONE, just like we all did. Since she couldn't do that with me anymore, I figured she was going to make sure I paid for it.

I pulled the comforter up over my head and tried to think about something else—anything else. It was dark and cold and empty beneath the covers. The world was going on without me. I was slowly dying, and no one was coming to rescue me. I didn't deserve to be rescued anyway because I had done this to myself and deserved to be punished for it. I begged for sleep. Instead, I got a severe case of the trots. Over and over, I rushed to the bathroom, until my poor butt was raw again, and bleeding from the disease of self-destruction. Even if I just had to pee, it stung like infuriated wasps. I ran to the bathroom the rest of the day, all day, and was so exhausted that I finally got a good night's sleep that night. And I did it without taking a Hydrocodone. I had to admit, I was proud.

The next day was Saturday, and I was glad. Fall Saturdays in the state of Nebraska always started out hopefully. It was game day again. Most Nebraskans hoped for a win for the Cornhuskers. At that point in my life, though, I didn't really care about the games. I just cared that I felt like doing something other than looking at the underside of the comforter on my bed. I didn't know if I would feel good enough to watch the game or not, but I was going to put my mask on and act like it.

I got in the pool in the morning, then painted my body into one of my huge pairs of jeans. I vowed that, after I got through my trip to hell, I was going to finally lose the weight I'd gained. I'd been vowing to do so for ten years, but had just kept packing pounds on. Now, it was different. Now, I had a huge battle to fight to change my life. I was going to dig my way out of the quicksand one handful at a time. When the sinking sand filled the scoop back in, I would pull another handful out with fervor. I wasn't going to let anything or anyone pull me under for good.

The battle that raged inside me, however, continued. Knowing that My Friend could easily move on without me was brutal. But even worse was the constant nagging that nothing I had done for her mattered. I fixated on that fact for hours, and the anger burned inside my head and chest like a Colorado forest fire. I needed a diversion, something to take my mind off of my agony and rage. The Nebraska game was just the ticket. I worked up the courage to go out to Lem's to see if the Huskers could pull out a win. Some of the Quilters were already there with their spouses. I tried to be present, to live in the moment, but it was difficult. All I kept thinking about was what My Friend was doing that day. My anxiety about it was chewing on my soul.

Carlie sat beside me again. Halfway through the first quarter, she asked how My Friend was doing, and my heart stopped. She hadn't heard what had happened?

"I, uh, don't know," I said. Carlie looked at me blankly.

"Oh," she said. "I just heard that she hasn't been feeling very well the last couple of days, and figured you knew!" I didn't say anything. I just nodded. Carlie looked back at the TV screen. Well, crap. Now, I would worry about what was wrong with My Friend AND what Carlie thought about my response!

I left at halftime because of sensory overload, and I knew what the score was, but couldn't recount any of the plays. Once home, I immediately sent My Friend an email and a text message to ask how she was doing. There was no sense in calling because she wouldn't answer the phone anyway. But I thought she might send a note back saying that she had sinus infection, or her legs were cramping again, or something. I checked my email obsessively, but by the time I went to bed at midnight, there was no response. I knew she didn't check her email every day, but the silence still ached to the core. That silence continued Sunday, Monday, and Tuesday of the following week. My Friend obviously didn't want me to know how she was doing, and wasn't going to relieve my worry by telling me. I had to force myself to think about other things. I still hadn't heard from my agent about the *Misty* book, so I tried to forget about that, too, and instead worked on this book and my novel. The rest of the time, I stayed in my pajamas, and tried to avoid looking outside. The anxiety constantly kicked my butt to the street, then drove by and splashed mud on my shoes.

The days were getting colder, the sky was cloudy and bleak, and all I wanted to do was hide from everyone, and push everyone away. I stayed in the house for three days, and won staring contests against my bottle of Hydrodocone several times per day. When the anxiety boiled in my blood like witch's brew over a campfire, I thought about how the pills had destroyed my health, mind, and life, and I arched my back against them. I hated them and loved them at the same time. I wanted one so badly, but my battle was now against them, and I refused to let them win. Every time I stared them down—whether it was for thirty seconds or thirty minutes—I walked away without taking one. I left six pills in the bottle every time.

When I needed something to eat during that time, I asked Randy to bring French fries or a malt from Frosty Queen, or I heated up the meatloaf and barbecued ribs that Cassie had prepared for me. Randy ate some when he was home, too. When he wasn't doing play-by-play, he and I sat at the dining room table, and even though my blood was thumping in my temples, I tried to pay attention to his stories about the store. He had earned that just for putting up with me for so long.

Wednesday, Sue called and asked me to go to a yoga class for seniors down at the Fitness Center. I knew I was out of shape and probably couldn't get through the class without running to the bathroom, but figured it would be good for me to get out of the house for a while. I had rotted away on my couch for days. I also knew that the bathroom at the fitness center was right beside the yoga room. So, I went.

The room where the yoga classes were held was gorgeous, with dark woods and a wall of mirrors. The instructor was fabulous. However, I had a hard time doing most of the poses because of my back and my sedentary lifestyle. I also hated looking at the wall of mirrors because I had let myself go so badly. I looked so old. The yoga was much harder than I had thought it would be, too. I tried to keep myself perked up, but it was such a chore! Would I ever get over the depression and the feeling of hopelessness? I knew I couldn't live this way forever, and hoped that I would snap out of it once the drugs were out of my system. But would I even live until then?

After yoga, I went to the pharmacy and got some new antianxiety medicine that Sandy had called in. I just kept looking for something—anything—that would relieve the relentless lightning bolts. However, the new medicine knocked me on my butt. I literally could not keep my eyes open, so I lay on the couch and slept from 12:45 to 1:30. One of the Quilters, Kathy Martin, called then and asked if she could come in to see me. I said yes, of course, but I was so tired that I could barely stay awake! She drove into town from her house in the country at 2:00 p.m., and suggested that we get some fresh air by walking to the end of the block. She helped me with my tennis shoes, which was mortifying because she was fourteen years older than I was. But, I sucked up my pride and headed out the door. I had to stop before we got to the end of my block just to stretch out my back and take some deep breaths. However, when we reached our destination, I felt better, so we continued on around my housing area, occasionally stopping so I could catch my breath. I felt like I was ninety years old. Kathy didn't have to stop at all!

As we finished the route and approached my house, Kathy said, "Do you have plenty of Halloween candy for tonight?"

"Oh my God, is it Halloween!?" I asked. Yep. It was Halloween! I hadn't purchased a single bag of candy. Kathy offered to go to the store for me, but I just didn't want to face trick-or-treaters. "That's O.K.," I said. "I think I'm just going to go downstairs and turn the light off." I just didn't care. I would've liked to have seen my little neighbor girl, Kendall, in her costume, but I hadn't seen much of her, or her mom and dad, in the previous year. That wasn't their fault either, it was mine. They were always out in their yard, tending to flowers out front, or swinging Kendall in her swing out back, but I had wanted to hide from everyone most of the time because I was so broken, and so much heavier than I had been previously. I was also crazily obsessed with the problems in my life. For those reasons, I usually pulled into the driveway, waved at Kendall, Tiffany, and Aaron, then ran into the house. I knew I appeared standoffish, preoccupied, and downright snotty. I wasn't that way at all. I was just lost.

Before Kathy left my house, I hugged her and thanked her for coming to see me, then I went back inside. I ran a glass of water and took it downstairs with me, so I could keep hydrated. I wrote my notes for the night, and tried to focus on the TV long enough just to say I watched something.

Randy was doing play-by-play on the radio for a playoff game somewhere in southeast Nebraska or northwest Missouri. When he came home, I asked him about the game, which didn't interest me at all. But it interested him, so I wanted to show my support. He told me about it, then said he was proud of me for all of the hard work I was doing, and encouraged me to keep going.

"I'm not quitting now!" I said, trying to muster some enthusiasm. I knew if I gave up, my life would be over. Literally. I would rather die than ever go through detox again. So, if I didn't stick it out, my addiction to prescription drugs would kill me. However, since I *was* going through it, I understood why so many addicts didn't make it. They weren't choosing drugs over their lives or families or children. They were doing anything they had to do to get rid of the withdrawal symptoms and the cravings! The cravings were worse than cigarette, ice cream, soda, food, coffee, and beer cravings combined. Detox was literally like being on fire, and I could now understand why some people doctor-shopped, pharmacy-hopped, and even robbed people to get out of it. I thanked God that I had enough hope and support to never do those things, but I understood why some people did. I had too much to lose, and my sanity was at the top of the list.

After Randy went to bed, I tried to go to sleep, too. I was so tired. Once again, though, sleep was elusive. I flopped onto my side, back, stomach, back, side, and finally gave up. I constantly looked at the clock, worried that I wasn't going to get any sleep. Would I ever sleep normally again? The last time I glanced up, it was 3:38 a.m. Good grief. Good night.

Chapter Eighteen

The next day was my appointment day with Brad again because I'd decided that I needed to see him twice per week. He and I had clicked so well that I looked forward to seeing him. I felt like I could tell him anything. There was no pretending with him, no holding back. He didn't mince words either, and I liked that. If I said something that was full of crap, he said, "That's bullshit, and you know it." He was exactly what I needed.

Before I went to my appointment, I dropped by my friend Jolene's house, in Nebraska City, and told her what had been going on in my life throughout the previous month. She and her boyfriend, Steve, were very supportive, and said they would do anything they could to help me through the rest of my journey. I had known that they would. I had such amazing friends. Why didn't I spend more time with people like *them*?

Jolene and I had once been very close, more than twenty years prior. We'd met shortly after she'd gotten a divorce and had started working at Peru State College, where I was working. I also followed the Peru State football team everywhere they played because Randy was the play-by-play announcer. So, one time, shortly after Jolene started working at the college, she signed up for a bus trip to an out-of-town game. She ended up sitting beside me. As the bus left town at 8:30

a.m., I cracked open a Busch Light, and asked her if she wanted one, too. We hit it off right then. We were both partiers, so we had an amazing time laughing and escaping reality. I adored her immediately.

After that, we followed the Bobcats every weekend for two years. We partied together, football season or not. We were also there for each other. We discussed our problems, and had a connection that was deep and without pretension. Another codependent relationship. Until, of course, I became smothering. She was completely broken because of her divorce, and I wanted to solve all of her problems, help her get through the divorce, and let her know how special she was. When would I figure out that most people didn't want someone to swoop in and solve all of their problems? It made them feel incapable of solving their own! Jolene was open and honest with me about that, so I backed off. I gave advice when she asked for it, shared my own frailties with her, and let her solve her own issues. We continued on as great friends. Now, twenty years later, I told her all about detox, then left her house feeling warm and fuzzy about the love that she and Steve had for me.

I headed on to my counseling appointment and sat down in the cushy chair in Brad's office. We talked at length about the bottle of pills that I had set on the counter. Brad said that, if I could set a bottle of Hydrocodone on the counter and tell the pills no, then I could put My Friend on the counter and tell her no, too. I could put ANYTHING on the counter and tell it no.

"I wasn't able to conquer the Hydrocodone on my own," I said. "I had to ask God for help." I saw Brad's forehead crease and his eyebrows raise. He leaned forward in his chair.

"Are you a Christian?" he asked.

"I used to be," I said. "Well, I still am, but I don't deserve to call myself that anymore. I walked away from God at age twenty, and haven't talked to Him much since. I got down on my knees this week when I couldn't take the anxiety anymore, but I haven't prayed since then. I don't deserve for Him to help me."

"Did the anxiety get better?" Brad asked.

"Well, I drank some Gatorade and took some medicine…"

"Did it get better?" he said.

"Yes," I said. "Yes, it did. It became more tolerable. I felt stronger and better able to fight it." I wanted to tell him about the incredible fortitude that I had felt, but like always, I stuffed it down inside. Why? Why did I always do that? I guess I was afraid that he would think I was crazy. Had I really heard a voice quote Philippians 4:13? Yes, by God, I had. But I couldn't tell Brad that. He would think I was nuts.

Lori! I thought. *You're in a counseling office! He already thinks you're nuts*! I shook myself back to reality. Brad smiled a big ole' grin.

"Lori, why do you think that you don't deserve for God to help you?" he asked. "Does your daughter lose or gain your love based on her actions, choices, or decisions?"

"Of course not," I said.

"Then why do you think God is any different? Why do you and so many Christians think that God's love has to be earned? And that we have to be 'good enough' for Him? His love is a gift that's freely given." I started crying then. Not just crying—sobbing. I wiped the tears off my cheeks with my sleeve, like a toddler. Brad handed me a Kleenex. "I've been wanting to ask you about your spirituality," he said. "What place do you want it to play in your recovery?"

"I'm not ready for all of that yet," I blubbered. "I can't go there. I will eventually, I promise. But I can't yet."

"Alright. But we need to investigate it at some point because it's one of the segments that will contribute to a balanced life. If you want to wait, then let's go back to your addictions. Very few if any addicts can set her drug of choice on the counter, have it in her possession, and say 'no.' But you have. Can't you do the same with Your Friend?"

"If it was that easy, don't you think I would've done it by now?"

"No," he said, "you're still leaving the door open! You're still waiting for HER to come back. You're waiting for HER to make a move. You're waiting for HER to decide what this friendship is going to be. You don't have to wait, Lori. Anyone who is worth everything you have to give would be in this room right now, fighting for YOU. Don't you see? You are fighting for her, but she isn't fighting for you! It is time for you to decide that you deserve more than this! It is time for you to break the bonds of codependency once and for all. Why do you always run after the love and approval of that one person who won't give it? You don't need anyone else's approval to be who you are. You don't need that one person with whom you can be yourself! Be yourself with everyone!" I buried my face in my hands.

"What if they don't like me?" I whimpered. Man, I hated crying in front of people. It meant I was out of control, and I hated being out of control.

"Then screw them!" he said. "You are a passionate, giving human being who takes care of everyone around you. You care more about other people than you do yourself, Lori. It's time to make YOU a priority. Do the things that make you healthy and happy. Make the changes that will give you the kind of strength you've had during detox."

"I just found that fight because I wasn't about to let her beat me," I said.

"Bull!" he said. "She isn't trying to beat you, Lori! She isn't paying any attention to you! You are beating yourself. Why? Because one person doesn't want to be friends with you? The one person you know who is more broken than you are? According to what you've told me, you have apparently done this your whole life. You find that one person who is drowning in his or her own problems, and you hoist that person onto your shoulders to keep their head above water. Before you met your husband, that person was a love interest. Since you finally found a healthy relationship, the subject of your codependence has always been a friend. You pour all of your time and energy into saving her instead of building yourself up. It's time to let her make her own choices, and for you to take care of you! What are you so afraid of?"

"I don't know," I whispered, wiping the pools of tears off my face, then dabbing at my eyeliner. "I always felt like I was destined for more, but....." I started crying again. "But maybe I'm afraid I'll fail."

"You aren't afraid of failure," he said, "because no one tries harder than you do. But something always holds you back. I think you're afraid of success. You know that God has something great planned for you, but you don't feel worthy of anything great. Besides, you want to take everyone you know on your journey with you—Your Friend, Jane and Misty, the rest of your friends and family, and God knows who else! Lori, they don't want to go! It's time for you to stop holding yourself back while you wait for everyone else to join you. It's time for you to work toward your own successes! You've raised your children! You have taken care of your parents! You've led communities and created events. What do you want to do with your life? Who do you want to be?" I felt the hairs on the back of my neck rise up. I was at a revival, and the Holy Spirit was present. The Southern Baptist choir had just finished singing, and now Brad was standing at the pulpit preaching, with a lot of ladies in hats shouting, "Hallelujah! You say it, pastor!"

"Who do you want to be?" he repeated. "Start thinking about that instead of that one friend you want to spend your time with. When you become who you want to be—who God wants you to be—then people will flock to you, Lori. The right people. People who want to be around your strength and determination. People who love and support you."

I looked up at him with puffy red eyes, and a blotchy, bloated face. He was right, damn it. I had given passionately and generously of myself to everyone, including My Friend and her daughter, who said they loved and adored me, but who had proven that they didn't. If it was so easy to cut me out of their lives, then they didn't care about me at all. But really, I had to accept responsibility for my part in the demise of our friendship, too. I had become smothering with My Friend, just like I had done with all of the subjects of my codependency since I was a young girl. Every time I'd gotten involved in a codependent relationship, whether it was a romantic interest or friend, I'd clung to that person. I wanted to please him, help her, save them both. I had to stop my pattern of codependency, or I would never reach my true potential. It was way past time that I put that type of one-sided relationship in my past for good, and start living my life in the moment, with people who truly loved me!

"O.K.," I said. "But I don't know how to do it. I still want her in my life. I still want to fix this."

"I'll help you with that," Brad said, "but it's going to take all of your strength and focus. All of it. You can't take care of other people right now, Lori. You have to focus on you." I nodded, but that was much harder than it sounded. "So, let's talk about your drinking," Brad said. "Your thirty days are almost up…"

"I know!" I said, excitedly, "and I'm going to celebrate with the Quilters. But first, Randy and I are going out for dinner with Cassie and Brian tonight, for her birthday."

"I said your thirty days are ALMOST up," Brad said. And he was right! I still had three days to go until thirty. Darn! "But Lori," he continued, "if you really want to make changes in your life, you need to give yourself a chance. What goals would you like to accomplish?"

"I want to get through detox and get rid of the pills for good, then lose the weight I've gained," I said. I knew that those two things would take most of my focus for at least a year, so I looked up at Brad for his response.

"One, two," he said. He was keeping track on his fingers, so he clearly thought more was coming. Then he smiled. I took a deep breath and thought about my long-term goals.

"I want to be a published author," I said. Three. "I want to be healthy and find a solution for my back issues." Four. Then he popped his fifth finger out.

"Number five—your codependency," he said. "And six, what about your spiritual life?"

"I do want to reclaim my spiritual life," I said, "but I need to overcome the rest first."

"You've got that backwards," he said, "but let's talk about the rest of it first. Close your eyes." So, I did. "Think back to the time when you were drinking heavily. Or when you were on all of your medications and were drinking four beers every night." I bit my bottom lip. "Do you see yourself accomplishing any of your goals while alcohol is in your life? Do you even see yourself conquering your codependency issues with Your Friend if you are drinking?" My body shook—and it wasn't from the withdrawals. I knew that, if I started drinking without the pills, I wouldn't limit myself to four beers. It would be balls-to-the-wall, and I would *start* with a twelve-pack. That would make my codependency issues even worse.

"Do you see yourself accomplishing your goals?" Brad repeated.

"No," I whimpered, letting the tears flow again. I crossed my arms in protection, and tried to cross my legs too, but I hadn't been able to do that in a decade. I just wanted to protect my inner self, to shield myself against the truth. I knew if I started drinking again, without medication, I would party like a college freshman. I had a great time when I was drinking. I couldn't deny that. Partying made me fun and funny. It helped me escape my problems and heartache, too. However, the day after I drank, my depression took a dive like a crashing plane, and my sense of worthlessness multiplied by ten.

I opened my eyes and looked at Brad.

"But life is too hard without it," I said. "I'm never going to make it through all of this, Brad. I'm not. I'm pretty strong, but I'm not strong enough for this."

"Maybe not," he said, "but God is. And look at what the two of you have already done. You already said you aren't getting through withdrawals on your own, right?" I nodded. The lump in my throat made it impossible to say anything. "And look where you are!" he said. "You've been clean and sober for how long? Four weeks?" I nodded. Then, I smiled. The next day would, in fact, be four weeks! It wasn't thirty days, but it was a month! I had nearly made it a month! That made me feel good. There were so many moments that I had nearly given up. I hadn't been able to take it day by day, I'd had to take it second by second. But I had done so. For a month!

"How does it make you feel to be able to say, 'I've been clean and sober for a month?'" I smiled. A big ole' proud smile.

"It feels pretty good," I said.

"Do you know how it will feel to be able to say, 'I used to be addicted to painkillers, but I've been clean for a year?' Do you have any idea how many people you will help with your story? You're a community leader, Lori. This problem crosses all socioeconomic boundaries.

People will listen to you!" I swallowed the knot in my throat.

"I'm not ready for that yet," I said. "I can barely get through my days right now. That's too much pressure."

"I know you're not ready," Brad said, "but my point is, without alcohol, you have a chance to completely change your life. You have a chance to end the depression that sucks you down, and the codependency that has kept you where you are instead of allowing you to fly. But if you go back to drinking, your brain cannot and will not heal, and life will continue down the same path that you've traveled since age nineteen, or maybe even earlier." His words sucked the air right out of me. I sighed heavily and closed my eyes. "That is what you won't survive, Lori," Brad said. "When you came here, I wouldn't have given you another year if you'd continued down the same path." And then he was quiet so I could let the message soak in. It was the same thing that Bob had told me when I saw him. I thought about their words. and knew that both the men were right. If I had continued down the path I was on, I wouldn't have lived another year. If I went back to it now, I would continue to be a depressed addict. And I guess I was starting to believe that I was a functional alcoholic. I nodded at Brad and bit the insides of my cheeks. I didn't want to cry again, but tears welled in my eyes.

"How am I going to do this?" I whimpered. My bottom lip shook. "This is going to take so much work, and I don't have it in me."

"By being honest with yourself and me," he said. "By coming here twice a week for now, and fighting for your LIFE the rest of the time. What you're doing isn't living. Lori, you're wearing yourself out trying to be everything to everyone! You don't want anyone to know that you're hurting because you think you have to be strong twenty-four seven, 365 days a year. You are not invincible, but you want everyone to think you are. You take on everyone else's issues while drowning in your own! It is wearing you out. In the past, you dealt with it by drinking, taking prescription drugs, and focusing on that one person you couldn't reach. Why? Because those things gave you excuses to stay where you are. You are obsessed about one person and what she thinks, or what she's doing without you. What about what YOU think and what you're doing without her? What about where you're going with your life? Live your own life and live it with passion! Do things you enjoy. Do things that make YOU strong!"

"Like what? I don't enjoy anything anymore!" I said. "And that boggles my mind! How can I not enjoy doing anything anymore? I used to love sports! Don't care. I used to love listening to music. I haven't turned on a radio or listened to a CD in ten years. I'm serious, Brad. I can't think of one thing besides going drinking, being with my family or friends, or watching my grandsons' ballgames, that I really enjoy doing anymore."

"Then until you do, you have to do whatever makes you feel better instead of worse. You will have to find those things on your own because they are different for everyone. And, at first, you're going to have to force yourself to do some things. Eventually, as your brain heals, you'll find things that you enjoy doing again."

"You mean, like, exercise?" I asked.

"If that makes you feel stronger," he said.

"It used to. I was an athlete, but I am so out of shape right now."

"Then that's a good place to start," he said. "I still recommend that you find a home church, and renew your relationship with God."

"I'm not ready for that yet," I said.

"You don't have to be 'ready,' Lori," he said. "God meets us where we are, loves us where we are, and forgives us where we ARE. He just won't leave us there."

That wasn't what I had been taught growing up. The Bible, based on my understanding, was a book of dos and don'ts. The church was like an extended family, and was supposed to guide its members on the correct path. Heck, one pastor had even told me that the church's primary responsibility was to point out sin in its members, and cast a sinner out if he refused to repent and sin no more! The pastor was talking specifically about a man who had been cheating on his wife, and said it was the church's responsibility to confront the man, then cast him out of the church if he continued the affair! But what about the Bible verse that says, "Judgment is mine, sayeth the Lord?" In my opinion, the main reason that people stayed away from church was because of judgmental Christians! People didn't want to be judged, or to feel unworthy! It was the same for me! When I figured out that I couldn't possibly measure up, couldn't possibly be "good enough," I turned my back on God and the church. My beliefs and values system told me that I couldn't be a believer AND a drinker. I couldn't go to church on Sundays after partying like it was 1999 on Saturday nights. If I wanted God in my life, I had to give up everything else. I knew I couldn't do that. I didn't want to do that! So, I had just given up God. And now, as a middle-aged adult, I was too hardened and ashamed to ask Him to take me back.

"Lori," Brad said, "God isn't sitting there waiting for you to come back. He's chasing after you. And none of your past matters to Him. None of it. If you repent and ask for forgiveness, it will all be wiped away. Do you remember the story in the Bible about the prodigal son?"

"Yes," I said, "I know the story."

"He asked for his inheritance, then left his father's home and squandered it all," Brad said. "He became homeless and said that even the pigs on his dad's farm ate better than he did. So, he buried his pride and went back to ask his dad to forgive him, and to ask if he, the son, could work for him. And when he went back, what did his dad do?"

"He came running," I said. "He killed the fattened calf, and had a big party for the son. But the older son was mad. He said that he had always been there, and that his dad had never held a party for him! The dad said, 'Everything I have is yours, but your brother was dead and is alive. He was lost, but now he's found.'"

"You are the prodigal daughter," Brad said. "It's time to go home. Your heavenly father is ready to come running, Lori."

"I'll deal with that when I'm ready," I said, sobbing again. "For now, I just need to get through this."

"Turn to Him, and He will get you through it," Brad said, "but until you're ready, it's my job to give you professional advice. And my advice is that you won't stay clean if you don't stay sober. At least until all of your detox symptoms are gone." I grimaced. I knew he had just added that last sentence because forever seemed impossible. But the bottom line was, I was going to have to stay sober. Ugh. I hadn't lived a completely sober life since I was nineteen and old enough to drink legally. I'd always thought alcohol helped me to be myself, to let myself out of the cage of perfection—that it helped me enjoy every moment, helped me to be present. How would I ever do those things without it? "Alcohol diminishes your ability to stay focused," Brad said. "It weakens your strength. And it has the same effect on the brain that narcotics do. If you drink right now, your chances of success are nearly zero."

"I can't go through this again," I said. "I won't. I would rather die."

"Then don't put yourself in that position," he said. I just sat there, feeling despondent. How was I ever going to do that? All I could see beyond that day was a gray canvas. I had no paints, no colors, nothing to make that canvas look better or brighter. "Look at it this way," Brad said. "When someone in your life needs your help or wants your care, you give them everything you've got, full speed ahead. Right?"

"Yeah," I said, "apparently, too much sometimes."

"Right now, the person who is crying for help is you," he said. "Treat yourself as well as you would a friend who needed you. If you truly want to be free of ALL of your addictions, then fight for your life. Toss away all of the substances, and together, we'll find YOU. Be who you are in God, and find out what He has planned for you. Who knows? Maybe His plan includes a book about what you've been through!"

"I told you I've been writing about this whenever I'm able, didn't I?" I said, sheepishly. "I would really have to put myself out there, though, and expose all of my weaknesses. Plus, I'm not even through detox yet, and the anxiety and depression are sucking the life out of me. I feel like I could fail at any time."

"Everyone who goes through it feels that way," he said. "You're already through the toughest part physically. Find your fight, Lori."

"I'm all or nothing. If I'm going to do this, I have to go all the way," I said. "I would have to completely transform my life. I'd have to finish detox, stay sober…lose all the weight I've gained, figure out how in the world I'm going to live without that codependent friendship…find a relationship with God again."

"Then go all the way," he said, "but for right now, let's concentrate on the first two things. You can't do all of it at the same time. When you feel strong enough, then you can start on other areas of your life. I want you to know what it's like to be free. Break those chains, Lori, especially the ones with the book, and with Your Friend. Your worth does not depend on the opinion of someone who is unable to give you the friendship that you want." I bowed my head and closed my eyes. The thought of that statement stung like a slap across the face. "It is not her fault, Lori. But it's not yours either. You want a friendship that she can't give you."

"No, I don't!" I said. "I just want to be treated like I matter! When she makes plans with me, I don't want to be ditched because Anastasia calls and wants to go somewhere! When My Friend treats me coldly, or ignores me completely, I want to know why!"

"You got too close to her," he said, "and you have given too much control of yourself to her! Your gifts probably made her feel obligated, indebted, and controlled. Every time you gave her money, she had to take it because she needed it. But she didn't want to need it! She doesn't want to need anyone! You have to let go of her. Let go of everything that has happened, and practice forgiveness, so you can be free."

"I don't think I can," I said. "She hurt me to the core. If I let go of it, then she wins."

"Forgiveness isn't for her, it's for you," he said. "The only way you'll be free is if you let her go." I knew that I could never do that on my own. Pssshhhaaww. Brad might as well have asked me to fly to the moon and live on the space station, where I'd be closed in and unable to get out. That would be impossible.

"How am I going to do this when I don't see a light at the end of the tunnel?" I asked.

"That's where faith comes in," he said. "You can't see it, but you have to believe that God can."

I can do all things through Christ who strengthens me, I heard the voice in my head say. I felt the fight or flight rise up in me.

"Maybe if I lose the weight I've gained and make some changes in my life, I really could help other people!" I said.

"You could help A LOT of other people just by telling what you've already been through," Brad said. I thought about it for a minute. He was right. I could help people by telling my story.

"O.K.," I said. "I'm going to try. I really am. I know we'll talk about it at every appointment, but at least until I get through detox, I'll continue to live without alcohol." He smiled happily. At least for the time being, he had talked me into staying sober.

My allotted hour was up, so he shook my hand, and stood up. That wasn't enough. I wanted a hug, so I wrapped my arms around him.

"Thank you," I said. "Thank you so much."

I walked outside, and the cool air felt great on my face. It was sixty degrees, and the sun was shining. I felt a wave of gratitude for the beautiful weather. I got in the car, took a deep breath, and took off. As I turned onto the highway and drove out of town, I felt something I had never felt before. Weightlessness. A sense of freedom. I normally felt like a hot air balloon that was tethered by stakes all around me—stakes of codependent relationships, food, drugs, alcohol, and claustrophobia, just to name a few. The claustrophobia was because of the incident in the hospital, but maybe it was also from being trapped inside myself—of not being who I was! The reason I enjoyed being with My Friend so much was because I let myself out when she was around. When we were together, we did silly things. We tried on funny hats and sunglasses when we were in stores. We bantered back and forth with teasing jabs. She was hysterically funny, and she said I was, too. Even while talking on the phone, we laughed until our necks hurt. But the only time I did those things with other people was when I was drinking. Otherwise, I felt like people thought I was weird or stupid. My Friend never felt that way. She always told me I was a blast to be around. And I knew she was. That's why I missed her so much. But my desire to be with her had become a need. I needed to be with her, to be needed by her, to help save her. And I was finally getting the message that that, in itself, was an addiction. I was not only detoxing from prescription drugs and alcohol, I was also detoxing from my need for that codependent relationship—in this case, my need to be with and save My Friend. I wanted to save her from her past by rescuing her future. No wonder I'd experienced the month from hell.

I drove south out of Nebraska City, toward Auburn. The wave of freedom washed over me again. I had a renewed sense of hope. Everything in the air just seemed lighter. I felt buoyant, like I really could break free from the tethers that had kept me from flying all my life.

Could I really do this? Could I break the chains of food, drugs, alcohol and people addiction? Could I lose the weight I had gained? Could I get clean, stay clean, and stay sober? I didn't see that happening, but I had to leap out in faith. Could I find a personal relationship with God again? Let go of the anger and resentment? Of the rejection? People-pleasing? Could I really live a healthy life, and be happy? Could I defeat my depression? Could I get to the place where I was comfortable in my own skin? Not only comfortable, but joyful?

Could I do *any* of that, let alone all of it? I would have to completely transform my life. It would require a lot of hard work that had previously been impossible for me. I had tried so many times before. I'd made resolutions, promises to myself, guarantees to others. But my depression had always pulled me back down into the pit. When it did, I lost the desire to do anything. Did I have the strength to overcome that debilitating feeling of hopelessness? For good? I had to face it, I didn't. Battling that kind of depression was something that no human being could do on her own. A fight that hard could only be fought through supernatural strength, commitment, and power.

I can do all things through Christ who strengthens me, the voice in my head said, again. Philippians 4:13 didn't say "I can do SOME things through Christ who strengthens me." It said, "I can do ALL things through Christ who strengthens me." When I had asked God for His help, He had shown up. He had walked beside me through the gates of hell called detox, and had fought for me, despite all of Satan's attempts to pull me back down. Through Him, I had found a fortitude that I'd never known, and I would use that to transform the other areas of my life!

I am going to do this, I thought. I had already been through the toughest days of my life, and if I could make it through thirty days of detox, then I could make it through anything. I could do this! I would do this! I looked at the beautiful blue sky and the green pastures turning brown, and tears rolled down my cheeks. But this time, they were happy ones.

"Lord, I'm turning things over to you," I said, as I drove down the highway toward home. "I can't do this on my own. I can't. I need you by my side, God. I want you by my side. I don't know what this is going to look like. I don't know how I'll find the strength to do the hard work every day. But I know, if I give it all to you, you will find a way. Let's do this, Lord. Let's go."

When I got home, I was still excited about transforming my life. But, that evening, my symptoms were wicked. I had actually expected them to be because I'd been out all day. I spent the evening running to the bathroom until the cuts bled. I had sneezing fits that made my eyes water and left me unable to breathe. My head and every muscle in my body ached.

The same things were true for the next three days. I crawled through those days with miserable symptoms and bottom-of-the-barrel depression. But I knew that it was Satan trying to pull me back down. I had given my fight to God, so the devil was going to fight harder for me than he had fought the prior thirty days. And man, was he giving it everything he had. I made it through those days, though, and celebrated my thirtieth day with a big ole' Frosty Queen malt, instead of the beer that I really wanted and had intended to have. I was proud—proud that I had made it through the first thirty days of the hell called detox. And grateful that God had given me the determination I needed.

I, Lori Kimball Gottula, had finally found the fortitude that allowed me to break some of the chains that had bound me for the thirty years prior—heck, my entire life. Finally, I had hope. After a lifetime of holding myself back and quashing the talents and drive that God had given me, I hoped and prayed that it really was my time to fly. But I knew that the only way I could do it was with God by my side. And I would soon find out that, by my side, He would be. Actually, He had been by my side throughout my first thirty days in the hell called detox. And the six Hydrocodone pills that were still left in the bottle were proof that Satan was no match for God and me. I was suddenly filled with joy, because my sky had cleared and I could finally see. God and I had already climbed the first step toward victory.

Epilogue

I wrote the majority of this book as the events happened, so my narrative would be fresh, real, and very raw. However, more than a decade passed before I sought publication because, as a habitual people-pleaser, I didn't want to hurt My Friend or make her or myself look bad in other people's eyes. But Brad finally convinced me that my story could be the key that unlocked someone else's prison, and that I couldn't help anyone if I didn't share it.

The story about my first thirty days was hard to write, but not nearly as difficult as it was to live. The words don't exist to fully describe it. Magnify everything I said by one hundred, and that may give you a glimpse into the terrifying torture that one lives while withdrawing from drugs, alcohol, and/or codependence. It is my hope that those who have loved ones who are fighting this difficult battle will understand more about the fight, and why their family or friends can't seem to get through to the other side. Thinking that it just takes thirty days is laughable. It takes much longer, and the emotional battle is much harder than the physical one. Our loved ones need support through the whole thing.

The demons with which I lived before and during detox were of biblical proportions. Breaking free wasn't the battle of David vs. Goliath, it was the battle of Lori vs. Legion. In the Bible, one man who was healed by Jesus was so consumed by demons that chains no longer held him. When Jesus called him out of the tombs where he lived, the man said his name was Legion because "we are many." That meant he had multiple demons. I did, too, and I had no idea they existed while I was living with them. I thought I was completely functional! I took care of my household and family, organized events, coached teams, directed plays, served on boards and committees, wrote works that placed in international contests, and nurtured relationships. I was able to hold things together when other people were around, and when Randy was home. I looked like I was living life large and in charge. But behind closed doors, I was completely lost. With Brad's help of treatment and self-discovery, I finally figured out that I was torturing myself with opiate addiction, functional alcoholism, food addictions, codependent obsession, people-pleasing issues, and guilt that made me depressed if I even *thought* I was disappointing someone. I spent my entire life chasing the affections of others, and particularly that one person who seemed to bring me the most excitement—excitement that was killing me, choking me, chaining me. I couldn't see any of it while I was in it. I also couldn't see any hope of getting out—not even after I hit rock bottom and knew that I had to change my life or lose it.

So, did I get out? I sure did. With the support of my husband, family, and friends, I did. With Brad's incredible advice and unending confidence in me, I did. With God's amazing grace and unconditional, unwavering love, I did. My climb out will be detailed in my second book titled, *Breaking the Chains,* but let me summarize it here, in hopes that you'll pick up the next book to join me on my journey, and more importantly, to help with your own.

After I survived the first thirty days of detox, I fought my way through two more weeks of unbearable daily symptoms. I went out occasionally when I could, but only for events like Jerry Joy's victory party on election day. Unfortunately, the event turned into a consolation gathering. Jerry lost the senatorial race by a slim margin because he was a Democrat in a mostly Republican state. Even though the

Nebraska legislature was unicameral, voters still voted along party lines. Many of Jerry's supporters were Republicans like Rod; people who voted for a candidate based on his or her achievements and ideas, rather than strictly voting party lines. But, there hadn't been enough. I attended his party for about an hour, then had to excuse myself because of sensory overload. I just wasn't able to stay anywhere for very long. Jerry continued to serve the people of southeast Nebraska in other capacities, and was crucial to some of the successes in our communities.

The intensity of my withdrawals began to taper off after the first six weeks, but I still experienced some symptoms every day. I was glad that I hadn't known how long the symptoms would last when I'd started, or I think I would have given up early on. When I was going through it, every minute was excruciating.

After my first six weeks, I had symptoms every other day. They didn't last all day like they had during the first six weeks, but I still struggled to go anywhere because of sensory overload. If I did anything outside the house, I usually paid for it the next day. But thank God the symptoms weren't as brutal as they had been the first six weeks.

When I celebrated three months of sobriety on January 5, 2013, I started a health plan on my own. My symptoms persisted a few days each week, then just a few times per month, for another year. They appeared out of nowhere, with no warning. But I was committed to changing my life, and I approached that commitment with the same fortitude that God had provided me through detox.

I decided that, to change my life, I had to give up the things that weakened me, and replace them with things that made me strong. In my humble opinion, that's why a lot of people fail during recovery and go back to their substances. When people give up mind-altering substances or relationships, they're left with huge holes. They have to fill those holes with things that make them strong, or they'll go back to the lives they knew, lives that are less frightening than the unknown.

I discovered six things that made me strong: a renewed spiritual relationship with God, exercise, counseling, spending time with people who loved me as I was, being outdoors, and getting involved in hobbies that kept me busy and eventually brought me joy. At first, I just had to keep myself occupied because there were very few things that brought me joy anymore.

In addition, the depression continued to stalk me. During the first several months, whenever I went to the grocery store, or downtown to get gas, I could barely get out of the car when I got back home. I didn't have the desire or will to do anything, even open the car door and walk twenty feet into the house! My whole body was anchored to the car. But I eventually put one foot in front of the other and made it inside.

When I first started the battle with my weight, I honestly felt as hopeless as I'd felt when I'd started detox. I had gained nearly one hundred pounds, and my depressive days were so horrible that I had very little hope that change was possible. I hated the way I looked, and wanted to hide in my house. I specifically hated my legs because my thighs looked like big bags of cottage cheese. So, I decided to focus on them first. I got in the pool every morning and worked my legs against the current. In the afternoons or evenings, I walked. As I said previously, when I took my first trek, I couldn't even tie my own shoes because my stomach was so big that I couldn't reach my feet. So, I wore tennis shoes with Velcro strips. I couldn't walk to the end of my block either, not without stopping part-way to stretch my back out, or rest because I couldn't catch my breath. That was a horrible feeling of defeat. I was so overweight that I couldn't even walk to the end of my block! There were times, too, that my pain level was an eight or nine on the pain scale when I started. I walked down the street with tears rolling down my cheeks. But I found that, if I just kept going, the pain lessened substantially. After several weeks of daily walks, I became a conqueror of the pain rather than a victim. When the pain tried to take me down, I found every ounce of fortitude I could to fight it. I just had to believe that, someday, my fight would pay off, and the pain would get better.

During my darkest hours, I recalled every reason for motivation that I could think of. Some days, that reason was being present for my husband, family, kids and grandkids, and being able to hold and play with any future grandkids that I might have. Some days, it was just believing that I could be well. Other days, it was revenge against My Friend. I knew that the revenge motivation didn't really make sense, but I convinced myself that, if I stayed in the pit and continued to decline in every way, then she had somehow won. It was the same principle as the "revenge body" motivation when someone got a divorce. *Oh yeah, you dumped me? Well, I'll show you! I'm better off without YOU.* At first, that reason was the one that motivated me most. It kept me going, got me into the pool every day, made me lace up my tennis shoes. But with Brad's help, I realized that *I* was the only reason that mattered. My health needed to be my top priority. Getting well was important. Revenge didn't matter because My Friend wasn't winning anything. Her life was hard. Her depression was often on the suicidal level. Trust me, she wasn't winning anything.

For the first year after she ended our friendship, I was cold and standoffish when we ran into each other in our small town. I tried to convince myself that I hated her for rejecting me the way she had, and for not caring when I was walking through hell. But I missed her so much. I begged God for a phone call, but none ever came. I felt like she was using the worst weapons I had ever had to battle—silence and indifference—and both made me angry, resentful, bitter, and bottom-of-the-barrel depressed. On those days, I had to force myself to get up and move. To exercise. To breathe. Sometimes, it took an hour to talk myself into simply getting off the couch. But then I walked or swam, prayed, and tried to think about other things. When I finished my workouts, I always felt better physically and mentally. One hundred percent of the time.

In late 2013 and early 2014, My Friend and I reconnected, but the friendship ended abruptly in April 2014 (ten days before my daughter's wedding). I thought it was because I had objected when she ditched me for Anastasia, but she said I was getting too close and suffocating again. I suppose from her perspective, I probably was. I enjoyed her company so much, and she said she could forget about her struggles for a while when she was with me, so I asked for too much time. She started being cold and distant, and when I asked why, she ended our friendship. It cut me to the bone again. Thankfully, Randy and my family members, and Brad were there to pick up the pieces. Brad, as usual, was brutally honest about the situation. He had warned me from the beginning not to become involved in the friendship. When My Friend cut me out of her life again, though, he was kind but firm. He said she wanted me around when she needed me but didn't want me around when she didn't. She had unbearable depression, and preferred to be alone; I assumed because she believed no one could understand her torture. I just had to accept that her life would continue without me and vice versa. Doing so took everything I had.

Today, I occasionally run into her, and when I do, we hug each other and talk like old friends who just haven't had time to get together. But we have no relationship beyond that. When I decided that I had to include her in this book, it took me more than ten years to publish it because I felt she had been through enough, and I didn't want to do anything to disparage her. I finally decided that I had to include her because her involvement in my life was crucial to my transformation. God used her to reach me. Without her, I never would have sought help. I probably would not be alive today. So, I have done everything I could do to ensure her anonymity. I haven't talked about her tragedies because I don't want her to be identifiable. My hope is that readers will see that she and I were two broken people who rarely let anyone else in. We got very close to each other because we were so much alike, but then she had to "go back to reality," (her words). That meant she had a blast with me, but had to return to the reality of her life. Her past was inescapable, and she was as broken as any human being could be. She couldn't give me the friendship that I wanted. But honestly, no one could have. She was just the latest manifestation of my codependent tendencies, and that type of relationship was more addictive to me than any of my other substances—opiates, alcohol, or food. Losing her broke me, so I hit rock bottom. Climbing out of that pit took everything I had, and everything God provided. I had to overcome heartache, frustration, anxiety, fear, and a level of rage that I had never experienced before. With God's help, I have done so. Now I have no desire for a codependent relationship of any kind. I finally realized that obsessive relationships suck the souls out of those who are caught up in them, so I have taken all steps necessary to maintain healthy, balanced friendships and relationships with everyone in my circle of trust. I also try to be myself with everyone!! Now, I have honest, open friendships and I feel alive with all of the people in my circle, not just one. Praise God!

Similarly, the *Misty* book, which I had hoped would be my first published book, never came to fruition. As I had surmised, our agent thought the book was too long and wordy, so he suggested that I hire a professional editor. I asked Jane and Misty if they wanted to continue the project, and they said they did, so I hired a professional editor. When she returned the book six weeks later, I rewrote the whole thing, and it took me six months. I turned it in to our agent, but by that time, my contract with him was near its expiration date, and he did not renew it. I never should have turned it in before it was ready the first time, but I felt like I had no other choice.

I continued to market the book through other avenues, and in the spring of 2014, I entered a short story version in a writing contest sponsored by Guideposts magazine. I also turned in an article about my own story. Guideposts' editors selected twelve winners who got to attend an all-expenses-paid writing workshop in Rye, New York. I found out in August that I was one of the winners! When I asked which of my stories had won, the editor who called me said that my own story had won, but that the magazine wanted to publish both articles in 2015. My contract with Jane and Misty was set to expire in October 2014, so I had to decide whether or not I wanted to take the chance that a well-known writer or producer would see their story and offer them a contract without me. After much thought, prayer, and advice from Brad, I decided that I was willing to take that chance if it meant something better for them.

Jane and Misty seemed happy about their story appearing in a magazine that had more than two million subscribers, but when Guideposts arranged a photo session with a professional photographer, the girls changed their minds. Shortly afterward, they decided that they no longer wanted to pursue the project. Although I was devastated that we had worked so hard on something that would never come to fruition, I fully understood and supported their decision. Sharing one's life and baring one's soul for all the world to see is very difficult. When that possibility became reality for them, both decided that they didn't want the attention.

Sadly, in 2018, Jane lost one of her other sons in a car accident. She had already lost two boys, so to lose a third was a tragedy of Kennedy proportions. Jane's son had accomplished more in his thirty-six years on earth than most people did in a lifetime, though. A lady's man with movie-star good looks, he had a wide circle of close friends who loved him dearly. And every woman in every room noticed him, young and old, single and married. He was strikingly handsome, outgoing, funny, inclusive, and mischievous. Just the kind of guy around whom everyone wanted to be. His funeral was so huge that it was held in a city auditorium.

I can't imagine the brokenness that comes with losing one child, let alone three. Jane's kids were her life. No parent should have to bury one child. To bury three is unthinkable. I pray for her every day, and I fully understand and support her decision to not share her life story.

Besides, God had other plans for me. This book. And the next one. And the next.

As I finish polishing this one, it's eleven years after I entered rehab. I have been clean and sober since that time, and have lost ninety-five pounds. I swim and walk every day, without fail. Both things have just become part of my daily routine. The first two pictures below are of me at age fifty-one. The third picture was taken at age fifty-five on a family cruise.

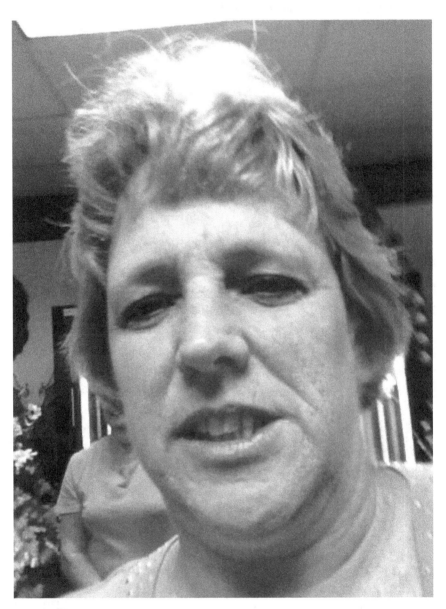

Me, age fifty-one

Me, age fifty-one, as big as Santa Claus

Me, age fifty-five

The following picture was taken at age sixty-one.

Me, in my pool room, age sixty-one

The thing I hope you'll notice most isn't the difference in the puffiness of my face or the crow's feet around my eyes. It's not the change in my complexion, the length or thickness of my hair, or the whiteness of my teeth. It's the difference in the light in my eyes. In the first picture, there is no light. The chains that bound me had literally stolen my soul. In the other pictures, I am free. Breaking my chains gave me back my light. It allowed me to experience joy again.

Do I still have back pain? Yes. But it is nothing like it used to be because I have become a conqueror rather than a victim. When the pain gets bad now, instead of lying on the couch and shoving chocolate donuts in my mouth, I lace up my tennis shoes and go for a walk, (yes, I can now tie my own shoes, too!). I refuse to let the pain defeat me or drive me to the couch. Instead, I drive the pain to the street. I am conquering. I am winning. On a beautiful morning in 2018, I even placed second in my age group in my first-ever 5K race. In July of 2023, I won my age division in the same race.

Me, walking in the 2023 Brownville,
NE Freedom Run
Sixty-two years old

The only reason I was able to do those things was because I stopped being a victim and became a conqueror. If you are counting the reasons why you can't get up and move, then you, too, may be in the chronic victimhood club; a club of which I was a member for twelve years. If your feet hurt and you can't walk, then swim, lift arm weights, paddle a kayak, do something, If your legs hurt, swim. Heck, get in the bathtub for thirty minutes and move your legs back and forth. Find SOMETHING that you can do. If you can't afford a membership to a gym, ask if you can clean the place in exchange for workout time. If you're a single mom or dad and don't have childcare, watch your neighbor's kids in the morning and let him or her watch yours for an hour in the evening. If you can't get to a gym, lift cans of veggies in your kitchen. If you don't have time to exercise, get up earlier or go to bed later. You can sleep when you're old and can't move. But if you don't move, that time will come sooner rather than later. Besides, once you start an exercise program, you won't WANT to sleep. You'll have more energy than you ever thought possible. No more excuses! Get up and move!

If I hadn't changed my life, just look at all of the things I WOULD HAVE MISSED:

1) All of God's amazing colors in His sunrises and sunsets!

Me, at sunrise, near Cabo San Lucas, Mexico

2) My daughter, Cassie's, wedding to Brian Shaw.

Cassie and Brian Shaw (photo by Todd Gottula)

3) Watching my oldest grandsons become incredible young men.

Left to right: Auston Hall, Preston Hall, Easton Hall

4) Getting to participate in one of the few pictures ever taken of my mom, me, my sister, Michelle Kimball, my younger brother, David Kimball, and my older brother, Mike Kimball. (Mike hates pictures so he doesn't pose very often, but did here in 2017). If I hadn't changed my life, this picture never would have been taken because I wouldn't have been alive. As of this writing, another picture like this isn't possible. My younger brother, David, died unexpectedly in December 2019.

Left to right: Me, Michelle Kimball (sister), Judy Kimball (mom), David Kimball (brother), Mike Kimball (brother)

5) Watching my youngest grandkids meet my great niece.

Left to right: Jasper and Lake, my grandchildren; Georgia, my great niece

6) Helping my mom recover from a 2015 brain aneurism rupture. The picture below is of her and me in 2023, eight years after her aneurism. She was eighty-three, I was sixty-two.

Judy Kimball (my mom), and me

7) My oldest grandson's wedding. Preston Hall married Macey Mathis on 5/20/2023 at Sylvan Lake, South Dakota, and this photo is of my family.

(Photo courtesy of Lynsey Prosser, of Lynsey Prosser Photography) *Left to right, back two*: Easton Hall and Auston Hall, my grandsons; *In front of them*: my sister Michelle Kimball, and mother, Judy Kimball. *To their left*: my step-daughter, Shanda Hall, and her husband, Andy; *In the center*: the beautiful bride, Macey Hall and my handsome grandson, Preston; *Next*: Todd and Kristin Gottula, my step-son and his wife; then me with my husband, Randy; and *at the right end*: my daughter, Cassie and her husband, Brian Shaw, and their two children, Jasper and Lakeleigh.

8) Growing old with my husband, Randy.

Me, with Randy, at Christ Place church

I would have missed all of these moments and millions more, if I hadn't changed my life! Even if I hadn't died from my addictions and dependencies, I would have missed these events mentally and emotionally. My back pain and mindset, my depression and anxiety, all of those things would have kept me from truly living my best life, with people who love me unconditionally.

I have always known, and realize even more so now, how fortunate

I am to have a family and friends who have always loved me, and a husband who never left my side. I have been blessed beyond measure.

Because I want to continue living my life out loud, I still see Brad on a weekly basis, but now it's at his own counseling business, College View Harmony Health, in Lincoln, Nebraska. His advice has been crucial to my recovery. Without him, I wouldn't be alive today. In addition, I used to be depressed five days out of seven. Now, it's maybe one day out of twenty. Brad helps me fight. I have included my perceptions of his advice throughout my second book, but my recommendation to anyone who needs to break chains of any kind is to find a counselor whose personality fits theirs. There is no shame in counseling. It has been imperative to my recovery. It has also been one of the leading reasons for my spiritual revival.

When I was a young believer, I worshipped God with reverence, but not relationship. As a result, I was always searching for something to fill the God-sized hole in my soul. I didn't feel worthy of God's love, so I searched in all the wrong places, and became addicted to things that eventually owned me.

When I hit rock bottom and realized the truth about my sicknesses, my eyes began to open, and I started seeing things more clearly. Then, an old and dear friend named Lore Dorsey invited me to go to church with her at Christ Place in Lincoln, NE. There, I found the God for whom I had searched all my life; the one and only God, who loves me without condition, and forgave me just because I repented and asked for His forgiveness. He accepted me simply because I believed. In 2015, I followed Jesus' command to be baptized. I had done so when I was eight years old because I wanted to commit my life to God way back then. However, I had been too young to fully understand. So, on January 11, 2015, I let the waters of spiritual baptism cleanse me.

My baptism on 1/11/2015, by Pastor Rick Lorimer

When I came up out of that water, I knew that I would give the rest of my life to God and His mission for me. This book is part of that mission. So is the next one. And the next. Today, I have a renewed passion and love for my savior, Jesus Christ. It is during my time with God that I find my greatest peace and strength.

My commitment to Christ has also strengthened my determination to attend church, or watch it online when I can't go. At the time of this writing, Christ Place is still led by pastors Rick and Wendy Lorimer, who are long-time friends of mine through Wendy's sister, Lore. Christ Place is a Bible-based church in Lincoln, NE, and its members not only welcome the lost and broken, but seek them out. The church believes in one mission—to see souls saved and lives changing. That mission has certainly been accomplished with me. It has apparently been accomplished with others, too, because attendance at Christ Place has soared since Pastor Lorimer took the lead position. That's because the church members wrap their arms around those of us who have finally realized that we will never be "good enough," and they help us see that God loves us as we are. He meets us where we are. He just won't leave us there. I am living proof.

In addition to church, I spend quiet time with God every day by praying, and reading His word. I have read through the Bible twice now, and am starting on my third time. I watch my favorite pastors on TV and online, and their sermons start my days off right. Other than my own pastor, my current favorite is Pastor Steven Furtick, who leads Elevation Church in Ballantyne, North Carolina. I watch or listen to one of his messages every day while I walk. His insight has helped me strengthen my relationship with God, and his encouraging messages have been crucial to my decision to publish this book and the next.

When I'm not focused on messages from favorite pastors, I listen to my "Jesus music." There are so many artists whose songs fill my heart with joy, and I am grateful for their incredible talents. I attend their concerts whenever my favorites are nearby. (I am always searching for new favorites!) In addition, I am addicted to *The Chosen*, the largest crowd-funded video project in history. It is about Jesus' ministry, and the lives of His disciples. I cannot recommend it highly enough. The

Jesus portrayed in this show is the Jesus I know, love, and follow. He's approachable, loving, giving, and kind, but firm. He's compassionate, and passionate. The producers have made Jesus and His disciples come alive. Dallas Jenkins and company, I cannot thank you enough.

Every day, I say a prayer like the following one, for anyone reading this book.

"Lord, my Father, I ask you to bless the person reading these words right now. Open his or her heart, Lord, and help the reader see that all things are possible through your Son, Jesus Christ, who strengthens them. Give the reader hope so that he or she can reach out and find help, Lord. Give him or her the strength to power through every day until freedom comes. In Jesus' most holy name I pray. Amen."

I pray also that my experience and triumph over my addictions will bring hope to the afflicted. I am living proof that conquering any kind of addiction is possible. Heck, with God's help, I'm conquering four! Prescription drugs, alcohol, codependent relationships, and food addictions. I'm still working on my people-pleasing issues, but I'll always be a work in progress. However, I'm proud to be where I am! Where I used to sit in my house day after day, avoiding people, experiences, life, and joy, I am now living life abundantly! I take pictures of local kids playing ball, and I give the pictures away. I attend Christian concerts, Broadway plays, local ballgames, and my grandkids' activities. I spend time with (and even wrestle with!) my youngest grandson and granddaughter. I help my mom, sister, daughter, and anyone else who needs me (when I can). And I enjoy life on the farm with my now-retired husband, who is no longer a workaholic! We are closer than we have ever been. I am living the life of which I dreamed. I have several more books planned after *Broken and Chained*, and *Breaking the Chains*, and I have also been traveling to give presentations about the transformation of my life. I have spoken in churches, schools, at conventions, and many more places. I hope to come to **your** city after this book is published. I want to meet people who have found help through my books. And I want to meet those who need hope that things CAN get better!

Transformation is possible for YOUR life. And it is possible for your loved one who is bound in chains. If it happened for me, it could happen for you, him, or her. I am truly changed, and I know you can be, too.

Live the life that you were meant to live. Join me as I detail my journey from darkness to light in *Breaking the Chains*, so you can see that there IS hope. Come and see what it is like to truly be free.

Me, age sixty-two, and free

Printed in the USA
CPSIA information can be obtained
at www.ICGtesting.com
CBHW071924250724
12177CB00023B/693